Citizens of Fear

Citizens of Fear

Urban Violence in Latin America

edited by
SUSANA ROTKER

in collaboration with
KATHERINE GOLDMAN

with an introduction by
JORGE BALÁN

 RUTGERS UNIVERSITY PRESS
New Brunswick, New Jersey, and London

Library of Congress Cataloging-in-Publication Data

Citizens of fear : urban violence in Latin America / edited by Susana Rotker in collaboration with Katherine Goldman ; with an introduction by Jorge Balan.
    p. cm
    Selection of papers presented during the Colloquium "Culture, Citizenship and Urban Violence in Latin America" held in Cuernavaca, Mexico, in 2000.
    Includes bibliographical references.
    ISBN 0-8135-3034-2 (cloth : alk. paper) — ISBN 0-8135-3035-0 (pbk. : alk. paper)
    1. Violence—Latin America—Congresses. 2. Urban policy—Latin America—Congresses. I. Rotker, Susana, 1954– II. Goldman, Katherine. III. Colloquium "Culture, Citizenship and Urban Violence in Latin America" (2000: Cuernavaca, Mexico)

HN110.5.Z9 V5248 2002
303.6'098—dc21   2001031781

British Cataloging-in-Publication data for this book is available from the British Library

This collection copyright © 2002 by Rutgers, The State University

A Project of the Center for Hemispheric Studies

Manufactured in the United States of America

Contents

             SÉRGIO ADORNO

The Stories

Chapter 9   A Small Mistake (chronicle)   *119*
             JOSÉ ROBERTO DUQUE

Chapter 10   Ciudad Bolívar: Brush Strokes against
             Death (chronicle)   *125*
             JOSÉ NAVIA

Chapter 11   The Drive-by Victim (chronicle)   *130*
             ALBERTO SALCEDO RAMOS

The Attitude

Chapter 12   State Violence in Brazil: The Professional
             Morality of Torturers   *141*
             MARTHA K. HUGGINS

Chapter 13   The Impact of Exposure to Violence in São Paulo:
             Accepting Violence or Continuing Horror?   *152*
             NANCY CÁRDIA

The Imaginaries

Chapter 14   The Social Construction of Fear: Urban Narratives
             and Practices   *187*
             ROSSANA REGUILLO

Chapter 15   Imaginaries and Narratives of Prison Violence   *207*
             YOLANDA SALAS

Chapter 16   We Are the Others   *224*
             SUSANA ROTKER

Chapter 17   Citizenship and Urban Violence: Nightmares
             in the Open Air   *240*
             CARLOS MONSIVÁIS

             References   *247*
             Contributors   *261*

Preface

CITIZENS OF FEAR is the result of a colloquium held in Cuernavaca, Mexico, to discuss problems of culture, citizenship, and violence in Latin America. The colloquium (actually three days in Mary Belfrage's marvelous house) had an interdisciplinary spirit from the time that its planning began in New Jersey, at the Center for Hemispheric Studies (CHS) and the Latin American Studies Program (RULAS) at Rutgers University. This spirit was the result of the need to try to create a space in which the different groups that work on the topic could encounter a common language that would be enriching for scholars and, even more importantly, for the community. For three days the languages of criminology, anthropology, social sciences, literature, psychology, politics, epidemiology, journalism, and culture tried to be mutually intelligible without the use of translators. There was, therefore, no desire to resort to using interpreters, even though both discussions and daily life together occurred in Spanish, English, and Portuguese. If any conclusion can be stated, it is that despite the linguistic and disciplinary barriers, there was increased understanding and enriched knowledge for all involved.

Two methodological criteria for this volume must be explained. The first is the definition of the topic. For practical reasons, it was decided that the project would be limited to the topic of urban violence in

Mexico, Colombia, Venezuela, and Brazil, since these countries share common characteristics and have been marked by the greatest recent growth of the problem. Violence in the countryside, guerrilla movements, and drug trafficking were not included so as not to try to cover more than what was possible within the framework of the colloquium and the book. If we have managed to define the new subjectivity, the new form of communal relationships, the citizenship of fear, it would be a great achievement.

The second criterion is that not all of those who attended the colloquium are represented in this volume, while some of those who could not attend are featured among the contributors. *Citizens of Fear* is not merely a compilation of the papers read during a conference: it rather is a book that offers important analyses of the topic, some of which were written by individuals who participated in the colloquium. Others did not come to Cuernavaca because of previous commitments, or, in one case the author had to travel to recover the body of a relative who was murdered after being kidnapped. In addition to the texts submitted by the participants after the colloquium, those of Alberto Concha-Eastman, Sergio Adorno, Jesús Martín Barbero, and Alberto Salcedo have been added.

It was decided that the prologue would be an introductory study of the subject of urban violence rather than a summary of the articles featured in the book out of respect for the value of each study and the intelligence of the reader.

Acknowledgments

ANA MARÍA BEJARANO, political scientist, coauthor of *Elecciones y democracia en Colombia* and *Al filo del caos*, and a specialist on the Venezuelan and Colombian constitutions, became the chronicler of the colloquium in Cuernavaca, with useful comments for every participant. Jorge Zepeda, recipient of the María Moors Cabot Award for Journalism (1999), also participated, as did Tomás Eloy Martínez, not only as director of the Rutgers University Program in Latin American Studies (RULAS), but as an essayist, *cronista*, cofounder of the *Fundación para el Nuevo Periodismo Latinoamericano*, and novelist who has authored, among other texts, *La novela de Perón*, *La mano del amo*, and *Santa Evita*.

Without the collaboration of Katherine Goldman (coordinator) and Boris Muñoz (press secretary) of the Center for Hemispheric Studies, both in Cuernavaca and in the research previous to the event, as well as its organization, the colloquium would not have been possible; nor would it have been possible without the support of Gabriela Mora, professor of literature of the department of Spanish and Portuguese at Rutgers and acting chairperson of RULAS, who dedicated invaluable time and effort as co-organizer of the colloquium. Beatriz Oropeza, from RULAS, always knew how to solve the practical problems.

I also want to recognize Rutgers University's support for the colloquium "Culture, Citizenship, and Urban Violence in Latin America," and that of the foundation of the Center for Hemispheric Studies, especially that offered by Richard Foley, former dean of the Faculty of Arts and Sciences; Ziva Galili, vice dean of the Graduate School; and Seth Gopin, director of Global Studies. I would also like to thank the individuals and organizations who provided economic support for this project at its various stages: the Ford Foundation, as part of its Writers at the Border program, Suzanne Bilello and the Freedom Forum, the Strategic Resource and Opportunity Analysis Allocations (SROA) of Rutgers University, the Program in Latin American Studies (RULAS), and Carl Kirschner, dean of Rutgers College.

Mary Belfrage's hospitality in Cuernavaca was essential to the original event's spirit of exchange and productive camaraderie. The translations of the texts from the original Spanish to English were provided by Katherine Goldman, Jennifer French, Heather Hammett, and Laura Middlebrooks; translations from Portuguese to Spanish by Clélia Donovan. Alejandra Marín is responsible for transcribing the recordings of the colloquium's proceedings, and Eileen Crowley edited the English version of the text in its entirety. Jorge Balán's generous offer to provide an introduction is greatly appreciated, as is the dedication of Marlie Wasserman of Rutgers University Press.

I would like to personally recognize Jean Franco, Erna von der Walde and my students, interlocutors of these reflections; and Richard Foley and Tomás Eloy Martínez, who gave their enthusiastic and concrete support to this project from the beginning, so that the social, cultural, and political urgencies discussed here could find a common space for reflection and publication, in an attempt to close the gap that tends to divide universities, researchers, and the community.

Publisher's Note

Susana Rotker had virtually completed her work on this book when she died in an automobile accident. Final details of manuscript preparation were handled by Katherine Goldman, Tomás Eloy Martínez, and administrators and staff from the Faculty of Arts and Sciences at Rutgers University. The publisher thanks Susana's family, friends, and colleagues for making this book a reality.

Citizens of Fear

Introduction

JORGE BALÁN

IMAGINE LOS ANGELES. I mean Los Angeles of the early 1990s, when in a single week seventeen thousand *saqueadores* (looters) and *incendiarios* (arsonists) were detained, and a much larger but unspecified number of undocumented Latino immigrants fled the city or were handed by the police to the INS for immediate deportation, following the most violent civil disturbance in urban America during this century. Imagine Los Angeles as described by Mike Davis in his *Ecology of Fear*, which tells the story of the "invisible" riot, "driven primarily by empty bellies and broken dreams, not by outrage over the acquittal of the cops who beat Rodney King."[1] In these Latino neighborhoods, where the worst California recession in five decades had brought unemployment, hunger, and a public health emergency, "the riot arrived like a magic dispensation . . . as a call to participate in the general distribution of wealth in progress."[2]

Davis also tells us the story of fear in the aftermath of the riots. Slumlords organize squads of armed mercenaries to exterminate crime on their premises. Wrought-iron bars and grates are installed in more than 100,000 inner-city homes, following the lead of liquor and convenience stores. Signboards saying "Have gun, will shoot" hang from some of these iron-barred windows. Schools, where students are regularly checked for weapons by metal detectors, look like prisons. Public housing projects are thoroughly controlled by the housing authority police, who seriously restrict residents' freedom of movement, routinely stopping and searching tenants without probable cause. The ecology of the inner ring in Los Angeles now shows "drug-free zones" and "gang-free parks," while neighborhood watch groups protect the blue-collar suburbs in the second ring. The more affluent live in gated neighborhoods in the outer rings. The new surveillance technology allows video monitoring of office buildings and shopping centers, while the rich spend fortunes on electronic guardian angels. At the edge of the city, the prison population, propelled by "zero tolerance" and the "three-strike rule," grows dramatically.

Now try the following mental exercise. Imagine cities of similar size, but with a median income per capita as low as one-tenth that of Los Angeles, such as Mexico City, Bogotá, Caracas, or Rio de Janeiro. Unemployment and precarious jobs, malnutrition, high-density housing and poor transportation, unsafe and irregular water supply are chronic among a majority of the population, not necessarily the result of an economic recession. Still, people have dreams. In fact, the poor include a large number of recent arrivals to the city searching for a better life. Many come from smaller towns or the countryside, pushed by lack of opportunities. Others come from neighboring countries where jobs are even scarcer and wages lower. A number may have escaped from the violence unleashed by rural guerrillas, armed forces, and paramilitary groups, drug lords, or a combination thereof. The urban ecology, though, may vary significantly from the classic U.S. city made up of rings, with areas relatively well demarcated by class and race boundaries and areas in transition, or as in a Los Angeles, organized to control violence and calm fear. Although the Latin American cities also have areas well defined by social class (as in Rio de Janeiro, with a southern more affluent zone and a northern zone with lower income and more polluting industries), the rich and the poor often live side-by-side in the better areas of town. Many of the poor make a living from selling all kinds of goods and services to the rich—washing their clothes and cars, keeping their gardens, guarding their streets. Public transportation is bad and often expensive. Dense settlements as close as possible to where jobs are available—on the steep hills or in easily flooded low areas or otherwise rejected urban spaces—are highly esteemed locations for the urban poor.

Let your imagination wander a bit further. Latin American cities that provide limited and inefficient public services with an obvious bias favoring the middle classes—not necessarily the upper-income groups, who have always resorted to the private sector for health, education, and security—are also attempting to balance the budget in the face of a fiscal crisis. Public employment, up to one-third of the formally employed work force, is under fire. Subsidized public services, even if essential, are reduced or privatized. Most children in the city attend school for at least a few years, but school days are short and further reduced by teachers' strikes in response to declining salaries and worsening labor conditions. Public hospitals and neighborhood clinics, a benefit of city life compared to life in the countryside, have gone into "cost recovery," although fees seldom resolve the lack of essential elements, overcrowding, and low-quality services. Private consumers demand more electricity, with the now widespread use of home appliances, including television, but power failures become more common and rates go up. Public transportation, always less than reliable, becomes more expensive as gasoline subsidies are lifted and services are privatized.

Now you need to really stretch your imagination. The city you are envisioning is also recovering from war. A special kind of war, a dirty war against internal enemies hard to identify, since they seldom wore uniforms and they spoke the same language and looked in all significant ways like the soldiers and policemen sent to annihilate them. The resemblance was accentuated by the fact that policemen and soldiers often were sent to fight without a uniform, responded to unwritten orders, and were not subject to any form of civilian control. In fact, armed men (at times, women too) on both sides resorted to looting, extortion, kidnapping, or other uses of their military might to sustain themselves. The war might have lasted a long time, maybe over a decade. Its end might have been announced publicly more than once, yet a peace treaty was never signed. The scars left by thousands dead or "disappeared," tortured, or imprisoned are reopened and memories of fear are reawakened by the continued presence of armed groups operating in the city. The war years have left a permanent imprint of mistrust in the relations between security forces, poorly paid and trained, and the population.

This exercise of imagination produces a composite view of many real Latin American cities, large and small, at the end of the twentieth century. These are the scenes of violence dealt with in this book. As in the urban United States, the action is reproduced daily on TV screens and in the press, for millions of viewers and readers. It mixes with scenes of fiction produced in Hollywood, often difficult to distinguish from reality. In fact, producers and market specialists in the media call both "entertainment." The culture of violence in the mass media feeds into popular imaginings and behavior in everyday life. The Latin American daily experience of violence is anchored in the open warfare between drug dealers and security forces that invades urban public space covered by the media daily.

Drug-free zones and gang-free parks, as well as closed-circuit surveillance in shopping malls, are for the upper-income groups only. The majority of the population has learned to survive in high-risk environments. Crime and violence, even if pervasive, are threats to be dealt with. Neighborhoods are often organized: squatters, tenants, or small property owners, shopkeepers and consumers, often associate to defend their rights and watch out for intruders. Regional associations, organizing migrant families from the same towns and villages, are powerful forces in some of these cities. It is not unheard of for organized neighborhoods to make deals with drug dealers to enforce some degree of order. Local governments and politicians recognize their strength, especially when elections are scheduled. Security forces, rather than protecting the populace, may often be seen as absent or, even worse, threatening.

Although cities also provide opportunities, intractable problems have accompanied rapid urban growth, threatening the social order in Latin American cities for decades. Urban violence, whether of a political nature (as in riots, insurgency, rebellion, or civil war) or based on ethnic, religious, or other local conflicts—and often mixed and confused with outright criminal behavior—fostered demands for security which fragile democracies could seldom meet. Authoritarian governments that followed these democracies, often seeking legitimacy based on those demands, reinforced perceptions of a widespread violent threat. As observed during the military dictatorship of Pinochet in Chile, the urban population might have been more afraid of the growth of delinquency and drugs than of unemployment or political repression.

Upon analyzing the authoritarian political regimes of the 1970s and 1980s, Latin American social scientists developed the concept of a culture of fear to describe the daily experience of confronting human rights violations in the Southern Cone. They saw the culture of fear not just as a product of authoritarianism but also as an element fostering its continuity.[3] As Norbert Lechner put it, "Authoritarianism deepens the vital need for order and presents itself as the only solution."[4] Authoritarian regimes responded to the fears by appropriating them. To justify police controls and the arbitrary use of power in everyday life, they created a climate of uncertainty and chaos.

The transition to democratic regimes and their consolidation in some countries initially fostered hopes for a decline in violence, repression, and generalized fears. Unfortunately, this has seldom been the case. On the contrary, there are indications that these democracies have dealt ineffectively with their citizens' needs and fears. Rooted in the daily experience of uncertainty and threat and reinforced by the lack of trust in the rule of law, fear became even more widespread in the urban population. Fear is now as much a threat to democracy as violence itself, since it may again justify repression, emergency policies that circumvent the constitutional rule, and, more broadly, alienation from the democratic political process.

For many people, living in a Latin American city today is a terror-filled experience. Where they look for the familiar and reassuring, they encounter now the dreadful and horrifying. Figures of authority, meant to protect, are seen as persecutors. Neighborhood streets, neighbors themselves, cannot be trusted. The schools, where mothers felt their children were nurtured and cared for, may suddenly be perceived as unsafe ground or the scene of violence. Even families, if one is to believe the unreliable statistical evidence on domestic violence, become less and less familiar, more and more terrifying. Fear, which at times can be a healthy reaction to danger, triggering self-protective behavior, instead produces paralysis. In the extreme, confronted with the too horrifying, people die of fear.

Urban residents of these fragile democracies have become citizens of fear. This is the underlying hypothesis of this collective effort led by Susana Rotker, building upon a rich diversity of disciplines, theoretical outlooks, and styles. The volume provides a wealth of description and thought-provoking interpretations of the contemporary urban scene in Latin America, with a focus on the various forms of violence and the subjective correlate of fear among its citizens. The book suggests the potential for a comparative research agenda on contemporary urban violence and fear, an agenda that could fruitfully use careful documentation and analysis in cities of the South as well as the North. Fear and violence, often evoked by governments and public opinion when dealing with organized crime, drug and arms traffic, and terrorism, have truly become global.

Susana Rotker and I discussed how best to introduce this scholarly product to the English-speaking public only days before her untimely death. We both felt that translation by itself, a difficult task indeed, was not enough. This introduction, with all its limitations, was meant to make this Latin American discourse somewhat more accessible to the North American reader.

Notes

1. Davis, *Ecology of Fear*, 372.
2. Ibid., 373.
3. Corradi et al., *Fear at the Edge*.
4. Lechner, *Los patios interiores de la democracia*, 90 (my translation).

Cities Written by Violence

SUSANA ROTKER

An Introduction

How do we talk about the fear in Latin America's major cities? Fear is as inexpressible a sensation as human pain, and yet there are places where fear is an experience of everyday life. One way of facing the fear of social violence is to approach the city as if it were a text: a text with omissions, repetitions, and characters; with dialogues, spaces, and periods and commas. It is a text written by the city's inhabitants, even though they cannot read it themselves.[1]

Numbers flesh out the story of fear in the cities: 15 out of every 100,000 inhabitants are killed each year in Latin America. This is a conservative estimate, as all averages are—one that lowers accuracy and betrays reality by including both the least violent areas and the most brutalized. Such a scandalous statistic becomes truly nightmarish if one considers that the death toll in Colombia rises to 100 for every 100,000 citizens. The feeling of civic helplessness is aggravated by the impunity of such aggression: in Mexico, for example, 97 percent of all reported crimes go unpunished.[2] This is the first evidence we have that the urban text of fear is written with bodies. Without the help of symbolic elaboration and language, the story fashions itself out of the numbers of the dead.[3]

Yet numbers do nothing but accumulate, and they are, therefore, a poor means of depicting reality, contradicting the inherited rationalist Enlightenment tradition in which the only form of knowledge was that of quantifying language.[4] With a little research, the numbers begin to pile up: about 140 thousand people die violently each year in Latin America; a street attack occurs every twenty-four minutes.[5] In Caracas, there are five thousand homicides each year, the same number of people that perish in earthquakes. It is estimated that each "Venezuelan between the age of eighteen and sixty will be the victim of seventeen crimes, four of which will be violent."[6]

Numbers are the first resource for communicating the experience of excessive social violence. Without them, one cannot believe the daily accounts of horror, but they quickly become hollow with repetition, like a worn-out song. In the face of impotent statistics, the testimonial steps forward as witness. When objective facts fail to tell the whole story, we resort to the most primitive and primal way of knowing, the subjective, the personal: this is what happened to me, this is how I survived.

Violence produces crises in all aspects of life, even in communicating.[7] Individuals search for ways to articulate their experiences, telling their stories again and again. Whether to exorcise their trauma or to explain the political and economic situation that caused it, the complexity of violence can only be fully comprehended when spoken of between two people—an apparent anachronism in the era of high-tech globalization.

In the face of violence, logic and morality are turned upside down. They acquire a rationality that goes beyond simple demarcations of good and bad. This is what Martha Huggins finds when studying Brazilian torturers, noting that they are viewed as state professionals. It is as if we could bridge the abyss between rational language and deteriorating meaning by anchoring ourselves in the language of subjectivity and emotions; such a contradiction thickens the fog of daily paranoia. In this haze there are few clear images: one is of a poor person, often represented within these social/textual imaginaries as a criminal. Yet the image of victim is reproduced in every social stratum, and not only because this reflects reality. Although wealth does not necessarily guarantee protection from violence, in a community of devastating need it is enough to appear rich by having more than others, whether it be a car, a job, a television, or a house in a neighborhood one step above the slums.[8] This is explained by one of the characters who appears in the chronicle "Trash Called Human Being" by Alberto Salcedo:

What I'm saying is that it doesn't seem to me like a man who
has a goddamn car is poor. We're the poor ones, we who were
born in shit, live in shit and know what shit smells like. Not
those sons of bitches who come around here driving cool cars,
challenging us on our own turf. The guy who wants to live
peacefully, let him go find peace somewhere else. Or do you
think that we're all happy and peaceful in this fucking country,
in this fucking world we ended up in? [9]

In the majority of countries over half the crimes committed occur
in big cities. Thus, it is the rare city dweller who has not yet been trau-
matized by a violent attack and who does not already have a list of pre-
cautions to take when "there is no other choice" but to go out—every
day. It is with this in mind that Carlos Monsiváis asks, "At what point
is violence assigned the role of *deus ex machina* as the fatal synonym for
urban destiny?"[10] The city has been transformed into a space of vulnerability and danger. Or, as Néstor García Canclini puts it: "It is evident
that the real city cannot be narrated, described or explained as it was
at the beginning of last century. The feeling of living together in the
capital was structured in terms of shared historical landmarks and an
approachable space—in everyday travels—by everyone in the city."[11]
It is the city as landscape for melodrama, assimilated for tragedy, like
the space of fatalism that presents itself primarily through the media,
as if there were no alternatives. This is how Monsiváis sees it, as the
space of an ethical response to violence that, diluted by melodrama,
has become complicit with violence.[12]

The Story

One out of every three citizens in Latin America has been directly or
indirectly victimized by violence; it should not surprise us that those
who inhabit the most dangerous cities in the hemisphere offer their personal experiences of suffering time and time again. This book includes
stories of urban violence by José Roberto Duque, José Navia, and
Alberto Salcedo. Written in the form of journalistic chronicles, they
bear witness to the immediate accessibility of the personal story at a
moment in which reality—and the analysis of that reality—seem
overwhelming.

It is important to note that the personal anecdote—especially the chronicle—can be understood as a first-hand elaboration, unlike the specialized studies on urban violence (sociological, criminological, anthropological, or cultural) that lamentably tend to be relegated to the field of the specialist and are thus incapable of opening up professional discourse. These chronicles are also a form of autonomization: a narrative performance that uses techniques of storytelling to show how much those very stories do not say.[13] Nonetheless, although the chronicle is an exceptional genre in which literature and journalism meet, it continues to occupy a marginalized place within literary and journalistic establishments.

Chronicles—and here we find one aspect of the extraordinary importance of chronicles written about violence—combine the urgency usually found in oral histories with an ingenious way of inviting a response or demanding answers. "Response" is used only in the sense given in this text: in the crisis of meaning produced by violence, spoken and marginalized forms of knowledge begin to weave new networks of representation that, ultimately, must be addressed—responded to. The media, with their tendency to magnify or distort the understanding of reality, in addition to their status as the only public space in which daily life is still represented to some degree, both do and do not enter into these new forms of representation. The chronicle makes itself at home within journalism, but it is not always a polite guest. Its hybrid form permits it a (potentially rebellious) value of autonomization in the system of representation while simultaneously allowing it to enjoy the prestige of the space in which it is published: the press as vehicle for exchange and identification, constructor and diffuser of discourses and symbols.[14]

It does not go without saying that the media has started to make up for the state system—at least in collective imaginaries—which has become incompetent when it comes to facing corruption and social violence. The media acts as both the prosecutor who makes accusations and the judge who responds to the very same charges, since the legal order operates with impunity, or, as Nancy Cardia says with more precision, with *selective* impunity. The media's role in the configuration of urban imaginaries, among them the imaginary of fear, is addressed by some of the most important communications scholars in Latin America, such as Jesús Martín Barbero, Carlos Monsiváis, and Rossana Reguillo. Cardia and Sergio Adorno also take into account the discrepancies between the current statistics and the images of young people that the media broadcast. Other trends include the sensationalist or populist media's tendency to single out immigrants as the cause of the fear, and the aforementioned systematic criminalization of the poor. In addition, the media often generate erroneous perceptions of crime. For example, as Ana María Sanjuán argues, reporting the week's crimes on Monday creates the illusion that important and violent crimes only occur on the weekends.

Imprecise data worsens the situation because the resulting sense of insecurity has a concrete impact on daily life. It is the inverse of the rational order, the tangible and the combatable; the impression multiplies the effects of violence. One of the most urgent tasks facing writers and researchers is to produce and disseminate precise data, simply because most Latin American countries have deficient mechanisms for reporting violence. It is certainly interesting to note that facts about violence are usually published in the form of public opinion polls, a few specialized studies (most of which, in turn, are based on the media and opinion polls), and, more recently, first-person accounts of violent crime, whether witnessed or experienced as its victim. Seen in this light, "rational" knowledge of violence is being created in part by these stories, by subjectivity.

The Crisis of Symbols

In a brilliant analysis of the "crisis of the popular," Jean Franco defines "crisis" in a way that is perfectly applicable to a society disconcerted by violence.[15] Franco points out that the "crisis of terminology" and the "placing in crisis of Enlightenment discourse" by the periphery and the marginalized are producing fissures in the order of Western knowledge. She also mentions—and this is what interests me in terms of these reflections—"the problem of representation within the neo-liberal societies, where social stratification is understood in terms of consumption and social movements are capable of surpassing class borders." In this reality, consumption has less to do with productivity than the symbolic exhibition of "the good life." People can no longer count on the upward mobility once supposedly gained by work and effort; the limits blur in the complicities of fear and insecurity. The other scandal, that of societies in which 60 to 80 percent of the population is malnourished, remains untouched. But like a powder keg ready to explode, no one knows which direction they will go in.

In this culture of transgression, corruption, and want, one can die over a pair of Nike sneakers. "You have to take care of your sneakers because that's your image," says one of those interviewed by Boris Muñoz and José Roberto Duque in *The Law of the Street*. He goes on to detail a murder caused by jealousy over clothes: "The thing with Chaveto was over some damn pair of Nikes. He had seen me a couple of times with my Charles Barkleys, my Bull Jacksons and my Black Points. I've always used brand names and I've never had a problem because of it." As Vallejo says in *La virgen de los sicarios*: "How can anyone murder for a pair of tennis shoes? you, a foreigner, will ask. Mon cher ami, it's not because of the shoes: it's about the principles of Justice that we all believe in. The person who is going to get mugged thinks it's unfair that they rob him because he paid for them; the one who robs him thinks it's unfair that he doesn't have a pair himself."[16]

The discourse has ceased to be that of class struggle and alludes now to the ephemeral possession of a few status symbols of well-being, made worse by the rise in drug use.

Citizenship

For an analysis of citizens' fear or, stated more clearly, the citizenship of fear, it is fitting to begin by focusing on major Latin American cities as representational spaces with a profound anchoring in the real. It is not necessary to gaze into the kaleidoscopic possibilities of terror because, in the face of the risk lived day to day with and in the bodies of those who practice the city (the expression is de Certeau's), what is real is that there are eighteen countries in this social space called Latin America, and the spectrum of terror does not cover all of them equally. Furthermore, people (the practitioners of urban space) continue living: in the midst of this undeclared war, people continue to celebrate their birthdays, visit each other, work, have children, and love each other as always. Habits and geographies are modified, tranquility or faith is lost, but some forms of happiness endure.[17]

What I am interested in narrating here is the very thing that makes it difficult to describe: the generalized sense of fear that taints Latin American capitals—that feeling that has continued to change the ways in which people relate to urban space, to other human beings, to the state, and to the very concept of citizenship. Capitals, like every text and space, are social practices. Perhaps because of this we should refer instead to habits of fear, habits or practices that have more to do with everyday worries. In addition to the insecurity produced by the possibility of being mugged or kidnapped, there are the added fears shared by the citizens of every country, rich nations and poor ones, due to globalization. These include job and income insecurity, health and environmental problems, hunger, the drug trade, ethnic conflicts, social disintegration, terrorism, and the migrations that disfigure cities, deterritorializing the sense of belonging that the former residents once had.[18] Raquel Sosa analyzes these problems in what was until recently the single-party political system of Mexico, attributing to it the responsibility for what she calls invisible power.

Today, circumscribing the topic of fearful citizenship presents a challenge to the way in which the terms of the ideological apparatus, the role of the state, and the formation of subjectivity have been consolidated up until now.

Perhaps instead of talking about fear, it is better to talk about *practices of insecurity* that redefine relationships with power, fellow citizens, and space. It is necessary, then, to analyze two ideas mentioned in the title of this book: fear and citizenship. Several concepts of citizenship could be used: from that which arose in the principles of the French Revolution, with its slogans of fraternity, liberty, and equality, to more modern notions of the right to represent or be represented by other members of the same community. More interesting, however, are the Aristotelean ideas we have inherited: it was known that very few societies are capable of true equality, and thus it was stipulated that only those citizens with the right to speak (a right defined by property, education, and gender) could belong to the *polis*, the governing body for defining laws, for deciding which ones to follow and which ones to enforce.[19] In antiquity the concept of *citizen* was built upon speech and (exclusionary) contracts in a society of equals, whereas the modern concept deals with a society of difference (also exclusionary) that, despite those differences, should be egalitarian and united.

It is thanks to Foucault that we think of citizenship as constructed by devices, mechanisms, and tactics of a rational and disciplinary society. One of the problems begins with a sense of latent irrationality, accompanied by shattered faith in social institutions that have ceased to function both in terms of solving problems and maintaining credibility. As Ana María Sanjuán explains, it is the loss of control caused by social violence that constitutes the principal threat to the democratic *ethos*. The topic of social cohesion appears to be the natural space for the control of social epidemics.

Other definitions of what it means to be a citizen are of interest to us here. Hannah Arendt affirms that every human being has a right to have rights; Elizabeth Jelin says that an ethics of citizenship rests on a premise of nonviolence, a premise that no one should suffer or be harmed.[20] Both definitions reveal just how fractured the concept of (and feelings about) citizenship can be in contemporary Latin America, even if we set aside the fact that the contracts of citizenship signed during the years of Latin American Independence in the spirit of the French Revolution never really implemented equality or extended citizens' rights to the entire population. If this were not so, the depressing rates of hunger, unemployment, and marginality in the hemisphere would not be what they are today.

Citizenship of Fear / Fearful Citizenship

The portrait of daily life in urban Latin America depicts a feeling of generalized defenselessness and the risk of paralysis (the stance that it is "better to do nothing" in order to avoid danger or, in the end, because it just isn't worth it). At the other extreme is the possible social production of repressive mechanisms to stem the loss of control. This last option is not a viable one: on the one hand, the social experience of authoritarianism in Latin America has always been lamentable, and on the other, people no longer believe in the honesty or efficacy of the police or the military. José Roberto Duque summarizes the abuses perpetrated by such parties in his chronicle, typically brimming with humor and pain, "Running into the Authorities Is All It Takes to Get to Heaven."

Conventional discourse has been exhausted and no longer serves convincingly to mitigate the extremely serious economic problems that besiege the continent. Nor does it ameliorate the even graver social consequences of corruption, decaying political parties and their traditional platforms, deteriorating institutions, lack of faith in the judicial system, unbridled consumerism inaugurated en masse by neoliberalism (citizens or employees who were once judged by their capacity to produce are now thought of as consumers), unemployment, job insecurity, and vulnerability to crime. The violence portrayed here only engenders paralysis, spurs on more violence or the need to find "something" or somebody, perhaps a charismatic leader carrying with him all the consequence of fantasy and disappointment. This "something" might in some way give coherence to the discursive order of political practice by fusing the representational with institutional structures, but only at great cost.

If the unraveling of the social fabric discussed here were to occur in a tribal society, an anthropologist would probably note the need to create a new kinship system to replace the dysfunctional one. In communities suffering from ever increasing social violence—especially during the last two decades of the twentieth century—change would have to begin with rethinking the social contract, the models of solidarity or the cultural/symbolic construction of a deteriorating system that produces more fissures than it fills. The fissures are structural, discursive, and political. But violence remains registered in the flesh itself. Violence rewrites the conditions of citizenship on the exposed body and creates the *potential victim*.

The urban situation compels even the theorists of discourse and the ideological structures of power to revise known postulates, because fear has created a new form of subjectivity. It is not the fear manipulated by the military, torturers, or dictators in order to reassert their control over the people; nor does that of the ideological models of unconscious social behavior suffice. A body's own wisdom and survival instinct against everyday fear serve more than mechanical discursive practices.[21] One perhaps oversimplified but illustrative example is the following: when a police officer yells for a passerby to stop, the passerby obeys because he has incorporated the entire system of laws and values that the uniform represents. But this is a poor example when the individual in question decides that he just doesn't feel like stopping (which can happen, and does), or when the passerby decides that it is as dangerous to stop for the police as it is to encounter someone who looks like a criminal.

Even in Caracas, where the police address pedestrians or drivers as "Citizen," the citizen has precaution inscribed in his body, from which a system of attitudes and responses originates. Body memory, as it is analyzed by Allen Feldman, involves a situation in which social space and the social body continually inform each other, both tied to violence and the dynamic problem of control and response ("agentism") in a nonmonolithic relationship of social markers such as class, ideology, or race.[22] Few places manifest the relationship between violence, space, and body as do jails. Yolanda Salas writes about the "blood strikes" of prisoners in Caracas who began protesting by sewing their lips together, refusing to eat. When they saw that their silence was useless, they started to cut themselves as a sign of protest against abuse. This chilling expression of protest has been described by Duque in his chronicle "The Innocents' Uproar," published in *El Nacional* on May 2, 1999: "A strike has broken out in the El Dorado jail. Nothing special; fifty inmates have declared a blood strike. And what is that? Well, you cut yourself up and if they don't meet your demands, you bleed to death. The prisoners had already patented the act of sewing their lips together in order to force a hunger strike, but the problem was that in addition to being unable to eat, they were also unable to talk."

Salas studies the compensatory system in jails; by doing so she revives the inmates' subjectivity and reveals them to be human beings who have been reified and animalized by cultural mechanisms of representation, that which Merleu-Ponty calls "giving shape to the world."

Let us return now to the common citizen, to the potential victim, to the one who ought to articulate this fear. *Potential victims* are all of those who could be killed at any given moment because they could fetch a big ransom, because they wear brand-name shoes, because the assailant—who made a bet with his friends—fired his gun by mistake. The potential victim is middle class, wealthy, or poor: it is anyone who goes out and is afraid, afraid because everything is rotting and out of control, because there is no control, because no one believes in anything anymore.

That no one believes in anything is, in reality, a way to allude to the definition of subjectivity in terms of its relationship to the state, to power, and probably to the institutions that constitute citizenship but that no longer guarantee the minimal right to move about or to be free from physical harm. And this is perhaps the most serious aspect of this crisis because, as de Certeau has asserted, the credibility of discourse is what makes believers act.[23] In fact, social practices depend on an ethical construct that is supported by what Zizek calls a certain "as if" (we act *as if* we believe in bureaucratic omnipotence, *as if* the president embodies the will of the people, *as if* truth could be found in the law). In the end, ideology is an illusion or a collection of cultural assumptions and practices that structure, camouflage, order, and simplify our social relationships as if they were effective and real.[24] This is a grave problem—and one that has still not been measured at the community level. When this as if stops being believable, what type of imaginaries, relationships, subjectivities will replace it?

Accustomed as we have been, in another era, to representing reality in terms of class struggle, and now in terms of ethnic or sexual minorities, we forget that going out into the street is a daily adventure in fear in many cities. We forget that today this fear shapes the most profound truths. It is an undeclared war that pits everybody against everybody else; it is a struggle of everyone for himself. As Jesús Martín Barbero so aptly puts it, you can't trust anyone who looks at you for more than a few seconds. This undeclared war is, in another sense, a civil war in which there are no safe spaces, no places of refuge, no patriotic slogans, no programmed proclamations, no directions, and no medium-range or long-term goals.

Before continuing with the idea of the citizen-victim, it is important however to stop briefly and consider this image of civil war. Elaine Scarry ascribes to wars both a body and a voice: the body is that which exposes itself, ready to hurt others and kill in the name of an idea. The idea belongs to what Scarry calls the voice: the language, the system of representation that authorizes, motivates, justifies, and mobilizes a war.[25] But social violence is, upon first reading, pure body: it *does not* have an organized voice that moves or justifies it, nor is it valued as a form of resistance. Resistance movements have one voice that allows them to shine and mobilize in defense of common interests, traditionally taking the form of strikes, marches, political groups, and even musicals. And yet, upon further consideration, social violence is a practical re-reading of urban spaces and of the terms in which citizens' rights are regulated.

If society can be understood in terms of the human body, in which every individual is a "member" (head, heart, legs, arms), what slowly emerges is a whole being, a body with its own illnesses, equilibrium, deviations, and abnormalities.[26] Cities, too, have their ailments, cancerous zones that should be excised, or at least isolated to specific neighborhoods. Modernity divided the large cities into clearly marked areas: high and low, clean and dirty. Although these zones still exist, they are overpopulated, with contemporary violence destabilizing all of their margins, penetrating neighborhoods, and erasing bodies and members.

Violence rewrites the text of the city and the rules of the game. It should be understood as a form of resistance that no longer attacks the powers that be, but instead crosses borders and space, erasing the boundaries that separate the outside from the inside. Steve Pile and Michael Keith propose the following analysis: the tactics of resistance have at least two levels of attack—one looks to the map of power, the other to the intangible, the invisible, the unconscious desires, pleasures, joys, fears, rage and hope, "the very stuff of politics."[27] This undeclared civil war in major Latin American cities clearly engages elements of fear and rage, but it is no longer a question of planting bombs or hiding in the mountains to take up arms against a dictator or corrupt government. It deals instead with a violence that resists the whole system, cracking it in a more profound way, at the heart of its social relations. As it makes victims of us all, this undeclared civil war obliterates spaces of difference and differentiation, making all of us experience injustice, insecurity, and inequality.

Several of those who collaborated on this book explain this by starting from the topos of the victim. Alberto Concha-Eastman defines the victim as "any person who has suffered a physical, mental or emotional injury, economic loss or substantial damage to his or her fundamental rights individually or collectively, through acts or omissions that violate laws that operate in each state." Eduardo Pizarro Leongómez—explaining the intensity of violence in Colombia and what he calls the partial collapse of the state in that country—insightfully uses the term "diffuse violence." Habits change, and, as Nancy Cárdia observes, people (the practitioners of the city) move elsewhere, stop using public transportation, retire from community life, and become more fearful of the stereotypical "stranger," "poor person," and "teenager." According to Rossana Reguillo, a community is created in three stages: fear is experienced individually, it becomes socially constructed, and, finally, it becomes culturally shared. She also alludes to geographies of fear: the practical, unpublished urban maps that inhabitants use to avoid historic districts or markets, drawn in accordance with the common knowledge of where danger lies. Young people are strangers in their own city, since shopping centers are the only places left to socialize besides the route between school and home.

Martín Barbero talks about the city as something strange, the denial of citizenry by the denial of the city, the redefinition of urban movement, and the reterritorialization of politics, the redefinition of citizen conduct. And so the central, unanswerable question of this volume remains: How does one conquer fear with civil solutions?

According to Plato, original and foundational violence is that which violates one's rights over one's own property; therefore, in order to be a citizen (in his words, an Athenian), one must refrain from using someone else's property without permission. These are old Western concepts: violence and property. But property and humanity should not be confused, whether in Plato's Athens or in the text written in the bodies of city dwellers who suffer the worst deaths and fear in the world due to a practical confusion of definitions—in this region where people sing, among laughter, mariachis, and love, that life is worth nothing.

The question for the community is not, therefore, how to think about fear or how to narrate it, but how to defeat it: body *to* body or body *with* body, and not body *against* body. In any case, there is no turning away, whether out of discomfort, indifference, or ineptitude. Because we are all, potentially, citizens of fear.

TRANSLATED BY LAURA MIDDLEBROOKS
AND KATHERINE GOLDMAN

Notes

1. De Certeau, *The Practice of Everyday Life*, 98.
2. According to Elena Azaola Garrido, of every one hundred crimes reported, fifty are investigated, eight end in arrest and prosecution, and only three end with a prison sentence. Thus the 97 percent impunity rate. See her article "Notes on Juvenile Delinquency."
3. In spite of the immensity of the problem in everyday life, up until now there has been on the continent little literary production that is concerned with or manages to condense in some way fear or social violence. The lack is significant; this investigation proposes to name some of the books, both to provide information to the interested reader and to recognize the authors. Literary production does not refer to studies, recompilations of documents, or interviews, obviously, if literature, by way of fiction, has successfully narrated any aspect of reality. A good example of what a text can achieve by penetrating the lives of marginalized neighborhoods without totally adhering to the norms of realism and mimesis is Colombian Laura Restrepo's novel, *Dulce compañía* (Sweet company). Although there are a few other literary works, they are not always known throughout the continent or have not all achieved the temporal synthesis of a collective imaginary of the 1970s and 1980s known as "magical realism," expressed so well in Gabriel García Márquez's Macondo in *One Hundred Years of Solitude*. Violence has supplanted the recognition of the collective identity of explanations of the "magically real," but nothing has replaced it. Even so, the coincidence or the switching of terms is significant: from the story "Un hombre muy viejo con unas alas enormes" we are left with Duque's chronicle, "Un hombre muy duro con unos hierros enormes," a story of a homicide assault.
4. A now classic study of quantifiable language is Jean Starobinski's "1789 et la langue des principes," especially page 22.
5. The numbers are overwhelming: a World Bank study of sixty-nine countries shows that Latin Americans are most worried about robbery and other crimes (see "Crime and Violence as Development Issues"). According to this study, 90 percent of the business owners interviewed have experienced crime as a serious problem; 80 percent admitted that they had no confidence in the state in terms of protecting their property or ensuring their personal safety. The most serious obstacles to investment and business are corruption, inadequate infrastructure, and robbery. The first of these, corruption, is simply another form of crime, differing only in that it is perpetrated by workers in the business sector. This statement on behalf of business people should not be considered an indication that they are the primary targets of social violence, although well-off people and most of the middle class may feel that they are more affected by violence. On the contrary, statistics show that the poor are the most likely victims. Perhaps there is an inverse relationship between age and risk, for risk increases notably as age decreases: young people of marginal neighborhoods are most vulnerable.
6. Domenico Chiappe and David González, "Los delitos aumentan y la denuncia disminuye" (Crime rises and complaints decrease), quoting the announcement by Luis Rivases, technical director of the National Security Agency. The following figures, no less significant, are added: the 630 crimes reported in Venezuela each day account for only 10 to 30 percent of all crimes committed. It is estimated that 70 to 90 percent of all crimes go unreported.
7. Violence reaches beyond the physical confines of the city. Organ theft, child

slavery, narcotic wars, millions of peasants uprooted at gunpoint in territorial disputes, the brutality of the drug trade, paramilitary groups, ethnic cleansing, and the desperate masses that illegally cross national borders looking for work and food are just a few of the many manifestations of violence.

8. Here I use the concept of the imaginary to mean a system of signifiers and symbolizations of a particular community, conceptualized by history, which is at once total and open. It is not the social imaginary in the Lacanian sense but that of Cornelius Castoridadis in *The Imaginary Institution of Society*, 56–61.

9. In a chronicle furnished by the author.

10. Monsiváis, "De no ser por el pavor que tengo" (If it weren't for my fear), 39.

11. García Canclini, *Consumidores y ciudadanos* (Consumers and citizens), 96.

12. See the essay by Monsiváis in this volume.

13. Among today's best writers on violence are Fernando Vallejo (Colombia), Juan Villoro and José Joaquín Blanco (Mexico), and Pedro Lemebel (Chile).

14. Ernesto Laclau and Chantal Mouffe see in autonomization the mutation of modes of representation or signifiers, a mutation that deauthorizes the ideological referents. See *Hegemony and Socialist Strategy*. The concept of autonomization that I use here—just as in the concept of imaginaries—coincides with that of Castoriardis and his value of opening, which he explains in *The Imaginary Institution of Society* in chapters 3, 6, and 7.

15. Franco, "La globalización y la crisis de lo popular" (Globalization and the crisis of the popular).

16. Duque and Muñoz, *La ley de la calle: Testimonios de jóvenes protagonistas de la violencia en Caracas* (The law of the street), 45, 40. Vallejo, *La virgen de los sicarios*, 68.

17. It is worth clarifying here if only to counteract—without denying all that has been said up to this point because that would be like trying to blot out the sun with a finger—the false image that the first world holds of Latin America as the traditional place of authoritarianism and barbarism. This is an image that doesn't take into account the fact that social violence has risen notably throughout the West, although the numbers may be directly related (not always, of course) to the level of prosperity the population is able to enjoy.

18. Job insecurity is also alarming: in Argentina, for example, where the unemployment rate is 20 percent, 60 percent of those who have a job fear losing it. According to the International Labor Organization, between 1971 to 1998—when regional governments liberalized laws regarding the movement of capital and commercial trade—seventeen countries showed a lower employment rate and lower salaries, and workers' buying power decreased 27 percent in the 1990s compared to the previous decade. Millions of *campesinos* remain without work, and hunger has increased. Traditionally an exporter of food, Latin America now must import it. In the last twenty years the debts of Latin American countries have increased four or six times. Although we must inevitably allude to economic and political policies, or try to look for explanations for instability or social violence, the objective of this essay is to try to think about or interpret—or better yet, to propose the need to find ways of thinking about or interpreting—everyday fear. Some especially useful studies about globalization are those edited by Brunner, *Globalización cultural y posmodernidad (Cultural globalization and postmodernity)*; Rorty, *Contigencia, ironía y solidaridad (Contingency, irony and solidarity)*; Bauman, *Postmodernity and Its Discontents*; and the impressive *Empire* by Hardt and Negri.

19. See "The Ideal of Citizenship" by Pocock, 29–52; also *Democracy*, edited by

Birnbaum, Lively, and Parry. Regarding the debilitating effect of authoritarian regimes on the concept of citizenship and civil society in the hemisphere, see Jelin and Hershberg, *Construir la democracia derechos humanos, cuidadanía y sociedad en América Latina (Constructing democracy)*.

20. Jelin and Herschberg, *Construir la democracia,* 124; Arendt, *The Origins of Totalitarianism.*
21. This is an example of the traditional Althusserian explanation of how ideology works. For more about the manipulation of fear as a form of power, see *Shamanism, Colonialism, and the Wild Man* by Taussig, 129.
22. Feldman, *Formations of Violence.*
23. De Certeau, *The Practice of Everyday Life,* 148.
24. Zizek, *The Sublime Object of Ideology,* 35–46.
25. Scarry, *The Body in Pain,* 62.
26. De Certeau, *The Practice of Everyday Life,* 142.
27. Pile and Keith, *Geographies of Resistance,* 16.

The Fears

The City

JESÚS MARTÍN-BARBERO

Between Fear and the Media

*I will speak of what I saw on the first day of the third
millennium of our era. I saw an open door and I entered
and saw the city . . . and yes, it was different: more
populous, swinging in the abyss, with video-clips that
exhorted couples to the demographic blessing of sterility.
And there were signs of plagues, death, weeping and
hunger. And there were more protests, more liberated
territories and occupied territories, more frustration and
resignation. And out of the corner of my eye I saw the
Beast with his seven heads and ten horns. And the people
applauded and took photographs and videos of him, and
recorded his exclusive statements, while the final knowledge came to me with a clarity that would turn hazy.*

—CARLOS MONSIVÁIS

In the Beginning There Was Chaos

IN CONTRAST TO THE narratives that identify chaos with disorder and
violence, chaos in the biblical tales precedes order and is designated as
that which will serve to form the cosmos, or in other words, the world.
Following that narrative of origins, the city is connected to Cain and
Abel. Cain, the murderer of his younger brother, Abel, has been condemned by God to wander and to wear on his forehead a mysterious
sign that, even as it marks him as an assassin, protects him from being
killed, and thus ensures that he who is condemned to err will build the
first city. Over time, men will try to construct a city that reaches the
sky but, condemning them again for their pride, God blurs the lan-

guages, hindering the construction of the city that will be built any-way, and that will be named Babel, which means confusion and disper-sion. In the Bible, the founding myths of the city could not be more expressive: while Cain's designates violence, Babel's designates disor-der. But, like chaos, both will also serve as the basis for the society that will find its form in the city.

Today, many cities seem damned by the gods, at least in terms of the abundant criminal influences that populate them and the confu-sion that marks them. But it is not only the number of murders or armed robberies that has made some of our cities the most chaotic and unsafe in the world, it is also the cultural anguish experienced by the majority of their inhabitants. When people live in a place that feels strange be-cause it refuses to know people and things, when one does not recog-nize oneself as from that place, one feels insecure. And insecurity makes even the most pacific people aggressive. Those of us who study the laby-rinths of urban culture do not limit ourselves to seeing only the injus-tice of the incessant reproduction of crime in violence. We see something else, something that leads us to consider not murder *in* the city but the murder *of* the city. The city dies when its memory is de-stroyed, when people are robbed of the reference points of their iden-tity, as has happened in Bogotá.

I arrived in that city in 1963, and when I walk there with my chil-dren now I realize that we are living in two completely different cities: the one that they see and the one that I remember. More than half of Bogotá is the city that I miss and a good part of the other half is the one I fight against. Few cities in the world have been so disrespectful to their memory. Of course crime grows, becomes professionalized, and scares us. But if fear makes us nervous and cowardly, it is distrust that makes us insecure. We do not feel insecure just because we are victim-ized. Perhaps the greater part of the aggressiveness that accumulates in this city develops in the opposite way: because we feel lost, we lack a sense of trust, and we accumulate a deaf rage—we don't even hear—against all of that which surrounds us. And this rage breaks forth with-out our even knowing why, shattering all of the learned and internalized urbanity. What urbanity or civility is possible in a city without ties of belonging?

The implosion of the private sphere represents the negation of citi-

zenship itself, since it begins with the negation of the city, which re-
lates back to the shrinking of the city as it is explored and enjoyed by
its inhabitants. The images of the city offered to us by the media, and
television in particular, corroborate this on a daily basis. Television is
the outlet that has become the vicarious but efficient link to a certain
mode of relating to the city. Some citizens of Bogotá distrust their city,
evade it, walk it as little as possible; for them, the images of the city
that television constructs serve, to a great extent, to reinforce imaginaries of fear. Until now the prevailing televised images of the city have
been incapable of going beyond the sensationalism and gruesomeness
of accidents and murders, of assaults and armed robberies. They are incapable of going beyond the chaos in which the camera—which cannot communicate even the most obvious criticism of the lack of
consideration for citizens' responsibilities—frequently delights.

The Labyrinths of Fear

In order to consider urban processes in Colombia as processes of communication, we must think about how the media has turned itself into
a part of the basic fabric of urbanity, and about how fears have recently
come to form an elemental part of the new processes of communication. Thus we see the need to confront two equally tenacious prejudices. One comes from the field of media studies, the other from experts
on violence and fear.

The first prejudice consists of the belief that one can understand
communication processes simply by studying the media, when what the
media does, what it produces in people, can only be understood in reference to the changes in urban modes of communication. In other
words, references to changes in the public space, in the relationships
between public and private, produce a new city where movement and
news are made more fluid, but less communication- and community-
oriented, every day—thus the ability to understand that the attraction
of television has much less to do with studying what television does
than with studying the processes and situations that compel people to
take shelter in the small space of the private and domestic and to project
security and protection onto it. If television attracts, it is, to a great
extent, because the street repels. The absence of the spaces—streets and

plazas—that facilitate communication makes television something more than an instrument of leisure. Television becomes a place of coming together, of vicarious encounters with the world, with people, and even with the city in which we live.

Confronting the second prejudice leads us to consider the idea that we cannot understand the meaning and magnitude of new fears by referring exclusively to the increase in violence, criminality, and danger in the streets. Since fears are fundamental to new modes of living and communicating, they are an expression of a deeper anguish, of cultural anguish. This anguish comes from two factors. First, it comes from the loss of collective roots in cities in which a savage urbanism—which also obeys a measure of formal and commercial rationality—slowly destroys, little by little, the landscape of familiarity in which collective memory might base itself.

Second, it is anguish produced by the way the city normalizes differences. It blames the media for homogenizing life when the strongest and most subtle homogenizing force is the city, which impedes the expression and growth of differences. We are left, of course, with the museums that fill up cities more every day: those places in which frozen differences are exhibited and to which we turn in order to nourish memory and nostalgia. By normalizing behaviors, the city, like buildings, erodes collective identities, blocks them, and this erosion robs us of our cultural ground and throws us into the void. This is where fear comes in.

Third, it is an anguish that comes from the order that the city imposes on us: it is a precarious, vulnerable, but efficient order. What is this order made of, and by what mechanisms does it function? Paradoxically, it is an order constructed with the uncertainty that the other produces in us, inculcating distrust in us each day toward those who pass by me on the street. Anyone on the street who passes by and makes a gesture that we cannot decipher in twenty seconds has turned suspect. And I ask myself if this other, converted into a threat on a daily basis, does not have a great deal to do with what is happening in our political culture, the growth of intolerance, the impossibility of that social pact that is so frequently talked about, the difficulty of recognizing myself in what the other thinks, likes, and has as his life horizon, be it aesthetic or political.

We could round out this reflection by saying that in Colombia, as perhaps in no other Latin American country today, the media lives on fear. This was evident in the last electoral campaigns, during which the threat of attack almost did away with the street theatricality of politics—which has been and still is, although reduced, its own particular space and form—making it project itself as and convert itself into a television show. Television is swallowing itself, devouring the space of communication that cannot be lived on the street.

But the media does not only substitute itself for public and city life during electoral campaigns. We can verify the disproportionate importance of the media industry in the country's daily life. In a country with such great structural deficiencies in housing, health, and education, we have a disproportionately developed media, both economically and technologically. But that disproportion—at least in terms of the importance acquired by what appears in the media—is proportional to the absence of institutional political spaces of expression and conflict resolution, and the lack of representation in cultural discourse of key dimensions of life and the majority's ways of feeling.

It is the reality of a country with a very weak civil society, a long political crisis, and a profound cultural schizophrenia that recharges the media's capacity for representation and excessive importance on a daily basis. It has to do with a capacity for interpellation that cannot be confused with audience ratings. This is not only because the ratings refer only to the number of sets that are turned on during a given program and do not take into account whether anyone is watching, much less who watches and how. It is also because the true influence of television resides in the formation of collective imaginaries, that is, a mixture of images and representations of what we live and dream, of what we have a right to hope for and desire, and goes far beyond the measurable hours that we spend in front of a television and the programs that we actually watch. It is not that the amount of time spent watching television or the type of programs watched do not matter, but that the political and cultural weight of television, like that of any other medium, is not measurable in terms of direct and immediate contact but can only be evaluated in terms of the social mediation that its images achieve.

A Bit of Context

In order to understand what has been stated thus far we must describe the new fears in terms of longer-lasting processes, such as those articulated by the new technological environment and the growing erosion of sociability—not of society in terms of institutions, but of sociability, that is, the sense of daily social relationships. In the first place, that erosion can take the form of the accelerated distancing between what Habermas has called the techno-structure and citizens' common life worlds. As underdeveloped as our societies may be, they are similar to the more developed ones in this respect. I refer to the process of autonomization of the technological sphere in relation to civil society as a whole, as if this sphere were controlled by a logic of its own to which the citizenry may not have access. Decisions regarding techno-scientific development are reserved for experts, who offer the excuse that only they understand the complex logic that governs these processes. Legitimated by this supposed autonomy, the techno-structure is retired from political debate even though it is precisely in that debate that many opportunities for economic and social development come into play, in which certain technological decisions can permanently affect the model of growth, the labor world, and cultural life. More and more, citizens have the feeling that all of that upon which job security, professional validity, even private identity is based has been mined by forces that completely escape not only their control but their comprehension. And the enormous acceleration of the operational capacity of science, which is the daily reduction of the distance between science and technology, or perhaps the speed with which science is translated in the technological sphere, has a lot to do with it. Even as knowledge is transformed into information, an abyss opens up between decisive knowledge and social life.

The second process in question—the overvaluing of information—suggests that this is true. Above and beyond the mythology of the "information society," there are fundamental transformations and formidable advances in the system of production, administration, and education. But, as Baudrillard has written, it as also true that "the greater the quantity of information, the less sense it makes." Each day we are informed about more things, but we understand their meaning even less. How much of the enormous amount of information that we receive about the country and the world is translated into better knowledge of others, of communication opportunities, and of the ability to act in our society in a transformative manner? On the other hand, information has begun to simulate social interaction and participation. Upon feeling informed about what is happening, I have the deceptive sensation that I am participating, acting in society, being a protagonist, when we know that the protagonists are others and that they are very few. If it is true that new technologies decentralize, it is also certain that they are not doing anything to counter the growing concentration of power and capital. We have information but its sense escapes us. We live in the euphoria of a type of participation that life itself shows to be a simulacrum.

The new technological sphere is producing an accelerated obsolescence of abilities and skills in the fields of labor and education, and this process is no longer limited to central countries. It is not simply a question of unemployment in terms of salaries, but of how automatization and computerization turn a good part of the adult population into mentally useless beings in that they are made incapable and unproductive. This adds another dimension to the generation gap. While until recently the space and symbol of knowledge was the elderly, while they were the memory of humanity and represented the time of beauty for centuries, today the elderly—that is, most adults—see their knowledge devalued to the point of having to simulate being young at any cost so that they will not feel displaced from a world that is legitimated by new technological knowledge and views. Now we find that the manner in which people relate to the technological sphere contributes to the gap: while it unsettles adults and makes them uneasy, young people feel that it is their natural sphere, their cultural and mental world.

What Do We Do with Fear?

How do people confront these fears, the anguish caused by the erosion of society that gives the city form? One way is the elite's response to estrangement, to the absence of roots that characterizes the urban world, by compensating for the cultural void with the search for aesthetic authenticities, by turning to traditional forms of organizing space, to old forms of furniture or weaving. And one looks to enter into contact with

that which sounds profound and seems authentic through this recreation of a primitive world. The hole in morality that technological
rationality opens with premodern frequency is filled with the magic of
the primitive or the cynical disenchantment of the postmodern.

A second type of reaction is that of those who search for new forms
of belonging. Since we no longer believe in great ideals, and given the
integral societal symbols' loss of value, the only option left is the immediate: the here and now. It is not that we have become unaware that
things are going wrong, or that we have lost the sense of a lack of justice, but the projects and utopias that oriented change have suffered a
collapse. And when they don't know what to do, people turn to living
with those beside them, with those to whom they feel closest, in the
best way possible. This is what Michel Maffesoli has called tribal
socialisms: marginal to institutional rationality, people return to old
communal impulses and fulfill themselves through precarious, vicious
groupings, marked more by the logic of identification than by identity.
They lack the longstanding status of ethnic or class identities and are
based instead on generations and gender, on professional or culture-
based communities. They seek out a modicum of heat in cities that grow
colder, more abstract, each day, and they look to build small islands of
warm relations where they can share their likes, gestures, fears.

The other observable reaction is that of the new urban movements,
which are constituted simultaneously by the daily experience of contradictory social demands and political institutions, and by the collective identities' defense of their own forms of communication. In their
own ways, the social, ethnic, regional, feminist, ecological, youth, consumer, and gay movements are giving form to all of the things that a
political rationale, which thought itself all-encompassing in terms of
social conflict, is not capable of representing today. Mobilizing identities, subjectivities, and collective imagineries in formation, overcoming dichotomies elided by the dynamics of economic transnationalism
and cultural deterritorialization, these new movements exceed the traditional sense of the political. And they are reorganizing it in cultural
terms. The new urban movements discover the cultural dimensions of
politics, they discover the political as a sphere for producing a sense of
the social, for negotiating interests and differences. The new urban
movements face a city made of flows and news with a strong dynamic

of the reterritorialization of struggles, of the rediscovery of those territories as spaces vital for culture. They are struggles that challenge what we understood as cultural identities because they articulate that which neither the politicians nor those who work in the field of culture knew how to articulate: the struggle for space—in terms of housing, services, and cultural territory—and the struggle for self-management against those now sophisticated forms of verticality and paternalism. Upon discovering the relationship between politics and culture—which has nothing to do with the old obsession for "politicizing" everything— the new movements discover difference as a space for deepening democracy and self-management. Thus the struggle against injustice is also the struggle against discrimination and diverse forms of exclusion, which is, at the end of the day, the construction of a new mode of being a citizen that allows all of us to recognize ourselves in others, an indispensable condition for communication and the only civil way of overcoming fear.

TRANSLATED BY KATHERINE GOLDMAN

The Facts

Urban Violence in Latin America and the Caribbean

ALBERTO CONCHA-EASTMAN

*Dimensions,
Explanations,
Actions*

THE VIOLENCE THAT Latin America and the Caribbean face is complex. It is a social and health problem, which, if not new, has recently acquired alarming proportions and dimensions in many countries. The South American continent boasts the highest homicide rate in the world, around fifteen for every one hundred thousand inhabitants, which in itself suggests a social crisis of serious proportions. The violence that is the subject of this study has a social dimension that differs from individual cases that follow pathological reasons. It is a social problem created by humanity, a product of society that has cultural, economic, and structural roots. For that reason, it is a problem that can be avoided, prevented, controlled, and abolished.

The subject is not only the concern and domain of the institutions and bodies that are formally responsible for attention to and the control, prevention, or punishment of acts of violence and insecurity. It is also the concern and responsibility of the many citizens who either live in fear of becoming victims, or who already have been victims, of acts that injure their person or security. Today, society in general, increasingly manifesting its discomfort with this situation, is probing its causes

37

and demanding solutions. Perhaps this preoccupation comes too late: if it had begun decades ago, the statistics might not rank many Latin American countries as "leaders" in violent acts.

Magnitude and Dimensions

Violence is exercised in state offices, schools, homes, and workplaces, on the street and in the countryside. Violence is exercised by the fathers who abuse, beat, and humiliate their wives and children; the youths who leave home and join gangs to rob, rape, assault, or kill; the members of organized crime who mug, assault, and murder; those who traffic in drugs—and all of its consequences—especially in urban centers; the state and the police who violate human rights; the public functionaries who abuse the rights of citizens soliciting their help; and, in extreme cases like that of Colombia, the guerrillas and the paramilitaries, who merge in the eyes of the defenseless campesino displaced from his home to the unfamiliar city. The conduct of corrupt politicians, leaders, and governors who are directly or indirectly enriched by the coffers of the state erodes ethics, norms, and the culture of coexistence.

A series of questions deserves an approach that is interdisciplinary and particular to each country or city. What is the dimension of the problem? Who is affected, and in what way? How grave does a specific society perceive this reality to be? What is insecurity, and what is violence? How do different members of society perceive them? How do the people who live in high-risk areas of the cities survive?

A World Bank study of the period from 1974 to 1994 demonstrates growth in the homicide rate of various regions starting in the mid–1980s.[1] Latin America is the region with the highest homicide rates. Although the rates for sub-Saharan Africa have also increased in recent years, Latin America's are still considerably worse. The lowest rates are in developed countries.

Why did acceleration occur during that period? There may be no single answer to that question, but it is striking that during those twenty years, the World Bank and the International Monetary Fund imposed increasingly demanding economic adjustment policies. In the cities, the poor population increased. The struggle for survival made the so-called informal economy—the range of activities in which persons without employment or job opportunities find refuge—grow. Drug trafficking and all of the illegal activities connected to it, including corruption and violence against the life and integrity of persons—acquired international dimensions.

Even without recourse to reliable, timely figures on the frequency of different forms of criminality in each country, statistics show that criminality has grown significantly in almost every nation in the region. The current situation can be summarized based on the victims:

VIOLENCE AGAINST CHILDREN

The World Health Organization (WHO) has defined the abuse of children as "child abuse or mistreatment . . . constituted by every form of physical or emotional mistreatment, sexual abuse, negligence or negligent treatment, commercial or any other kind of exploitation that results in real or potential damage to the health, survival, development, or dignity of the boy or girl with whom the abuser has a relationship of responsibility, confidence, or power."[2] Abuse includes international, social, institutional, and intra- and extrafamilial interpersonal abuse or neglect.

There are no studies that offer a real picture of the dimensions of abuse worldwide. The WHO has estimated that nearly forty million children between the ages of zero and fourteen suffer mistreatment or abuse and require attention and social and health care.[3] It is clear that the magnitude of the problem surpasses common suppositions.

There are some studies that give us hard numbers. In Colombia, 49 percent of women with a history of abuse said that they also abuse their children. In Costa Rica, a poll of university students showed that 32 percent of women and 13 percent of men had experienced some form of sexual abuse during their childhood; those abuses occurred between the ages of five and ten. In 1988, the National Task Force on Child Abuse in Jamaica received 3,033 reports of abuse, the majority of them cases of sexual abuse, especially against girls.[4] The Study of Attitudes and Behaviors coordinated by the Pan-American Health Organization (PAHO) determined that in Latin America between 3 percent and 27 percent of children are punished with objects by one of their parents, and up to 34 percent are beaten with the hand.[5]

It is recognized that intrafamilial violence against women exercised by their domestic partners makes the children victims as well, either as direct recipients of a parent's anger or as witnesses to the situation. Finally, in urban zones boys and girls in and off the street suffer violence at the hands of the state and society, as well as of their families. Their fundamental human rights to education, shelter, food, clothing, love, and recreation are denied; besides having suffered violence in their homes, they live in an environment that consents to and teaches them various forms of criminality.

VIOLENCE AGAINST WOMEN

Violence against women has been defined by the United Nations as "every act of gender-violence that produces, or can produce, lesions or physical, sexual, or psychological suffering. It includes the threat of such acts, coercion, or the loss of liberty, be it in public or private life."[6] Its magnitude is to a large extent unknown or hidden. Differences in methodology and in the definitions of the types of injuries or aggressions in many studies make comparisons invalid. When the definition of abuse is restricted to physical or sexual violence and psychological aspects are disregarded, violence against women is reported less frequently than it actually occurs. Women's groups and national and international networks against the abuse of women and children are making efforts to unite and increase awareness about gender equality.

Velzeboer-Salcedo compiles facts from various Latin American countries that show the magnitude of this problem:

(1) Gender-based violence causes more deaths and disabilities among women between the ages of fifteen and forty-four than cancer, malaria, traffic accidents, and wars;

(2) between 20 and 60 percent of women have been hit by their domestic partners, in many cases severely;

(3) the cases that are reported are the minority;

(4) a high proportion of pregnancies among adolescents is the result of forced sexual relations.[7]

In a study of Nicaraguan women, Ellsberg points out that violence was more prevalent against women with the following risk factors: more than five children, a history of violence in either the wife's original home or her husband's, poverty, residence in an urban zone, youth, and low education level.[8]

Every form of gender-based violence is a violation of the victim's human rights. So it was understood and recognized at the World Conference on Human Rights held in Vienna in 1993, a conference that led to the formulation of two key documents of international influence: the United Nations' Declaration on the Elimination of Violence against Women (1993), and the Declaration of Belén do Pará (1995) of the Interamerican Convention to Prevent, Sanction, and Eradicate Violence against Women.[9]

VIOLENCE AGAINST ADOLESCENTS AND YOUTHS

Deaths and injuries among young people represent an average thirty to forty years of potential life lost for each fatality. According to Weaver and Maddaleno, 28.7 percent of all homicides that occur in the Americas are against youths between the ages of fifteen and twenty-four. In ten countries of the region with populations above one million, homicide is the second-largest cause of death in the fifteen-to-twenty-four age group. By country, the homicide rate among young people has alarming dimensions: per 100,000 inhabitants, Colombia had 267 youth homicides; Puerto Rico, 93; Brazil, 72; Venezuela, 69; Mexico, 41; United States, 38; Panama, 32; Ecuador, 26; Trinidad and Tobago, 21.[10]

Youths are not only victims, they are also the most frequent aggressors. In some countries of Latin America and the Caribbean and in Colombia, Peru, and Venezuela, young people in juvenile gangs are responsible for a large portion of the violence and perception of citizen insecurity. Although they are not the only aggressors, they are the most infamous. According to a recent report of youth organizations that work to prevent juvenile violence in El Salvador, between thirty and thirty-five thousand young people are involved in gangs known as *maras*. Preventative or rehabilitative programs should focus their efforts in a participatory form, work with young people, listen to them, know their concerns, and plan concerted actions.[11]

HOMICIDES

Despite flaws in information gathering, there is a consensus on using homicide rates to compare violence among countries. In table 4.1 is a comparison of the crude homicide rates registered in diverse countries of the Americas in two periods, 1988–95 and 1994–97, calculated on

Table 4.1
Crude Rate of Homicides in Countries of the Americas (per 100,000)

Country	Last available year from 1988–95	Last available year from 1994–97
Argentina	4.2	4.1
Brazil	17.8	23.5
Canada	2.1	1.6
Colombia	76.3	73.3
Chile	3.0	3.1
Costa Rica	3.7	5.3
Cuba	7.3	6.6
Dominican Republic	n.d.	12.2
Ecuador	12.6	12.3
El Salvador	39.9	40.9
Guatemala	25.3	2.2
Guyana	n.d.	11.0
Jamaica	1.8	1.3
Mexico	17.6	15.1
Nicaragua	6.1	6.4
Panama	9.7	12.7
Paraguay	9.3	11.6
Peru	2.9	n.d.
Puerto Rico	23.2	22.4
Trinidad and Tobago	8.0	11.1
United States	10.1	8.2
Uruguay	4.3	4.4
Venezuela	11.2	13.5
Average	14.7	14.7

Source: Figures based on *Basic Indicators, Situación de la salud en las Américas* (Health situation in the Americas), Oficina Panamericana de la Salud (Pan-American Health Office), 1996, 1998.

the basis of the cases registered in the countries and reported to PAHO.[12] Each year between 110,000 and 120,000 persons are murdered in this region. In more than ten countries, the rate per hundred thousand inhabitants is in or near double digits. According to these figures, Colombia has the highest homicide rate in the region, nearly double El Salvador's and five times that of Brazil. In Brazil we notice an increase; Colombia and Mexico, in contrast, show slight decreases. According to the statistics reported, homicidal violence has increased in Panama, Paraguay, Trinidad and Tobago, and Venezuela. Puerto Rico shows rates above 20 per 100,000 inhabitants. Peru shows similar rates, especially for the period in which the guerrilla group Sendero Luminoso (Shining Path) was active.

Subsequent studies have corrected a few of these figures. In El Salvador, after a careful review of forensics archives, it was concluded that the homicide rate in 1995 was 139 per 100,000 inhabitants and decreased to 90 in 1998.[13]

In Jamaica, the homicide rate rose from 24 to 45 per 100,000 between 1991 and 1996; the Department of Forensic Medicine established the homicide rate in Honduras at thirty-six per one hundred thousand.[14] In Guatemala, a similar investigation determined that the rate is approximately 32 and in Nicaragua approximately 15 per 100,000. The Division of Criminal Policy of the Ministry of Justice in Argentina calculated—by reviewing statistics on the accused—that the homicide rate for 1997 was 8.8 per 100,000, almost double that shown by official reports.[15]

URBAN GROWTH

The unplanned and accelerated growth of large cities in Latin America has caused changes in the rural to urban relation. In Central America the population has grown from 353 million in 1980 to 506 million in the year 2000. This is a 30 percent growth in population at an average rate of 1.5 percent per year. The proportion of the populace living in urban areas surpassed 65.1 percent in 1980 and 75.6 percent at the end of the twentieth century. Today Argentina, Brazil, Chile, Cuba, French Guyana, Uruguay, Venezuela, and some Caribbean islands have already exceeded that figure. Colombia, Mexico, Peru, Puerto Rico, and Trinidad and Tobago are close to the average. In Belize, Costa Rica, El Salvador, Guatemala, Guyana, Haiti, Honduras, and Surinam, just under 50 percent of the population is urban. The urban populations in other countries fluctuate between 55 and 70 percent.[16]

What is the role of urban growth in the generation of violence? The changes in population structure are due not only to natural growth (births minus deaths), but also to the effect of migration from the country to the city. In Latin America, at least two factors help explain this migration and its relationship to the increase in violence. The first is the legitimate response to the desire and right to seek new opportunities on the part of residents of the countryside or small towns. These individuals move to peripheral urban areas and, astonished and angry, find that the social opportunities they had dreamed of are tremendously elusive. The second group that has "migrated" has done so involuntarily, forced out by armed conflicts or other forms of violence. These individuals were compelled to abandon their homes, their plots of land, and their few movable and immovable goods to seek refuge in urban centers in order to save their lives. They are displaced by wars, victimized by confrontations between insurgents and the army or paramilitaries. So it was in Peru, El Salvador, Nicaragua, and Guatemala, and so it is today in Colombia, where it is estimated that between 1.2 and 1.5 million campesinos and indigenous persons, many of them children or mothers with babies, inhabit abnormal urban spaces, soliciting alms, trying to sell whatever they can at traffic lights and shopping malls. All are struggling to survive, unable to worry about dignity or decorum.

This phenomenon can be observed in various cities, but it is not the only source of violence. Nor should the poor, or poverty itself, be stigmatized as if they were the fundamental or only causes of violence. Even where the indicators of violent acts are higher among low-income sectors, especially in developing countries, the aggressors are certainly a minority among them. White-collar criminals, gangs, and organized crime form a different category of violent individuals.

Theoretical-Conceptual Approaches

Clarifying some definitions will make the discussion more precise. Violence is an intentional use of force or power with a predetermined end by which one or more persons produce physical, mental (psychological), or sexual injury, injure the freedom of movement, or cause the death of another person or persons (including him or herself).[17] There are three basic components to this definition: the intentionality of the use of force or power; the infliction of injury; and the pursued end, behind which stands the exercise of some form of power, be it at the level of the home, the public, or the group. Violence expresses itself in diverse forms; the classification system adopted should allow for the clarification of the phenomenon's complexity and the proposal of preventive actions based on the multicausality that defines it. (We will return to this idea shortly.)

Another term that must be discussed is "citizen security." This is understood as the right of all citizens—understand *all*—to move freely and without fear, to know that their objects and belongings will not be taken from them, that they will not be fraudulently stripped of their goods, that they will not be intimidated, and that they can trust other human beings as they trust persons close to them. This concept is frequently used in polls on victimization in order to determine the prevalence of or city residents' perception of their experiences as victims. These two problems, violence and citizen insecurity, are distinguished in their definitions but frequently overlap in practice.

Finally, a victim is any person who individually or as a member of a group has suffered physical, mental, or emotional injury, economic loss, or substantial deterioration of his or her fundamental rights through acts or omissions that are in violation of the laws operating in each particular state.[18]

The perception of violence and insecurity varies from the housewife who is afraid to open the door of her home to a stranger for fear of being robbed, to the adolescent or young woman who must travel streets where she fears she will be raped, to the shopkeeper who passes a discreet, scrutinizing look at the pair of unfamiliar customers whom he hurriedly identifies as thieves and his potential murderers, to the hundreds of residents who seek the protection—which is at times only psychological—of security gates around their homes or decide to live in residential developments patrolled by armed guards, to the bankers or jewelers who are historically victims of assault.

The population is a collective victim. The population recognizes the problem, feels and lives it, and demands solutions that may or may not include its own participation. We all feel that we are affected by violence and insecurity. This prevalence is demonstrated in the PAHO-coordinated "Multicentered Study of Attitudes and Cultural Norms about Violence, ACTIVE." Through polls of 10,821 adults in seven cities in Latin America and in Madrid, the study documented and demonstrated the extent to which violence and insecurity are perceived and endured in our region. When asked if they had suffered any kind of violence in the last twelve months, the percentage of participants that responded affirmatively was: San Salvador, 38.5; Caracas, 30.6; Salvador de Bahia, Brazil, 28; Cali, Colombia, 27.4; Río de Janeiro, 17; San José, Costa Rica, 15; Madrid, 13.7; and Santiago, Chile, 10.6. The average for Latin American cities was 34 percent. More simply, one in three persons has suffered some form of violence intentionally produced by another person. Cruz points out a similarity between the homicide levels and the indices of victimization found in these cities.[19]

Classification

A classification of types of violence appears in table 4.2. While it may not match each country's particular statistics regarding the intensity and types of violence, it is generally concordant with the different forms of violence present in the region. A careful analysis by country or by city would permit us to identify the particular situation of each one with more precision.

Violent acts are motivated by diverse causes. There is a component of power, domination, or supremacy behind most of them. Motives vary according to the type of violence committed. Interpersonal violence may result from a desire for vengeance; it often arises in conflicts over debts or issues of personal control. Many times the causes are unknown.

Economic motivation may reveal itself through the actions of groups with little or no organization, or through those of organized groups wishing to exercise some kind of power, be it political, social, or territorial. Political violence motivated by anxieties over power, ideas, or social vindication affects society in general as well as those who directly exercise violence.

Risk Factors, Multicausality, and Theoretical Focuses

Violence is a phenomenon with multiple causes, in which the different factors that generate it or facilitate its occurrence interact. Three interrelated explanatory levels are proposed: structural, institutional, and situational or direct. The three levels are connected in such a way that if the chain of transmission cannot be broken, it is less likely that the situation will be controllable. One level and one factor influences the others as an intrinsic dynamic connects the different levels.

In order to counter structural violence, states must favor and create spaces that allow citizens to enjoy the advantages of development and democracy. These advantages, of course, include education, social justice, equity, the right to work and food, and respect for human rights. The structural factors that envelop the whole of society and impact its

Table 4.2

Classification of Violence by Motive, Type, and Actors in Latin America and the Caribbean

Motivation	Type of Violence	Victimizers	Victims
Interpersonal or social: domination, revenge, control, debts, disagreements, unknown intimidation	Domestic or intra-familial: physical, sexual, verbal, psychological deprivations, neglect	Male partners, fathers, relatives, friends, acquaintances	Female partners, children, seniors, relatives
Economic: crimes with little or no structure	Fights: injuries, homocides	Gangs, acquaintances, unknowns	Friends, acquaintances, unknowns
	Homicides, rapes, robberies	Common delinquents, gangs members	General population, members of gangs or groups
Economic and power: organized crime	Homicides, magnaticides, injuries, assaults	Drug-traffickers, organized gangs	Leaders, judges, journalists, citizens, gang members
Politics:	Magnaticides, homicides, massacres, kidnapping, injuries	Guerrillas, para-military troops, government forces	Peasants, rural residents, guerrilla fighters, soldiers, police

members in general depend upon the macroeconomy and social and developmental conditions. The abuse of power and politics on the part of representatives of the state for individual interests, the loss of social ethical norms, and corruption are causes of violence. All of these damage the social fabric, the basis of coexistence, and the peaceful resolution of conflicts.

Institutional factors underlying violence are those which, by their essence, favor both the occurrence of acts of violence and passive attitudes on the part of victims. The higher the level of impunity, the more the cycle of crime repeats itself, because those who commit crimes and are not punished feel freer to act unlawfully. Low levels of education and social control lead to primal responses to conflict. Lack of confidence in the police and in the justice system discourages many citizens from turning to them in search of support or a solution to problems of violence, and leads many to take the law into their own hands.

Women who suffer spousal, psychological, physical, sexual, or economic violence live in circumstances that put them at greater risk for similar occurrences. Most are women who repeatedly suffer this type of violence, often at the hands of their partners.

Direct or situational factors in acts of aggression are those which, under specific circumstances, facilitate the carrying out of a violent act. It has been conclusively demonstrated that the abuse of alcohol and narcotics is associated with violent behavior; this abuse is not the basic cause, but it favors the occurrence of violence. Bearing and possessing firearms is an initial or facilitating factor, given that it increases the possibility and risk of their use. The exaltation of violent behaviors in the media distorts reality and models violent responses to interpersonal conflicts, which may be imitated without the imitators measuring the consequences of such an action.

These concepts are summarized in table 4.3. (The arrows show the interrelationships between various levels.)

Ratinoff maintains three hypotheses regarding sources of urban criminality:

(1) population dynamics related to high urban growth and migration rates;
(2) the relationship between poverty and crime, given the extreme vulnerability of the urban poor to diverse types and forms of violence and insecurity, as both victims and victimizers;
(3) the conduct or ethical option of behavior, a choice that is by nature individual and not necessarily related to poverty or the effects of the economy, whose incidence can be observed in all social strata and in all professions.[20]

There is no social or productive sector that is not affected by criminality, in particular when it occurs in situations that are difficult to control, as Ratinoff defines them.

For his part, Mockus proposes a focus that comes from culture and that serves both to explain why acts of violence occur and to propose solutions to the problem. In brief, he recognizes a "divorce among three regulatory systems of behavior: law, morality, and culture." Such a separation is expressed in a "lack of moral or cultural approval of legal obligations and cultural and/or moral approval of illegal actions." To resolve the social conflict created by the ruptures of behavior-regulating systems, his proposal centers on the re-education of adults through the pro-

Table 4.3
Violence: Interrelationships

	Structural Factors	
Social and economic inequality		Lack of governability
Poverty		Weak democracies
Loss of ethics and moral values		Human rights violations
Corruption		

↑

	Institutional Factors	
Lack of social responsibility		Impunity
Lack of faith in police/ justice		Exposure to violence
Distrust in institutions		Decomposition of the family

↑

	Direct or Facilitating Factors	
Possession of firearms		Role imitation
Alcohol/drug abuse		Promotion of violence in the media
Free time without free space	⇒	Multicausality

gram Citizenship Culture (Cultura Ciudadana), translated into government action. This project consolidated the basic philosophical idea that inspired the government program that Mockus developed as mayor of the Colombian capital. Modernity, for Mockus, is characterized by a clear and massive invitation to each individual to constitute a system of rules of their own that allows each of them to govern themselves according to their own understanding (moral autonomy).

Ethical and cultural factors deserve specific treatment, given that they are fundamental to understanding the phenomenon that concerns us. Social ethics is a category of behavior that is intertwined with social control. Social control is understood as those norms and criteria by which citizens choose respectful conduct and coexistence because they believe that such norms are valid, and that they apply to all members of society and provide for the respect of individual and collective rights. But in order for this situation to occur, it is not enough to have laws or regulations that punish whoever transgresses them (a measure that is unnecessary for many) but it requires a community in which members have socially learned the values of respect, coexistence, and tolerance.

Violence generates changes in social behavior, producing an erosion of social capital, which is understood as the combination of social and organizational relationships that make possible collaboration and cooperation among distinct levels of society in order to improve its level of development and harmony.[21] Social capital is "learned" in familial, educational, and social environments, and from the behavior of directors and leaders. Human beings tend to identify with different kinds of role models, and, unfortunately, some identify with those who act outside the law. All of those who have public responsibility are special objects of the population's gaze. Their social roles are not limited to completing their bureaucratic duties; respect and deference to the laws and norms that govern society are expected of them.

Nevertheless, when political leaders, governors, military officers, clergy, or business people become involved in and commit criminal acts—be it directly, by appropriating public funds (as in administrative corruption), violating human rights, committing fraud in political activities or indirectly, by endorsing these practices or suppressing criticism of them out of personal interest—forms of control and social ethics are inevitably ruptured. In some Latin American countries this type of behavior has affected social ethics. In one way or another, sectors of the population have erroneously interpreted this criminal behavior as an example to be followed. The discrepancy between what is said and what is done is not understood, but the resultant logic is clear: if the pillars of society do not respect the norms that they themselves have created, why should those who have not had access to the benefits of society abide by them?

The effect extends and aggravates the problem. The so-called mules or drug couriers are the most typical example of this situation. They agree to carry a pound of cocaine, despite the risk of being arrested or killed in the attempt. Their ethical convictions are of another dimension: they will do anything to acquire money and relief from poverty. Of course, such reasoning does not justify criminal acts, nor does it apply in every case; nor are we facing the total and general transgression of social norms. But it does play a significant role in the occurrence of crime.

Prevention and Alternative Actions: The Focus of Public Health

The historical evolution of procedures used to confront violence can be summarized in three stages: repression and control, prevention, and the recuperation of social and human capital. Repression and control is intervention by the police and the judicial system. It is based on the intimidation effect on potential aggressors of incarceration and the loss of rights with which the state punishes those who break the law.

Prevention is the inter-sector response to the multicausality of violence. The need to confront violence from a wide, preventative perspective has recently been recognized and is broadly accepted today. Diverse sectors dealing with the assistance, rehabilitation, care, and control of victimizers and victims of violent acts should unite their efforts to that end.

The recuperation of social and human capital requires intervention through a broad commitment on the part of citizens, leaders, clergy, communicators, educators—society as a whole—to fight to revitalize ethics and social control.

The three levels are developed simultaneously, and the better the relationships among them, the greater the possibility of success.

The advances that have been made in public health in the control and prevention of illness and the promotion of health apply equally to the problem of violence. In short, it is necessary:

(1) to characterize the problem according to the basic, intertwined variables of person, place, time, circumstance, and situation;
(2) to identify causes, associated behaviors, and risk factors;
(3) to propose interventions and evaluate them;
(4) to extend interventions to other sectors and disseminate them.

The purpose of preventative health actions is to avoid the occurrence of violent acts or the exacerbation of their consequences. The promotion of healthy behaviors and life habits and the prevention of events injurious to communities and the individual take primacy among the tasks of public health.

Prevention is essential to the mission of the PAHO, especially primary prevention. Primary prevention seeks to encourage social and individual environments of respect and tolerance, of social values and personal conduct that favors nonviolent conflict resolution. In other words, our efforts are directed toward preventing the occurrence of the violent act. For example, macro-strategies designed to diminish poverty, seek social equity, improve education, and recover ethics and social control are part of this level of prevention.

Secondary prevention applies when a violent act has already occurred; its purpose is to avoid new or more serious episodes. Examples of this kind of secondary prevention include programs for identifying persons who seek health treatment for violent injuries and are actively linked to crisis intervention programs, through which solutions to the situations that preceded the violent event are sought.[22] Multiple projects concerning violence against women form part of this level of prevention, including programs such as the Programa Polygono Industrial (Polygonal Industrial Program) and Homies United in San Salvador or Parces in Cali, Colombia, in which juvenile gang members seek out and analyze different life options.

Tertiary prevention is applied in the area of public health to avoid more injury to those who have an established illness and to improve their quality of life. In the case of violence, rehabilitation is directed toward those serving jail sentences. Rehabilitation programs should focus on teaching productive activities and psychological resocialization. Tertiary prevention is of special importance in the case of youths detained for minor infractions who, in the absence of rehabilitation programs, frequently spend the period of confinement perfecting delinquent behaviors.

To conclude, I cite the criteria that underlie PAHO strategies for confronting violence:

(1) violence stems from multiple causes and should be met with polyvalent strategies;

(2) it is necessary to improve and maintain up-to-date information on the characteristics and circumstances in which acts of violence occur;

(3) prevention should be privileged above repression, emphasizing projects directed toward the causes in order to avoid the occurrence of violence (primary prevention);

(4) interventions, projects, or decisions by authorities, academic institutions, and nongovernmental organizations should be made with due planning, follow-up, and evaluation of their results;

(5) communities (at the local, municipal level) should have an active role in the projects and a clear right to propose, modify, and actualize their development;

(6) civil society (understood as the social sectors that are not part of the apparatus of state, government, military forces, legislators, judges, and magistrates) has the responsibility and the right to support and implement preventative actions and projects;

(7) local conditions and communities must shape the design of policies, inviting members of the community to think imaginatively and to develop collective proposals that reach and affect the largest groups of the population;

(8) vulnerable groups, that is, those with the greatest risk of victimization, must receive special assistance.

TRANSLATED BY JENNIFER FRENCH

Notes

1. P. Fajnzylber, D. Lederman, and N. Loayza, "Determinants of Crime Rates in Latin America and the World," *World Bank Latin American and Caribbean Studies* (Washington: World Bank, 1998).
2. *Report of the Consultation on Child Abuse Prevention* (WHO/HCS/PVI/99.1, March 1999), 15, 17.
3. *Protocol for the Study of Interpersonal Physical Abuse of Children: Child Health and Development* (Division of Family Health, WHO/FHE/CHD/94.1, 1994), 15.
4. K. Hofman and I. Levav, *Child Maltreatment: A Plan of Action for the Reduction of Violence Against Children* (Washington: PAHO, 1998), 7, 8.
5. Various authors, *Rev Panam Salúd Pública/Pan Am J Public Health* 5, 4–5 (April–May 1999).
6. L. L. Heise, J. Pitanguy, and A. Germain, *Violence Against Women: The Hidden Health Burden*, World Bank Discussion Paper No. 225 (Washington: World Bank, 1994), 3.
7. M. Velzeboer-Salcedo, *Violence Against Women in the Americas* (Washington: PAHO/HDP/HDW, November 1998).
8. M. Ellsberg, "Prevalencia y características de la violencia conyugal hacia mujeres en Nicaragua," *Memoria Seminario Taller Modelos en construcción para la atención integral a la violencia intrafamiliaar y el rol del sector salud*, Programa Mujer, Salud y Desarrollo (Program on women, health, and development), Managua, Nicaragua, November 12–14, 1997 (OPS/OMS, 1999), 338–343.
9. L. Guido, "Deconstruir la violencia intrafamiliar: Estado y sociedad civil: Rol del sector salud," *Memoria Seminario Taller Modelos en construcción para la atención integral a la violencia intrafamiliar y el rol del sector salud*, Programa Mujer, Salud y Desarrollo (Program on women, health, and development), Managua, Nicaragua, November 12–14, 1997 (OPS/OMS, 1999), 14–48.
10. K. Weaver and M. Maddaleno, "Youth Violence in Latin America: Current Situation and Violence Prevention Strategies," *Rev Panam Salud/Pan Am J Public Health* 5, 4–5 (April–May 1999): 338–343.

11. A. McAlister, *La violencia juvenil en las Américas/Juvenile Violence in the Americas*, OPS/PAHO, ASCID/SIDA, Kellog (September 1998).
12. *Situación de salud en las América: Indicadores básicos de Salud* (OPS/OMS, 1996, 1998).
13. J. M. Cruz, L. A. González, L. E. Romano, and E. Sisti, "La violencia en El Salvador en los años noventa: Magnitud, costos y factores posibilitadores," Instituto de Opinión Pública. Universidad Centro Americana José Simeón Cañas, BID. Working papers, R–338 (BID, Washington, October 1998), 6.
14. G. Gordon, T. Durant, E. Ward, K. Lewis-Bell, and D. Ashley, "Understanding the State of Accidental and Violence-Related Injuries in Jamaica," July 1999 (mimeograph).
15. M. Ciafardini and H. Olaeta, "Homicidios dolosos en Argentina. Ministerio de Justicia, División de Política Criminal," 1999 (mimeograph).
16. *Situación de Salud en las Américas. Indicadores básicos de Salud* (OPS/OMS, 1999).
17. This definition of violence is adapted from the one developed by M. L. Rosenberg and J. Mercy in "Assaultive Violence," in Mark Rosenberg and Mary Ann Fenley, eds., *Violence in America, A Public Health Approach* (New York: Oxford University Press, 1991), 2:14–50.
18. *United Nations Victims Assistance Handbook* (New York: United Nations, 1998).
19. J. M. Cruz, "La victimización por violencia urbana: niveles y factores asociados en ciudades de América Latina y España," *Rev Panam Salud Pública/Pan Am J Public Health* 5, 4–5 (April–May 1999): 259–267.
20. L. Ratinoff, "Delincuencia y paz ciudadana," *Hacia un enfoque integrado del desarrollo: ética, violencia y seguridad ciudadana*, working papers (BID, Washington, 1996), 3–25.
21. D. K. Runyan, W. M. Hunter, R. S. Socolar, et al., "Children Who Prosper in Unfavorable Environments: The Relationship to Social Capital," *Pediatrics* 101, 1 (1998): 12–18.
22. E. DeVos, M. A. Goetz, D. A. Stone, and L. L. Dahlberg, "Evaluation of a Hospital-Based Youth Violence Intervention," *Am J Prev Med* 12, supp. 2 (1996): 101–108.

Colombia

EDUARDO PIZARRO LEONGÓMEZ

*Toward an
Institutional
Collapse?*

IN THE LAST TWO OR THREE YEARS, the terms used in the world press to describe the difficult and complex situation of Colombia have multiplied. These designations—which reflect more uncertainty and ignorance than an understanding of what really occurs in the country—range from the "Latin American Vietnam" or the "new Bosnia" to the "new Kosovo." At the same time, the risks of the "colombianization" of various countries are discussed throughout Latin America with a tone of increasing and evident concern. This expression is used from Mexico to Argentina, passing through Ecuador and Venezuela. A recent example is found in the article "¿Rumbo a la colombianización de México?" (Toward the colombianization of Mexico) by columnist Darío Ibarra, published in a Mexican newspaper.[1]

These expressions are a reflection of the uncertainty that exists, both in international circles and in the Latin American context, with respect to Colombia's future. In spite of the multiple types of violence that affect the country, my discussion here is limited to the analysis of political violence, guided by some basic questions: Is Colombia on the verge of institutional collapse as a consequence of the multiple faces of violence affecting the country? What are the current characteristics of political violence? Is there a strategic equilibrium in Colombia between the armed forces and the guerrillas? Has paramilitarism made the transition to right-wing guerrillas? Is a politics of peace viable today?

Institutional Stability and the Partial Collapse of the State

The interesting article "El espejo colombiano" (The Colombian mirror), by Marco Palacios, a researcher at the prestigious Colegio de México, is a rigorous attempt to describe the drama that affects Colombia and, at the same time, to call the attention of leaders and the Mexican people to the risks that the nation will face if it gets further caught up in the vicious circle of violence.[2]

Palacios draws an interesting contrast between creative violence, which served as a catalyst for freedom and democracy in the English and French Revolutions, and the destructive violence that pervades Colombia today. While the earlier experiences with violence allowed for the creation of a more democratic and just order, the many faces of violence that traverse Colombia are destroying the social fabric and creating widespread institutional disorder.

Violence is similar to the phenomenon of inflation: once it becomes hyperinflation, it exceeds state control and, in an uncontrollable spiral, destroys the country's economy. The same occurs in the case of hyperviolence: once it is born, violence overruns the judicial system, the penal system, and the police and military authorities, destroying everything in its path—work ethic, the minimum norms of cohabitation, and respect for life—like an enormous cyclone. Is the hyperviolence that affects Colombia driving it to the point of no return?

In general terms, three basic components have characterized Colombia over the last four decades, since the Frente Nacional in 1958: recognized and praised macroeconomic stability, equally acclaimed institutional stability, and, in contrast to the first two characteristics, high levels of violence. In effect, Colombia is the only country in Latin America that has maintained economic growth over the last forty years. Along with Mexico, Costa Rica, and Venezuela, it was one of the four nations that managed to avoid the military coups that ravaged the continent in the sixties and seventies. But, at the same time, Colombia held the hardly honorable title of being one of the nations with the highest levels of violence in the world.

Is this situation changing? Are the recessive signals seen today indicative of serious future economic instability? Was the political crisis under the administration of Ernesto Samper merely prelude to a severe institutional crisis? Will the violence that affects the country increase inexorably? In other words, if economic and political stability have served to cushion the impact of violence, what will happen if this double shock absorber fails?

The comparisons published in the international press about the future of Colombia—if current levels of violence persist—with the war in Bosnia and with the Vietnam War are wrong. Neither ethnic conflagration nor the war that was fought between the two cold war superpowers in small countries is comparable to the Colombian experience. From this perspective, given the superimposition of the various faces of organized and diffuse violence, Colombia's risks are those of an erosion of institutions and the social fabric that could hasten the partial collapse that the Colombian state is suffering and affect both institutional and economic stability in the next few years.

In 1978, North American researcher Paul Oquist published *Violencia, conflicto y política en Colombia* (Violence, conflict, and politics in Colombia), which is one of the most outstanding studies of the period of violence that the country faced between 1946 and 1953. In this study, Oquist coined the controversial term "colapso parcial del Estado" (partial state collapse) to refer to the impact of the various modalities of violence on state institutions during those years. This collapse manifested itself concretely in the breakdown of parliamentary, police, juridical, and electoral institutions; the loss of legitimacy of the state among large sectors of the population and the concomitant use of high levels of repression to ensure obedience to the state's orders; the contradictions within the armed apparatus of the state that reduced the effectiveness of high levels of repression; and the physical absence of public administration in the large and important areas of the nation.[3]

Fifty years later, Colombia is suffering from a similar situation. Our precarious state, facing challenges and demands that exceed its capacity to control and manage, is experiencing a partial collapse of some of its key institutions, such as justice and security. On the other hand, some institutions maintain their consistency, as is the case of the agencies responsible for the management of macroeconomics and foreign affairs. The principal indicators of this partial collapse are the loss of the weapons monopoly, the multiplication of armed actors who challenge state authority, high crime levels, high levels of impunity, and the lack of state presence in many sectors of the country. In many of these regions a "praetorian system" has been configured, defined by Samuel Huntington as "one in which different social segments confront each other directly in order to resolve conflicts involving the distribution of power and resources, in the absence of institutions or legitimately accepted bodies that would carry out the functions of mediation and the rules of the game in order to resolve the conflict."[4]

Could this lead to a generalized partial collapse of order in the coming years? In specialized journals, attempts have been made to outline common characteristics of those nations in which a "total collapse of the state" has been experienced, such as Somalia, Afghanistan, or Bosnia-Herzegovina. Nine central characteristics were identified in the three cases: strong demographic pressure, a massive refugee movement, economic growth aligned with ethnic segmentation, a long tradition of revenge and reprisals, a profound delegitimization of the state, a severe economic crisis, a progressive deterioration or elimination of public services, a demonstrated incapacity for implementing legal norms, and security apparatuses operating as "a state within the state."[5]

Despite the presence of many of these characteristics in Colombia today (such as the brutal displacement from rural areas to the cities or the existence of strong paramilitary groups), there exists a notable difference. In the three cases mentioned there were strong collective ethnic, linguistic, religious, or ideological identities.[6] Because of the absence of this factor, it is quite improbable, from our perspective, that a generalized civil war will be produced in Colombia. The risk is that the continuation and even deepening of this serious social imbalance could, in the medium term, call into question the institutional stability of the country in both the political and economic realms.

Negative Stalemate

For more than a decade, there has been a "negative stalemate" between the armed forces and the guerrilla in Colombia. This concept, which I coined a few years ago, differentiates itself from the more commonly used "military stalemate" (or strategic equilibrium), which is not appropriate when describing the Colombian conflict's unique characteristics. The term was initially proposed by General José Joaquín Matallana in a study that opened a sharp debate in the mid–1980s (*Paz o guerra: alternativa en 84*). According to Matallana, the guerrilla lacked the ability to defeat the army, and the army lacked the resources needed to defeat the guerrilla, which led to the need to search for a negotiated end to the armed conflict.

In Latin America, the notion of "strategic equilibrium" was born of the Salvadoran experience. A few years ago, the U.S. Congressional Research Service stated that

> at that point, after eight years of civil conflict in El Salvador, it seemed that we had arrived at a moot point: none of the parties had shown signs of being capable of overthrowing the other militarily or of offering alternatives that would lead to the end of the war. The majority of the observers believe that, except in the case of an unexpected change in the circumstances that provoke or maintain the war . . . , the two sides seem capable of continuing the struggle at the current rhythm indefinitely.[7]

The notion of a military stalemate, on the other hand, affirms that even if the armed forces have momentarily lost the tactical initiative on the battlefield, they maintain clear strategic superiority. Nonetheless, military success is improbable for all of the groups in the conflict because of many factors. Among these elements is the wretched Colombian geography (which is perhaps, of all of the countries on the continent, the one that most lends itself to a prolonged rebel war), the distance between the war fronts in a country fifty times larger than El Salvador, and, most important, the existence of a vast strategic rear guard (colonized zones both in the center of the country and on the borders, such as the extensive unpopulated areas along the already sizable borders with Venezuela, Brazil, Peru, Ecuador, and Panama).[8] Under

these conditions, the heartrending war that Colombia faces could be
prolonged indefinitely (as it has been for five decades), unless the peace
process currently underway is successful.

The Guerrilla Groups

The guerrilla movement, whose initial nuclei arose ten years before the
Cuban revolution, was born in a context that did not favor its chances
for moving toward revolutionary success.[9] Regardless, as a result of many
factors (the long experience of guerrilla battles, the relative closure of
the Frente Nacional, the precariousness of the central state, and its incapacity to measure and channel the social conflicts in rural societies),
the conditions for the consolidation of these rebel forces were created.
In this way, a "chronic insurgency" phenomenon was produced that was
similar in its general characteristics to the experiences in the Philippines
and Guatemala, countries in which the guerrilla also achieved consolidation without power and nonetheless reached their final objectives.

The guerrilla groups, which came into being in a precocious manner compared to those of the rest of the continent and were consolidated by leaps and bounds between the end of the 1960s and beginning
of the 1980s, took up almost all of the space in the left-wing democratic opposition. This brought about an early political militarization
on the part of left-wing groups. To a certain extent, the war ceased to
be a prolongation of politics by other means and was converted into a
long-term substitute for political action. In the left-wing political subculture of Colombia, the military confrontation forms a part of its rep-
ertory of action alongside other methods of social and political action.
The "combination of all forms of the revolutionary movement" has constituted the strategic heart of the communist family (FARC, Partido
Comunista, Unión Patriótica) since the 1960s.

After a period of decline and crisis during the 1970s—during which
the guerrilla was at the point of disappearing—reorganization and a
strong and renovated expansion was produced after 1980. This expansion, whose roots are complex, was achieved, among other reasons,
thanks to the resources of the drug trade and oil company taxes.

What is the current strategy of the guerrilla groups at the military
level?

First, the centrifugal strategy—which is the model of multiple fronts, an increased number of men, and diffuse expansion throughout the nation's territory—continues. It is a strategy of expansion from the colonized zones toward regions with dynamic economic activity (petroleum, gold, carbon, agricultural industry) and the country's most important administrative and political centers by way of the calling up of urban militias. Comparing the number of military actions undertaken by guerrilla organizations in the last few years, one discovers that 173 municipalities were registered in 1985, a number that rose to 437 in 1991 and to 622 in 1995.

Second, to sustain this strong guerrilla expansion, rebel groups look to diversify their financial resources, aided by the weak demarcation of borders between politics and crime. The traditional depredation of their "internal enemies" via kidnapping has been maintained, while the use of extortion against drug producers and traffickers as well as the petroleum, mining, and agricultural industries has multiplied.

Third, given the fact that succeeding by means of strategic military action and sustaining continuous military action is impossible, both the FARC and the Ejército de Liberación Nacional (ELN, National Liberation Army) have decided to augment their influence in local areas. This influence is not only directed at territorial control over areas of strategic value (such as the Serranía de San Lucas for the ELN or the Llanos de Yarí for the FARC), but also at municipal power structures. In effect, political-administrative decentralization, the transfer of resources to municipalities, and the popular election of mayors have given armed groups, both left wing and right wing, incentive in terms of gaining political control and access to municipal economic resources. This is what has been referred to as "armed clientelism."

Fourth, what is the guerrillas' attitude toward peace? From my perspective, a vision of accumulated military power with the goal of a radical transformation of society and state still predominates in the heart of the guerilla. But, in the absence of other real possibilities for military triumph (given, among other factors, the disappearance of the old socialist field and, by extension, the existence of a hostile international environment), the guerrillas maintain the "salvadorization" of the country as a strategic goal, that is to say, the transition from a "negative stalemate" to a strategic equilibrium in order to negotiate with the state as equals.

Guerrilla or Narcoguerrilla?

Since former U.S. ambassador Lewis Tambs coined the term "narco-guerrilla" more than a decade ago, the debate about the appropriate-ness or inappropriateness of this vision of the rebel movement has not abated.

The notion of a narcoguerrilla implies at least two things. First, it implies the existence of a strategic agreement between the guerrilla and the drug cartels, given the similarity of interests as much in terms of confronting the state as in regard to marketing illicit drugs. Second, the guerrilla has moved from being a political actor to a criminal one in that private economic interests have superseded political ideals.

The consequences of accepting these two postulates are clear: given that conducting negotiations with political actors is the only viable choice, the criminal decomposition of the guerrilla groups obliges the state to give them exclusively military and penal treatment. Thus, peace negotiations would be excluded from the outset.

From my perspective, both postulates are false. In regard to the first, the geography of the armed conflict in the country reveals at least two different situations: in regions where the guerrilla is a hegemonic ac-tor, it imposes a tax on the various agents involved with the produc-tion and marketing of illicit drugs. In other words, a pragmatic coexistence between the guerrilla, especially the FARC and some divi-sions of the ELN, and the drug traffickers exists in these regions. This coexistence provides the guerrilla groups, particularly the first, with the immense majority of their economic resources. Second, in regions where the rural narco-paramilitary action is hegemonic, drug traffickers mili-tarily confront the guerrilla in order to impede the payment of war taxes. Coexistence or confrontation is not determined by a supposed strate-gic accord, but by the strength of military forces in various regions of the country.

The very possibility of a *profound* identity is antithetic to the in-ternational experience. It reveals, on the contrary, the eminently con-servative character of the mafias given their predilection for a weak state and an open market economy. In Italy, the Mafia always maintained tight relations with Christian Democratic political leaders. Thus a stra-tegic agreement between the drug mafias and the guerrillas, supporters of a strong state (the "dictatorship of the proletariat") and a centralized economy is unthinkable.

With regard to the second point, the line between politics and crime is very unstable in Colombia. The guerrilla does not escape the national scourge that is drowning us in a sea of corruption and criminality. More than in any other place in Latin America, the Colombian guerrilla has practiced crime in a systematic manner in order to finance itself (kidnapping, extortion, *gramaje*) since its inception.[10] Without a doubt, these practices have their origins in the era of violence, during which the principal leaders of the FARC were born, particularly the organization's symbol, Manuel Marulanda Vélez. This attitude, which is condemnable in every way, coexists, in spite of everything, with a discourse that is political in nature and with politicized military leaders.

For all of the reasons mentioned, I believe that the term "narcoguerrilla" is not only inadequate but also inconvenient for the country. This position, however, does not impede a condemnation of the marriage; their coexistence has reached a level of comfort at which the guerrilla and drug traffickers have resided together in various regions of the country for years.

Paramilitary Groups: Self-defense, or Right-wing Guerrillas?

At the 1999 meeting of the German Association of Research on Latin America (Hamburg, November 25–27), there was an interesting debate about the role of irregular groups in the continent's counterinsurgency war. Since the end of the 1970s, various armed organizations have emerged in Colombia in reaction to the guerrilla groups that began to be reactivated during the same period, with the express purpose of filling the gap that the state had left in its weakened capacity for counterinsurgency.[11]

According to analysts, it is important to differentiate between paramilitary groups and death squads. The first, although they constitute irregular forces, are structured forces, with central commands and known functions. The second, informal groups, are flexible in structure and lack a known base or composition. Their formation specifically responds to the need to protect the identity of their members when they carry out clandestine operations. Examples of the former include the Patrullas Armadas Civiles [PAC, Armed Civilian Patrols] in Guatemala, the Contras in Nicaragua, the Rondas Campesinas [Rural Patrols] in Peru, and the Autodefensas Unidas [United Self-Defense Forces] of Colombia. Examples of the latter are the death squads that beset the Southern Cone, which were generally composed of members of state intelligence agencies. These groups still exist today, no longer oriented against rebel groups but instead against common crime, and they are responsible for the "social cleansing" operations that are so common in cities like Rio de Janeiro and São Paulo.

What functions have paramilitary groups fulfilled in the context of armed conflicts in Latin America? In the first place, the birth of these groups had the objective of developing a military apparatus at the service of the state or of the elites at a lower cost than expanding the regular armed forces. The Guatemalan state, for example, would never have been able to put together an army of 900,000 soldiers, the number of PAC militias during the war. In the second place, these groups constituted a decisive instrument in the counterinsurgency strategy, especially in rural areas. Given the inability of the region's weak states to control the territory, the "paras," in their various modalities, were able to make up for the absence of a parallel para-institutional order on the part of the state. Third, these groups constituted a local intelligence instrument (the guerrilleros of the FMLN were called "the ears") that complemented state agencies. Fourth, their existence allowed regular military forces to avoid the dirty work and thus diminished the international costs implied by human rights violations. Lastly, they allowed the state to confront the guerrilla using the very methods of an "irregular" war.

Colombia is the only country in Latin America where these two types of criminal organizations persist. How can this be explained? Why is there more evidence of cohabitation than conflict between the army and the paras? Are the paramilitaries part of the state's counterinsurgency strategy, as in the case of the PAC or the Rondas Campesinas in Guatemala and Peru? These questions are at the heart of the current debate in Colombia.

Since the end of the 1970s, different groups of armed organizations have formed in Colombia in response to the revival of guerrilla groups during the same period. The express justification for their existence is to try to fill the void created by the state's weak capacity for counter-insurgency.

During the first stage, the majority of the cases involved regional self-defense groups financed by landowners and local politicians. But as time passed the groups gained the capacity for mobilization and offensive action, due to the support of the drug mafias or the *esmereldas* (emerald miners), which allowed them to acquire a certain organizational complexity. Finally, in the past two or three years, under the leadership of Carlos Castaño and his Autodefensas of Urubá and Córdoba, they have been trying to move toward a type of right-wing guerrilla, complete with a central command and coherent discourse. This was the creation of the Autodefensas Unidas de Colombia (AUC).

The structure of this organization on a national level raises certain key questions about the current importance of these armed actors. As long as there is no clear rating of these groups as political actors or common criminals on the part of the state, it will be impossible to define a coherent political approach to dealing with them.

Are the self-defense groups making the transition toward a rightist counterguerrilla model, supplied with a political discourse, territorial control, and solid bases of social support? Has a coalition of self-defense groups unified under the name of the AUC, as an Estado Mayor Conjunto, and, as such, should they be considered one actor? If this were the case, would all of the groups that form the whole share the same principles or, to the contrary, is there a multiplicity of disparate groups, some politicized and others more criminal, some distant from drug trafficking and others subordinate to it, hidden behind the term?

Are We Moving Toward a Right-wing Guerilla?

That which most strongly marks the recent documents of the AUC is probably its political character, in other words, its intention to project an ideological justification for its counterinsurgency actions. This discourse could be synthesized as extreme-right authoritarian populism.

During the 1980s, at the height of the cold war, the United States began its unmitigated support of the armed organizations that fought against leftist governments. The Contras in Nicaragua, UNITAS in

Angola, and the mujahideen in Afghanistan were the most successful movements. These were right-wing guerrillas that boasted a coherent discourse that served to challenge their adversaries in terms of political legitimacy. In the AUC's search for the recognition of self-defense groups as political actors, the construction of a coherent discourse is fundamental. It is no longer a question of criminal movements defending interests divorced from any utilitarian character (for example, protecting the illicit drug laboratories), but instead a movement that has collective ideals. To what extent are the hundreds of old guerrillas from the EPL, the FARC, and the ELN sharing their ranks with agents of this transformation?

With a great deal of astuteness, the AUC states that the final objectives of its movement (agricultural reform, solving the problem of the displaced, overcoming poverty) are not different from those of the guerrilla, except in terms of the political perspective that motivates each. This is the rightist, populist characteristic of their proposal, which is intimately related to the landowning sector's offers to propose an important land bank within the framework of an eventual peace negotiation.

The extremist character is obviously determined by the modes of action of these groups, founded on generalized terror, selective murder, and massacres. In other words, this is a vertical and authoritarian order, in which a perverse friend/enemy dynamic dominates. Carlos Castaño's naked elegy of a politics of devastated earth in Mapiripán (Meta), in which dozens of campesinos who supposedly collaborated with the guerrilla were killed by firing squad without any formal judicial process, is one simple example.

A Unified Actor?

One of Carlos Castaño's principal goals is unifying all of the self-defense groups under the Estado Mayor Conjunto, a national organization of contra-guerrillas.

The self-defense groups have very diverse origins. Some were created by groups of landowners and local politicians tired of the criminal excesses of the guerrilla in regard to kidnaping and extortion. Others were born of drug traffickers like the "disappeared" Gonzalo Rodríguez Gacha, who refused to pay war taxes, the so-called *gramaje*, to the

FARC. Others were called up directly by state officials under the auspices of the counterinsurgency war. Finally, others were constituted by known leaders of the emerald mines.

In spite of the self-defense groups' varied origins, I believe that the framework that allowed for their considerable expansion has been the immense agricultural counterreform that the drug traffickers have led in the country, through which a new class, enriched by illegal means, has replaced the old landowning class.

The complex geography of the self-defense groups prompts me to doubt the hegemonic character of the AUC. There are too many differences on the level of politicization and autonomy with respect to the drug trafficking groups. While some groups, like that of Carlos Castaño, look to construct a legitimating political discourse, others act with a purely delinquent and openly criminal mentality.

Political Actors or Criminals?

One of the characteristics of the different governments that have come to power since 1977, the year of the first paramilitary groups' insurrection in Magdalena Medio, has been ambiguity in regard to their characterization and treatment of those groups. Not only has there been constant vacillation between their being recognized as political actors and their being judged as criminal groups, but the various levels of state government have different relationships with these groups.

First, some sectors have supported and even openly incorporated the mechanism of counterinsurgency into the armed forces. It is impossible to know if this position has had the support of military leaders. Regardless, it would be ridiculous to deny the support that these groups have enjoyed on the part of many officials, brigades, and battalions from various regions of the nation. Second, some sectors consider these groups a necessary evil given the armed forces' poor performance. Even if they are opposed to the groups, they do not consider it convenient to dismantle those groups that have succeeded in paralyzing the advance of the guerrilla in some areas of the country. Third, some sectors of the state think that these groups should be unhesitatingly confronted with official military force, given their openly criminal character. Finally, there are those who believe that these groups should be recognized as part of the conflict, in other words, as political actors that should be involved in negotiations parallel to those that will take place on the road to peace with the guerrilla.

In my opinion, the majority of those at the heart of the state hold the second opinion, which is pragmatic coexistence. Given the pressure of both national and international denunciations, open support is seen as inconvenient; but, given the armed forces' inefficiency and the paramilitary's already proven capacity for combat, their dismantling is not seen as desirable. The slogan for this sector of the state might be, "Neither help them nor fight them."

The paramilitary groups currently have four to five thousand troops. This means that they have an apparatus similar to that of the ELN, spread out across twenty-five war fronts. Their resources come from two fundamental sources: landowners and drug traffickers. To a certain extent, their force is derived from the logistical support of many members of the armed forces and the police, as well as almost complete impunity with regard to their actions.

Institutional Breakdown

Colombia cannot, from any point of view, continue on the road to the privatization of war and of citizen security, which implies a governmental loss of the monopoly on arms and justice that grows more serious each day. Pragmatic coexistence with paramilitary groups constitutes two absolutely condemnable policies that, far from diminishing the dimensions of the conflict, make it deeper and more widespread.

The state should decide to fight them without hesitation, like common criminals, or open the door to their eventual incorporation into civil life by recognizing them as political actors. With each passing day, the second option becomes less feasible: how can amnesty be offered to groups that commit more and more crimes against humanity each day, and that, at least on principle, are excluded from a politics of forgive and forget?

Future Prospects

What are Colombia's future prospects with regard to the conflict? Will external military intervention be necessary to prevent a worsening of the conflict? Is a negotiated plan viable? To respond to these questions, it is necessary to make some basic observations.

First, time is running out for all of the armed actors who defy the authority of the state. Tending to erode the already precarious margins of legitimacy that the armed groups currently have are, on the one hand, the growing mobilization of the international community in favor of a negotiated outcome to the Colombian conflict and, on the other hand, the important mobilization of the national community that was expressed, for example, through the ten million votes cast in October of 1997 in favor of a politics of peace.

Second, there is an economic barrier to the expansion of the rebel movement. Even though the ELN's and FARC's internal plans for the next few years include doubling the number of troops and fronts, as well as strengthening their military structures, it will be very difficult to achieve these objectives given the limitations of their economic resources unless they transform themselves into drug cartels. That is to say, in some way they are repeating the experience of the Maoist guerrillas in the poppy triangle in northern Myanmar.

Third, there is a growing military barrier. On the one hand, the paramilitary advance in the north of the country is destroying with blood and fire the ELN's support bases, and it is probable that the paras will displace this guerrilla group from its strategic sanctuaries, particularly the Serranía de San Lucas. On the other hand, the current reform of the armed forces will allow them to remedy their tactical insufficiencies with respect to the FARC, particularly in the south of the country.

Military Intervention or International Mediation?

Colombia finds itself in the eye of the hurricane. It has not managed to overcome the rebel conflict that constituted the crux of the international agenda in the era of the East/West confrontation, and it should respond to the exigencies of the post–cold war world agenda: human rights, environmentalism, an end to corruption and illicit drugs. Thus its international vulnerability deepens each day.

At the same time, the overlap of past and present conflicts deepens its internal vulnerability. Not only has the already chronic climate of violence that has plagued the country for several decades become worse in the last few years, but indicators of human rights have deteriorated, and corruption, the drug trade, and environmental destruction have increased.

In this way, Colombia has become a problem country for the international community. We are moving from the status of solid Western ally in the cold war period to a situation of isolation and condemnation. In this regard, it is indispensable to recall the transformations suffered currently in terms of the national sovereignty and the sacrosanct autonomy of nations. Both the United Nations and various developed nations defend the opposite position today, the right to intervention for humanitarian reasons. The result of this has already been seen: Bosnia, Somalia, and Haiti are only a few examples. In light of these lessons, it is necessary to tirelessly insist on the need for the internationalization of peace, and not that of war.

The successful and celebrated negotiation between the Guatemalan government and the UNRG (Unidad Nacional Revolucionaria Guatemalteca, Guatemalan National Revolutionary Union) finally allowed the convulsed Central American region to find peace and begin urgent work on a plan for economic development, political democratization, and regional integration. In the cases of El Salvador and Guatemala there was the mediating presence of the Group of Friendly Countries and the United Nations. The role of this multilateral organism was strategic not only in terms of peace but also, and equally, in terms of the later process of national reconstruction, as guarantors of the completion of the agreements.

Colombia finds itself in a time of dangerous conflict escalation and in the middle of a climate of deep mistrust, which will make a solution that is limited to internal actors improbable. I do not believe that the Colombian society can tolerate another round of negotiations that, from the outset, seems destined for failure because of the members' stubborn insistence on looking for personal benefits or petty victories. I also do not believe that our economy can continue to resist the many costs of the confrontation. Both the direct losses and the loss of international competitiveness are driving us toward an unmanageable situation.

If we do not boldly play the cards dealt us in order to accomplish peace, Colombia will be the only Latin American country that enters the new millennium in a worse situation.

TRANSLATED BY KATHERINE GOLDMAN

Notes

1. In Ibarra, "¿Rumbo a la colombianización de México?"
2. Palacios, "El espejo colombiano."
3. Oquist, *Violencia, conflicto y política en Colombia*, 184.
4. Samuel Huntington, *The Soldier and the State: The Theory and Politics of Civil-Military Relations* (Boston: Harvard University Press, 1956), quoted in Moneta, *Fuerzas Armadas y gobierno constitucional*.
5. Baker and Ausink, "State Collapse and Ethnic Violence."
6. The number of displaced in Colombia in 1997 had already reached a terrifying 920,000 people, which, according to the CODHES, exceeds the number of displaced generated by racial conflict in Rwanda, Burundi, and Zaire (900,000), the war in Bosnia-Herzegovina (345,000), and the total of Chipre, Afghanistan, Myanmar, and Iraq (510,000). But, in contrast to these countries, in which the displacement was generally directed toward other nations, in Colombia it is generally an internal displacement to marginal areas that lack public services, which is even more serious and of even more catastrophic consequence.
7. Cited by Benítez in "La ONU y el proceso de paz," 84.
8. The Colombian guerrillas, especially the Fuerzas Armadas Revolucionarias Colombianas (FARC, Revolutionary Armed Forces of Colombia), founded a centrifugal strategy over the past decades (dispersed fronts throughout the country). Today this is combined with a centripetal strategy (the concentration of fronts in order to attack military objectives in a joint manner). See Rangel, *Colombia*.
9. See Pizarro, *Insurgencia sin revolución*.
10. *Gramaje* refers to the various taxes that the guerrilla charges to cultivators, processors, and marketers of illicit drugs (marijuana, coca, and poppy.)
11. See in particular Ignacio Cano's presentation, "Policía, paramilitares y escuadrones de la muerte en América Latina."

Terror and Violence in Mexican Political Culture at the End of the Twentieth Century

RAQUEL SOSA ELÍZAGA

IN THEIR EVALUATIONS of the prevalent political conditions of peripheral countries, international organizations customarily consider Mexico a nation that has begun to consolidate its democracy. This positive evaluation is based on the occurrence of periodic elections and the presence of diverse political parties that eventually led to a change of government, in opposition to a regime that has managed to stay in power for seventy years.

The fact that it has been recognized that drug trafficking has penetrated the highest strata of government, leading to the continuous illegal use and diversion of public resources and the constant violation of human rights, has not fundamentally altered this conclusion. For the sake of stability and the well-being of the economic regime, it becomes more important to emphasize the elements of continuity than to condemn the violence and manipulation that the regime uses to sustain itself. A large body of specialized literature in Latin America and the United States tends to underrate the role that violence plays in the public life of countries that, like ours, have experienced dictatorships, wars, the deterioration of the population's living conditions, inequality, extreme poverty, and exclusion.[1]

The so-called governability of most Latin American countries stems not from the widespread exercise of the population's democratic rights but from a program of control based on the conviction that any state negotiation or mediation with organizations comprised of the masses ultimately threatens the existing system.[2] Ongoing political instability and disintegration play important roles in the distribution of wealth, which is based on both the development of a country's production capacity and its acquisition of large illegitimate gains from exporting raw materials, drug trafficking, selling arms, and state-level corruption.

This essay bears witness not only to the limitations of the electoral processes in Mexico, but also to the way a state party's regime, allied with the most dubious economic and political interests, threatens to subvert democracy through violence against citizens and organized communities.

The Substance of Violence: The State and Economic Power

A succession of governments has held office with neither restrictions on nor protection against adjustment programs, economic and commercial initiatives, financial deregulation, and the privatization of government enterprises. They have become obsessed with the growth and control of inflation and deficit reduction. These governments abandoned any pretense of creating lasting conditions for the well-being of the populace many years ago. They opted for control rather than the compromise previously accomplished through compliance with the demands of the labor, farmer, and professional unions and public sectors, and they gave exclusive priority to their relationship with big business and finance, national and international.[3]

After more than seventeen years of tension, the current administration is in a liminal situation, both in the federal sector and in the state sectors. Sustaining an alliance between financial groups, combined with the need to maintain political control of a population victimized by rising costs, has led them to undertake operations of great importance in order to hide irregular banking practices that guaranteed the status of the defenders of financial capital in public administration, starting in 1994.

In recent years, embezzlement in the banking industry has cost the country about twenty million dollars. The embezzlement not only lined the pockets of bankers themselves, but also funded electoral campaigns with millions of dollars of manufactured credit (supported solely by bank administrators' signatures) and contributed to foreign currency laundering, the creation of phantom businesses, and the accounts of officials who were involved in embezzlement in places as far away as Switzerland, Australia, or the Cayman Islands.[4]

The accused embezzlers' efforts to escape justice involved burdensome state expenditures and negotiations. Upon analyzing the private debts that were to be converted into public debt at the end of 1998, Congress forbade the disclosure of all knowledge of the concrete operations along with the first and last names of those responsible for the embezzlement. The accusations presented to the office of the republic's attorney general by the Democratic Revolutionary Party (PRD) were ignored. Proposals to convert the losses associated with banker embezzlement were attacked and dismissed by the organizers of a citizens' council. Although the council amassed three and a half million votes against the legitimization of fraud, the oldest opposing faction, the National Action Party (PAN)—some of whose best-known directors were involved in the bank salvage program—gave in to governmental pressures when the time came for discussion and approval by the Office of the Deputy. In an "act of patriotism and responsibility" (as defined by their directors), the PAN approved the conversion of the embezzlers' debts into public debt.

In reprisal, the PRD reduced the debt capacity of the government of Mexico City (headed by Cuauhtémoc Cárdenas) by more than one billion pesos and withheld federal funds. The Canadian corporation hired to perform an audit was forced to submit its report in spite of receiving only the most cryptic information on each embezzlement case.[5]

The evident link between economic and political power made it impossible for the administration to maintain the facade of democratic methods of inquiry into the government's actions. The government now readied itself to confront new crises, organizing its armor with an eye on the upcoming elections.[6]

The Dismantling of Public Resistance: Big Brother's Actions

In Mexico's social politics, maintaining collective control is based on two fundamental mechanisms: continually cutting social services to reduce expenditures, and instituting programs to combat poverty that divide communities and dismantle resistance. Year after year, Congress has authorized minor increases in social spending that hide a decrease in the percentage of the GNP and related per capita spending.[7] Congress has also approved legal reforms that reduce the low-income population's access to social services such as education, health care, and insurance, in order to gradually dismantle public institutions and pave the way for their privatization. This policy is enhanced by low-profile public assistance programs that guarantee the approval of loans by diverse international organizations.[8]

Programs instituted to combat poverty have brought with them a complete reorganization of the relationships between the state and communities. During Carlos Salinas de Gotari's presidency (1988–1994), farmers' and migrant day-laborers' social and political organizations were to be replaced by solidarity committees directly dependent on the executive branch. The goal was to stimulate collaboration in the form of economic support for the inhabitants' production in regions where the opposing party had received the majority vote in the presidential elections.[9] In a second phase, during Ernesto Zedillo's presidency (1994–2000), the programs were reorganized with the specific objective of dismantling the channels through which their host communities could articulate responses and grievances.[10]

The process used for distributing aid was as follows. Women from each community were selected to operate the program, and detailed information about the members of their community (family make-up, income bracket, living conditions, and political preferences) was demanded of them. On the basis of the information gathered by these women, a list of priorities was mapped out that assumed the distribution of economic assistance in all cases, along with the offer of temporary employment, support for the construction of housing, and the granting of health services and educational funding—subject to the acceptance of a political and electoral commitment to the government party.[11]

The insufficiency and misuse of programs focused on the poor become evident if we consider that, according to CEPAL (Comisión Económica para América Latina y el Caribe, Economic Commission for Latin America and the Caribbean), 43 percent of Mexican households (close to fifty million people) are poverty stricken, or that more than half of the country's inhabitants suffer from malnutrition, particularly among the indigenous populations. One also has to take into account the degree of polarization produced by the concentration of wealth in the hands of a few and the country's widespread poverty.[12]

Nevertheless, the use of poverty as an instrument of political control has been relatively efficient, largely because it uses an ad hoc apparatus whose successful operation depends on variable political decisions (usually a function of electoral results). It is restricted to specific time periods and—to the extent to which program operators are among the beneficiaries originally targeted by the program rather than employees paid by the state—does not generate additional expenses, permanent commitments, or the possibility of alliances forming among its operators. In a strict sense, the granting of economic assistance is a decision made by an invisible and unrecognizable "above." The operatives can be renewed as many times as necessary, and the selection (purging or expansion) of beneficiaries is processed independently of the criteria suggested by those who supply information and work in exchange for their own survival.

The invisible tie between power and the poor results in the extraordinary capacity of the state to exercise control through blackmail and threats against those who aspire to join the program, who wish to temporarily participate, or who may have already been excluded. Big Brother's decisions admit no appeal, and the sensation of helplessness that they produce is undoubtedly much greater than the effects of poverty itself.

The Pressure of the Media:
The Nonexistent Truth

Given the presence of an objective and free media that allows for a great diversity of opinion, censorship of the news has been refined by controlling time allotments and the context of news bulletins. Information is presented, albeit briefly, about almost everything that occurs, and different points of view have a place, however small. The result, however, is the blurring of the magnitude of events, for audiences receive no information in the form of image, sound, or text about the differential importance of testimonies, the degree of actors' involvement in the events, and the individual or collective responsibility in the decision-making process. The larger truth disappears behind the multiplicity of minor truths or little white lies. When all events seem flat and distant, it is impossible to establish an order among them or to formulate a relatively well-founded position.[13]

Official discourse is transmitted without criticism, even when it directly contradicts reality. The only possible solution to the country's problems—repeated to the citizenry daily—is the defense of national unity and sovereignty, and whatever allows us to systematically confront adverse international circumstances. The repetition of the lie obliges communications administrators to superimpose ideological positions over every critical opinion, which is obligatorily filtered. Time and again, absolutely unconnected parallel discourses confront each other and result in the ratification of the government's positions on the terms initially proposed.

During elections the television consortium, the press, and the radio benefit from the multimillion-dollar resources of those who influence public opinion with media-based campaigns. Through them, candidates and hopefuls substitute staged debates for the real exchange of points of view, a few "tough" slogans for real positions and demands; through repetition, the public buys these as believable and acceptable. Lacking any emotional or intellectual ties to their messages, politicians are presented time after time to an audience presumed to be ignorant of previous information, lacking in proper judgment, and predisposed to favor their particular points of view. The resulting impoverishment of public discourse can only in the end exclude a real audience that is much more avid for criticism and responses than the "protagonists" are in a position to admit.[14]

The Use of Force: A Permanent Resource

As is true virtually throughout Latin America, the so-called democratic consolidation in Mexico has been accompanied by the increasing use of the armed forces to resolve internal conflicts.[15] Since 1994, the support of North America, an increase in military forces, and weapons modernization have been sustained.[16] They operate in concert with campaigns against drug trafficking, the harassment of Zapatista-affiliated populations in Chiapas, the frontal attack against the armed "Erpista" and "Eperrista" groups in Guerrero and Oaxaca, and territorial control in disaster situations, such as earthquakes and floods.[17]

Studies conducted by independent human rights organizations suggest that a national policy does exist regarding the use of public force. The territory's military occupation is carried out under the following specific conditions, which lie outside every constitutional norm. The army installs itself in communities that are considered to be "high risk" and secures operatives close to the population, localizes and controls productive activities, antagonizes social organizations and political independents' activities, conducts arbitrary interrogations and arrests, and controls provisions and community services. Everything is done in accordance with the counterinsurgency program dating back to the 1970s that was used in various Latin American countries.

The major use of funds occurs when these forces suspect that armed rebel groups are present. In these cases, a radius of not less than three square kilometers is defined through special operations. Within these parameters, the entire population is forced to surrender and the directors or members of the independent organizations are apprehended without order or legal justification. These individuals are tortured, forced to sign declarations that associate them with armed activities, and sent to state prisons to await judgment, a process that can take several years. Additionally, a vast horizontal network of political assassinations, most of which have been concealed within intercommunity confrontations, is set up to induce collective terror and paralysis.[18]

In the states of Guerrero and Oaxaca, where the violence has intensified over the past few years, military action is complemented by the so-called Mixed Operation Brigades that place the state and federal judicial police and the public municipal security forces under the orders of and the jurisdiction of the army. "Rastrillo" operatives—whose presence coincides with sites designated to receive benefits from the programs designed to "combat poverty"—have been placed throughout the country's indigenous areas.

Beginning in 1996, army and Mixed Operation Brigades operatives were supplemented by paramilitary groups, particularly in the country's indigenous zones. These groups, trained and armed by the military and the state forces for public security, were developed in communities where the opposing social or political organization is in the majority, and where PRI supporters have been expelled or marginalized from collective decisions. The functions of paramilitary members include the destruction of harvests, the assault and rape of women, attacks on defenseless populations, and selective en masse assassinations.[19] The event that fostered awareness of these groups took place in December of 1997 in Acteal, Chiapas.[20]

One of the independent human rights organizations that has most carefully systematized the information regarding the civil and political rights violations of unarmed populations registered a national total of 4,068 cases between December 1995 and October 1998. It affirms that in more than 80 percent of the cases in which perpetrators have been identified, they are members of public security outfits or the armed forces, while most of the victims are members of social and political organizations, particularly in rural areas.[21]

One of the most significant characteristics of such brutal force is the absence of a justifying discourse like that offered by the military leadership of the dictatorships or in support of the wars of the previous decade. The coldness with which operations designed to guarantee "public security" are carried out contrasts extraordinarily with the number of dead, injured, detained, and disappeared during the neoliberal period. If impunity itself constitutes a stimulus for the repeated human rights violations carried out against a defenseless population, what is peculiar is the absence of arguments that might be used to convince the rest of the population that the use of force is justified.

Neoliberalism has replaced the concept of the enemy or the political adversary with the "transgressor," "criminal," or "terrorist." These propagandistic terms elicit fear while precluding punishment for those who carry out state-sanctioned illegal activities and absolving them from any political repercussions for their actions. The reorganization of public security during the last fifteen years in practically every region tends toward a suppression of vocabulary and naturally attempts to do the same with the conscience, legitimizing alternatives to the authority of the state to preserve order.[22]

As in the best periods of Emile Durkheim's influence on sociologists, and in the worst of the U.S. Pentagon's strategies, "anomie" is perceived as dysfunctionality with respect to a system in which the majority of citizens are integrated.[23] It merits no consideration and, as a result, it is easy to promote the most brutal actions against anomie. Whoever raises a voice in protest against the uncontested and uncontrolled use of force on behalf of their peers does nothing but defend criminality, an accusation repeated in Mexico as well as in other countries, particularly against defenders of human rights.

The Disarticulation and Division of the Resistance

Electoral and political opposition activity grew consistently in 1997 and 1998. Regions that had no significant organized force and had not required special action by the state because they were not part of the geography of misery, such as Zacatecas, Baja California, Nayarit, or Tlaxcala, were converted into opposing blocks beginning with the victory of opposition parties in elections in the nation's capital. Suddenly, a fifth of the population found itself beyond the ruling party's control. This forced the government to establish support for municipal and state elections in Veracruz, Chiapas, Michoacán, the State of Mexico, and Guerrero. In the last three cases, the security forces' actions and the massive distribution of goods and services from programs to combat poverty were barely adequate to ensure the defeat of opposing candidates.

In Veracruz, where a political alliance was formed between the government and one of the country's richest impresarios, the work of dismantling the opposition was accomplished through the division of its major party, brought about by running as a candidate an obscure individual recently discharged from the government and presumably connected with drug mafias. In Chiapas, the combination of counter-insurgency strategy, the conflict between the PRD and the Zapatista Army for National Liberation (EZLN), and the fortuitous occurrence of Hurricane Paulina (which allowed the army to control areas previously governed by the opposition) helped officialdom to triumph by a wide margin.[24]

The strategy of encouraging internal division has been partially successful. It has played a significant role in the annulment of the PRD's internal elections, the breakdown of attempts at alliance between the PRD and the PAN, the orchestration of an alliance between the PAN and the PRI in Congress, and even the confrontation between student and professorial factions in the strike at the National Autonomous University of Mexico (UNAM). It has begun to split the alliance forged in Chiapas comprised of all opposition factions that participated in the 2000 elections. The split may reverse itself during the next presidential race and the change of government in Mexico City.

Nevertheless, these politics place the country in a dangerous situation. The administration of instability as an ongoing condition could include ruptures in the official sector, the discrediting of the opposition's spokespersons, and the loss of control over public finances, clearing the way for a political and economic crisis of tremendous proportions. The ruling politicians favor the following scenario: no real dialogues or eventual negotiations between the government and the opposition; the use of the army and paramilitary forces to silence the noncompliant; the disruption of mediations between social and political organizations; political and electoral control of populations immersed in extreme poverty; and draining the treasury indefinitely to support interest payments on a debt accrued by dishonest bankers, drug traffickers, money laundering, and state corruption.

The Limits of Violence

Among the conditions for the effective use of violence and terror is one that translates into neither its permanent use nor the independent use of hegemonic control. Throughout the neoliberal years, during which no strategy for responsibly overcoming the economic weakness in Latin American countries was implemented, governments and financial organizations have been intent on turning instability into the most promising expeditor of high earning indexes. The indefinite postponement of change, the exclusion of the majority, and the indiscriminate invitations for economic, political, and military intervention have become dangerous components of collective life.

If arms dealers and drug traffickers constitute the most important actors in the reorganization of society, if the destruction of the communal tapestry seems to be a convenient form of achieving the goal of relegating the opposition to the margins, the decline of each country's economic capacity, the continual decrease in stable job opportunities, the increase in poverty, and the deterioration of general living conditions will limit the ability to incorporate the migrant work force into other regions and other countries, particularly the United States. None of these therefore can be considered long-term solutions. A blind eye should not be turned to these ticking time bombs: while short-term policies generate revenues, in the long term, their destructive potential increases and threatens to invade other spheres.

Violence and terror are high-risk measures because they profoundly affect the system of political relations, culture, and social life of each of our countries. In Mexico, we can confirm this without hesitation: a culture is incubating that implies contempt for the rights of others; the search for privileges above or against the law; the undervaluing of work as a means of gaining financial wealth; the discrediting of criticism and knowledge as paths to overcoming collective problems; the mistrust of all authority; and the lack of a sense that there might be peaceful resolutions to conflict, individualism, and the destruction of nuclear solidarity.

The use of force to suppress or divert political conflict is directly contrary to every model of the construction of citizenship as it is understood in the traditional sense of "equality under the law," or, as we prefer to define it, the simple exercise of individual and collective rights. No citizenship can be based upon inequality, extreme poverty, exclusion, or authoritarianism. Furthermore, it is useless to think of education as a means of promoting acceptable behavior if practices and institutions that govern the social order remain unchanged, as demonstrated by the strike at UNAM.

It is impossible to restore the value of work as the legitimate means of survival in society, the need for bonds of solidarity, and confidence in the collective ability to find peaceful and positive resolutions to conflict if steps are not taken to transform the organization, management, and supervision of public life. This means an insistence on the construction of an order based on the true recognition of diversity, the full exercise of citizens' rights, and the production of goods and services that guarantee, first and foremost, compliance with the population's needs.

Similarly, it becomes indispensable to work toward the reform of judicial systems that have, until now, replicated impunity by way of corruption; the purging and setting of boundaries for the police and military operations whose orientation has been exclusively guided by counterinsurgence doctrines; the reform of penal codes and laws for public security that, up until now, were directed toward severe sanctioning of society's legal transgressors, but not of the government or economically empowered groups.

Even in the face of the deterioration and desperation in which the policy of violence places us, the import of tradition and community practices can still be recognized. The search for the consolidation of collective identities is based on the defense of dignity; the struggle for the expansion of collective rights, particularly for the indigenous communities; and the formulation of development initiatives that presuppose a policy for the effective elimination of poverty, as well as the search for peaceful and lasting resolutions to conflict.

It is possible that these measures may still not be enough to shape a new orientation toward collective life and that the severity of the crisis may postpone or obscure its influence on Mexican society. Nevertheless, in my opinion, they constitute the only imaginable salvation when we are faced with the destruction that is the result of excesses of authoritarianism, extreme and illegal concentration of wealth and power in the hands of a few, and exclusion of the majority. The potential of this alternative to reconstruction is less today, while its strength is decreased and largely fragmentary. We hope, for everyone's benefit, that the possibility will not disappear in the early years of a new century.

TRANSLATED BY HEATHER HAMMETT

Notes

1. See Manuel Antonio Garretón, "La democracia entre dos épocas. América Latina, 1999," *Revista paraguaya de sociología* 28, 80 (January–April 1991): 23–37; Fernando Calderón and Mario Dos Santos, "Hacia un nuevo orden estatal en América Latina. Veinte tesis políticas y un corolario" (Santiago de Chile: Fondo de Cultura Económica/ FLACSO [Facultad Latinoamericano de Ciencias Sociales], 1991); Norbert Lechner, *Cultura política y democratización* (Santiago de Chile: CLACSO [Centro Latinoamericano de Ciencias Sociales]/FLACSO, 1987); Augusto Varas, *Transición a la democracia* (Santiago de Chile: Asociación chilena de investigación para la paz, 1984).

2. For an analysis of this subject, consult the following studies by Raquel Sosa Elízaga: "Descomposición política, militarización y resistencia popular en México," in Margarita López Maya, ed., *Lucha popular, democracia, neoliberalismo: protesta popular en América Latina en los años de ajuste* (Caracas: Nueva Sociedad/ Universidad de Central de Venezuela, 1999), 65–78; "Violencia política na América Latina: contradicão ou consequencia da política neoliberal?" *Cadernos do CEAS* (Centro de Estudos e Ação Social) 173 (1998): 11–20; "Violencia política y terrorismo del Estado," in Ruy Mauro Marini and Márgara Millán, coords., *La teoría social latinoamericana. Cuestiones contemporáneas* (Mexico: Ediciones El Caballito, 1996), 4:141–148; *Conciencia colectiva y control social en Emile Durkheim* (Mexico: Dirección General de Publicaciones/UNAM, 1998).

3. Lucio Oliver, Eduardo Ruiz, Irene Sánchez, and Raquel Sosa, "Neoliberalismo y política: la crisis mexicana," *Estudios latinoamericanos* (Centro de estudios latinoamericanos de la facultad de ciencias políticas y sociales de UNAM) 4 (1995): 115–138.

4. Andés Manuel López Obrador, *FOBAPROA: Expediente abierto* (Mexico: Grijalbo, 1999).

5. While Michael Mackey pocketed twenty million dollars to carry out the audit of the FOBAPROA without producing a single significant piece of data, the total fiscal cost of the bank's debt was estimated at between 600,000 million and one billion Mexican pesos at the end of June 1998. In the farewell project of the year 2000, the government proposes designating 59,300 million pesos for deposit in the bank salvage fund. See Gerardo Flores, Victor Fuentes, et al., "Debate de la semana: ¿Informe, revisión, auditoría o qué?" *El financiero*, July 31, 1999; Carlos Fernández Vega, "Expediente FOBAPROA: ¿Cuánto valen los empresarios rescatados?" *La Jornada*, July 31, 1999; Carlos Acosta and Agustín Vargas, "Comienza el calvario del IPAB," *Proceso*, September 19, 1999; Antonio Castellanos, "Prevén la transferencia," *La Jornada*, November 12, 1999.

6. The World Bank and the International Monetary Fund express their confidence in the Mexican government, whose estimated growth in 1999 was 3 percent. During that year they granted loans for $5,200 million and $4,200 million respectively. See Jim Cason and David Brooks, "Crecimiento negativo para América Latina," *La Jornada*, April 8, 1999; David Aponte, "Ya utilizó el gobierno," *La Jornada*, October 31, 1999; Rosa Elvira Vargas, "Anuncia el BM préstamo," *La Jornada*, October 12, 1999.

7. Between 1998 and 1999, the amount of money from the federal budget that was allocated to education was reduced by 3.8 percent, and to health, 4.4 percent (the lowest spending for social programs since 1992). Spending for defense increased by 2 percent. For the year 2000, an election year, on the other hand, increases of between 4 and 8 percent will be seen for social programs.

See "Informe: país de contrastes. ¿Quiénes somos los mexicanos?" *Reforma*, July 22, 1999; Mireya Cuéllar, "En 1999, el menor gasto social," *La Jornada*, January 10, 1999; Antonio Castellanos, "Gasto programable del sector público por clasificación sectoral económica," in Ernesto Zedillo, *V Informe de gobierno* (Mexico, 1999).

8. Laurell, "Social Policy Issues in Latin America," 221–240, and *La reforma contra la salud*.

9. J. Molnar and J. Weldon, "Electoral Determinants: Consequences of National Solidarity," in Wayne A. Cornelius, Ann L. Craig, and Jonathan Fox, eds., *Transforming State-Society Relations in Mexico: The National Solidarity Strategy* (San Diego: University of California at San Diego, 1994), 123–142. In the same volume see Denise Dresser, "Bringing the Poor Back In," 143–165.

10. Three million homes in the country are included in the social assistance program (PROGRESA), which includes grants and dietary support. The selection of beneficiaries according to priority includes the States of Chiapas, Oaxaca, Guerrero, Veracruz, and Hidalgo. Luis Guillermo Hernández, "Cambia estrategia presupuestal contra pobreza," *Reforma*, November 22, 1999. See also Julie Boltvinik, "Evolución heterogénea de la pobreza en México, 1979–1995" (a paper given at the international conference "Confronting Development: Asserting Mexico's Economic and Social Policy Changes," University of California at San Diego, 1999) and "La agudización de la pobreza en el regimen neoliberal" (a paper given at a conference entitled "Neoliberalismo y resistencia popular," May 18, 1998; published in Mexico by the Secretaria de Formación Política del Partido de la Revolución Democrática, 1999, 81–88).

11. Mexico: Secretaria de Formación Política del Partido de la Revolución Democrática, 1999, 2.

12. According to economist David Márquez Ayala's calculations, 10 percent of the wealthiest households account for 38 percent of the total earnings, while 32 percent of the poorest households (with earnings lower than three minimum-wage salaries) receive only 9 percent of the total wages. See "La distribución del ingreso en México," CEPAL, *La Jornada*, November 15, 1999; Luis Guillermo Hernández, "Fractura al país la desnutrición," *Reforma*, October 17, 1999; Ivonne Melgar, "Aumenta pobreza en México," *Reforma* CEPAL, July 17, 1999.

13. Delvi Crovi, coord., *Cultura política, información y comunicación de masas* (Mexico: Asociación Latinoamericana de Sociología, 1996); Florence Toussaint, *Democracia y medios de comunicación: un binomio inexplorado* (Mexico: La Jornada Ediciones/Centro de Investigaciones Interdisciplinarias en Ciencias y Humanidades, UNAM, 1995).

14. The internal pro-PRI campaign for presidential candidacy of the Institutional Revolutionary Party (PRI) and for the government of the federal district concluded on November 7, 1999. On a day of empty ballot boxes, ten million votes were registered and accusations of irregularities were reported in local and federal electoral processes.

15. According to a CEPAL report, military spending in Latin America increased from $13.5 to $26.5 million between 1990 and 1998 (*El Universal*, October 29, 1999). In Mexico, expenditures on national security, the armed forces, and the Department of Justice have increased from 1,228.4 million pesos in 1987 to 30,540.4 million in 1997; see E. Zedillo, "Anexo: gasto programable del sector público," in *V Informe de gobierno*.

16. According to data from the secretary of national defense, close to five thousand

Mexican military personnel have attended courses abroad, more than half of them in the United States, between 1978 and 1998. The Mexican army is currently at 170,000 members. Beginning in October 1999, the Preventive Federal Police was added to their forces, with combined elements from the army and the police, personnel from Central Investigations and National Security, from the Police of Federal Roads, and the customs police. See Jorge Alejandro Medellín, "Está en riesgo la capacitación antidrogas," *El Universal*, November 13, 1999; Jorge Luis Sierra, "APFP, la nueva contrainsurgencia," *El Universal*, October 29, 1999.

17. Gilberto López Rivas, Jorge Luis Sierra, and Alberto Enríquez del Valle, *Las fuerzas armadas mexicanas al fin del milenio. Los militares en la coyuntura actual* (Mexico: LVII Legislatura, Grupo Parlamentario del PRD, 1999); Carlos Fazio, *El tercer vínculo. De teoría del caos a la teoría de la militarización* (Mexico: Joaquín Mortiz, 1996).

18. Comisión Mexicana, *Las consecuencias de la militarización*.

19. Centro de Derechos Humanos Miguel Agustín Pro Juárez, "Informe annual," (1999).

20. Centro de los Derechos Humanos Fray Bartolomé de las Casas, *Acteal*, 1, 2. The December 1997 event was the massacre in rural southeastern Mexico, where the Zapatistas' rebellion began, which occurred when government forces confronted villagers whom they accused of collaborating with the EZLN and committing terrorist acts.

21. Centro de los Derechos Humanos Fray Francisco de Vitoria OP, "Informe annual" (1997–98), 996.

22. Area de Análisis Político, "Ley de Seguridad Pública," 1, 2.

23. Sosa, *Conciencia colectiva*.

24. In 1998 and 1999, the official party once again began to increase its percentage of votes, which climbed to 49 percent. See Instituto Federal Electoral, *Resultados de las elecciones estatales y municipales*, 1998, 1999.

Democracy, Citizenship, and Violence in Venezuela

ANA MARÍA SANJUÁN

IN VENEZUELA THE OFFICIAL HOMICIDE rate for 1999 showed an increase of 20 percent from the previous year. The increase was even greater in the city of Caracas, where the number of homicides reached the hundred mark on some weekends and particularly bad days. Scarcely two decades ago that figure would have been the total number of homicides in the nation's capital during an entire year. The figures on homicide are imprecise because, among other reasons, not all statistics in the country are given the same importance. While it is possible to establish the effects of macroeconomic weaknesses on the nation's finances from day to day, it is more difficult to ascertain the real number of victims of violence, perhaps because the majority who suffer from this phenomenon belong to the most vulnerable sectors of society; in other words, they are poor. With its causes and consequences, the current state of uncontrolled social violence in Venezuela constitutes the principal threat to the ethos of democracy in aspects as central as ethical standards, the expansion of human rights, and the predominance of public liberties and the state of law.

Venezuela ended the twentieth century undergoing a series of complex processes of political, economic, and social transformation. In the country's current situation one observes the simultaneous exhaustion of a model of economic development and its modes of state intervention within a more general framework of politico-institutional restructuring intended to broaden and strengthen democracy for society as a whole. Taken individually, each of the changes is extremely complex; the transformations in progress do not always converge, and they themselves unleash tensions, social and political antagonisms that translate into a new series of conflicts. The growing collective awareness of the gravity and profundity of the crisis accelerates the social imperative to break with the past, radicalizing society's agenda of demands.

In the social realm, the crisis expresses itself in a growing fragmentation and heterogeneity, in the exacerbation and extension of relative poverty, and in the displacement of the public sphere as a privileged forum for participation and expression of citizenship. In this new environment, violence and personal insecurity are fundamental concerns for the majority of citizens, as shown in the public-opinion studies periodically undertaken in Venezuela's most important cities. The fear of becoming the victim of a violent crime, which is constant for the majority of the country's residents—independent of social position, gender, education level, or work situation—has doubled in the last five years.

The problem of violent criminality is foremost on the list of citizens' concerns, leading to a polarization of collective perceptions of the phenomenon. Through its wide repercussions, the real or symbolic increase in violence creates skewed perceptions and extreme simplifications, which combine to widen the breaches in society. The power of images of violence, lived and consumed without mediation, provokes opposing positions on their possible causes, among which socioeconomic factors are privileged, confusing the visibility of some of its variables with the true problem, its multicausal origin, and thus with its consequences. In this way the social and institutional attitude toward violence itself can become another of its causes.

This essay will present some of the characteristics that define democracy and the pursuit of citizenship in Venezuela, as well as their possible influence on social violence. The magnitude and characteristics of this violence will be analyzed, in turn, through the normative and legal contexts that regulate everyday life and social conflicts in the country.

The Context of Violence in Venezuela: Deficiencies of the State, Democracy, and Citizenship

In what is described as its restricted or minimalist version, democracy is understood in many Latin American countries, among them Venezuela, as the achievement and maintenance of a political regime based on popular sovereignty, which is expressed through free and competitive elections. Other constitutive characteristics of democracy include the real possibility of alternation in power, a place for the participation of political minorities, political and partisan pluralism, and popular representation and participation in public matters.[1] Nevertheless, the absence or precariousness of fundamental principles and mechanisms of democracy—such as institutional respect for the state of law, civil authority over military forces, and citizen security, as well as the basic minimal conditions necessary for the exercise of civil, political, and social rights—has allowed for the survival of an institutional absurdity: democracies in which the majority of the population lacks citizenship.[2]

According to its original definition, citizenship "essentially consists of assuring that each person is treated as a full member in a society of equals."[3] Citizenship has been divided into three distinct rights: civil rights (those necessary to ensure individual liberty), political rights (rights of direct or indirect participation in political power), and social rights (the right to well-being, education, health, minimum salary, and social services in general).

Modern citizenship is considered a combination of rights and obligations that are foreseeable and valid for each member of the political community. These rights and obligations can only be fully exercised in a given political and social community if the juridical and legal framework is established by universal criteria, if the state of law maintains validity equally among all citizens—regardless of their social position—and if there are sufficient constitutional guarantees that public powers will protect rights and be held responsible for their own deficiencies. Similarly, if private relations are to develop peacefully, it is a necessary condition that governments, like leaders, respect the constitution and laws, and that the state enforce norms with universality and predictability.

Since the mid–1980s, an atmosphere of profound disequilibrium has developed in Venezuela that affects life in a variety of ways. While economic transformations are not negligible, political life has seen the most extraordinary changes in recent years. In ways that have yet to be determined, both economics and politics have affected the development of the state in its primary function as the arbiter that corrects inequities and pacifies social relations.

Venezuela's democracy could be characterized as a polyarchy due to the clear presence of elements like elected public authorities, open and clean elections, universal suffrage, the right to compete for public positions, freedom of expression, alternative information, and freedom of association.[4] Despite its achievements after four decades, the political regime shows signs of vulnerability, such as a precarious and low degree of institutionalization, the prevalence of an authoritarian political culture, the corrosion of republican values, an extreme asymmetry of political powers in favor of the executive branch, and an abysmal difference between the legal country and the real country, which stems from the state's inefficiency and recalcitrance toward its responsibilities.

These characteristics weigh heavily on political and social life and prevent satisfactory responses to demands for the expansion of democracy, spaces of public participation, and the rights of citizenship that have been heard among the population since the early 1980s. Nonuniversality of rights and difficult access to the legal order lead to social violence and a culture of illegality that primarily affects the most vulnerable. The rectification of these problems fills out the agenda of political reform, since the current ineffectualness of the state of law with regard to the poor majorities and the elite's systematic subversion of the rule of law have resulted in a high tolerance for legal instability, which has culminated—after periods of declining republican principles and values—in a crisis of authority.[5]

Given its structure and preeminence over the economic and social sectors, the state has had a determining influence on the consolidation of democracy and citizenship in Venezuela. Diverse factors have affected the state's efficiency in its principal functions, and its legitimacy in the process. The proportion and duration of the nation's fiscal crisis drastically affected the state's ability to perform basic tasks, especially those related to "the promotion of collective well-being through the redistribution of funds in salaries, health care, education, social security, and justice." The state's limitations in guaranteeing order and public security, as well as the subsistence-level conditions of vast sectors of the population, have dangerously widened the socially and politically excluded fringes, eroding its already precarious legitimacy even more. Reduction of the state's role through policies such as the redistribution of national territory and the breakdown of traditional mechanisms for including less-favored segments of society have affected the guarantee of universal access to essential public health services and judicial order, making the exercise of citizenship impossible for the most vulnerable elements of the population. The crisis of legitimacy that faces the Venezuelan state has also eroded its ability to maintain a legal monopoly on violence and the use of instruments of coercion, occasioning an exponential increase in criminality and urban violence in the nation's main cities.

As a consequence of the economic and political crisis and the state's inability to fulfill some of its fundamental functions, Venezuela's social situation has worsened considerably over the last fifteen years. After almost three decades of upward social mobility and the system's demonstrated capacity to include majority populations in services such as education and health care, the failures of Venezuela's state-based development model and the investment-based petroleum economy put an end to traditional mechanisms of social integration, reversing, moreover, many of the social gains that had been achieved in the first stage of the democratic regime. Indicators of the dispersion and distribution of income suggest a sustained increase in inequality, since income redistribution has been increasingly regressive in the last decade. Other problems are only partially captured by statistical indicators focused on revenues and persistent inequalities: the feeling of precariousness, the growing sense of insecurity, and the attenuation of social bonds that have developed along with the real inaccessibility of many of the benefits of society, such as justice.[6]

In peripheral areas of Venezuelan cities—where the poorest live—the state's deficit is expressed not only in the lack of infrastructure, health care, or education, but also in its incapacity to promote and initiate minimal social regulations and to valorize their legality. In practice this means a democracy characterized by what O'Donnell calls "low citizenship-intensity." The existence of a political democracy and the acceptance of some of the rights associated with it do not preclude the violation of the fundamental civil rights of the majority of the population on the part of public agencies responsible for maintaining social order. The fragility of institutions designed to guarantee respect for civil rights nationally, and the lack of mechanisms to guarantee civil control over the actions of the armed forces or the police, make evident the preeminence of authoritarian traits in Venezuelan political culture, the weakness of democratic values, and the insufficiency of the state in providing law and order. This situation fosters violence in the negotiation of the conflicts inherent in social life.

Thus, in the poor areas where structural difficulties inhibit the creation of organic relationships with state institutions, the absence of old establishments capable of regulating conflicts is much more marked.[7] That absence increases the degree of social disorganization, favoring informal or alternative justice systems that feed the cycle of violence. The impossibility of practicing justice eliminates an excellent space for socialization in the public sphere, one that would lead to the long-term development of democratic values and the skills and traditions of citizenship.

The pervasive violence in almost all areas of social life—private as well as public—directly affects democratic governability and stability, since it generates an environment of insecurity and instability and has negative repercussions for the reasonable and harmonious development of public institutions. This is due to the fact that the resources necessary for consolidation and institutional modernization are instead directed at the struggle against criminality and violence, limiting the renovation of public institutions as well as their efficacy in the continuity and planning of activities. The elevated level of violence in Venezuela not only limits institutional development, but also erodes the social legitimacy of public and private institutions, which come to be perceived by the population as ineffective or inadequate in their response to society's needs. From there, incorrect perceptions about the efficiency and capacity of the democratic system and its institutions can develop, as well as a series of social and political attitudes favoring quotas in political participation and democratic control of the nation instead of a reduction in the rates of social violence.

For the majorities, being vulnerable to violence and incapable of accessing justice directly aggravate social exclusion, so that citizenship itself has the appearance of privilege. In Venezuela, this lack is evident not only in social and economic inequality, but also in the recurrent violation of civil and human rights that the less fortunate sectors of the population frequently suffer.

Albeit to a different extent, the international process of globalization has also impacted a social totality already disarticulated and fragmented because of poverty: for the vulnerable, globalization increases the perception and reality of exclusion. The variable velocities at which members of different social sectors move in Venezuela show, in practice, that a relatively low proportion of the population is hyper-modernized and hyperintegrated into the vertiginous consumption and logic of globalization. Meanwhile, much larger social groups at the center of a complex process of social reordering pursue economic practices of survival and experience a total lack of citizenship. Individualism, lack of optimism and faith in the future, and the abandonment of the excluded are also inherent and constitutive facts of contemporary Venezuelan society that influence shared expectations and the self-image of the country and its vision of the future.

The state's crisis, the accumulated lack in civil, political, and social citizenship, and the political system's inability to negotiate the totality of society's demands permit multiple expressions of violence to take place, which in turn negatively affect the conditions necessary for the recuperation of democracy and the improvement of the social bond.

Violence in Venezuela: Dimensions, Modalities, and Characteristics

The most relevant characteristics of the manifestations of violence in Venezuela allow us to define the problem as social and predominantly urban. Despite the enormous deficiencies in the reliability and quality of official statistics, studies of criminal behavior are unanimous in recognizing marked increases in the number of crimes reported, especially violent crimes such as homicide, robbery, and car theft. In addition, research undertaken in emergency services at public hospitals in Caracas report a sustained increase in care given to trauma victims, especially youths, women, and children.

Violence in Venezuela finds various expressions, not only in urban criminality, but in a series of social behaviors. The distinction between crime and violence becomes crucial in this case, since these two social phenomena coincide on certain occasions but can also exclude one another. They coincide when a crime—so the penal codes used in nearly every country explain—is committed by using violence.[8] When this is the case, acts of violence—including battery, homicide, kidnapping, rape, and other crimes against people—are combined with crimes against property such as robbery or theft.

There are, however, sociocultural factors that tend to normalize a number of daily behaviors by representing them as part and parcel of private interpersonal relations inseparable from the area of the affective. Familial or interpersonal violence (between spouses, against offspring, children and adolescents, the elderly; collective brawls) that the penal code recognizes as criminal only in its most extreme occurrence should also be considered among these collective or individual behaviors.

Crime is the transgression of a group of norms imposed by the state. Violence marks the limit of social conflict and can even include the direct action of the state.[9] In the case of Venezuela, the magnitude of crimes has increased significantly. But the growth of social violence has been exponential.

Figures speak eloquently of the explosion of criminal violence over the last fifteen years. While in 1982, 22 percent of crimes against property involved violence, in 1998 the proportion rose to 49.6 percent, with homicides increasing by 200 percent. In Caracas, homicides have increased by 506 percent over the last ten years.[10]

Studies suggest some patterns in the characteristics and circumstances of the occurrence of violence. For example, theft and robbery generally occur in public spaces, at any hour of the day or week, at the hands of a stranger. In urban zones where the risk of homicide is high for young adults between twenty and twenty-four years of age, the risk of theft is relatively low. Higher rates of robbery and theft, personal injury, and transit accidents are found in areas of higher socioeconomic levels, whereas homicide rates are higher in the peripheral areas.

Interpersonal conflicts (brawls, fights, assaults) take place, for the most part, in the victim's residence or in a public place near his or her home; more occur on Fridays, Saturdays, and Sundays between six and twelve o'clock at night than on other days of the week. The victimizer is generally an acquaintance of or has some relationship to the victim. The use of firearms in violent acts has increased alarmingly, being present in between 70 and 95 percent of homicides.

On the other hand, domestic violence in all social strata almost always occurs in the home, occurs at every hour of the day, and increases somewhat on weekends. There is a slight tendency toward trauma, and a direct family member is frequently responsible. Women and children are most vulnerable to this kind of violence. Although there is a lack of conclusive evidence here, too, it is recognized that approximately 60 percent of emergency attention directed toward women in one of the most important Caracas hospitals is in response to cases of domestic violence, and that the number of women killed in the last five years due to severe trauma makes up 9.7 percent of the total, as opposed to only 0.3 percent for men.[11]

In the last ten years, 69 percent of homicide victims were between fifteen and twenty-nine years old. In the same interval, the average rate of mortality by homicide for this group was 222 per 100,000 in Caracas alone, so that since 1993 homicide has constituted the leading cause of death in the country for men between the ages of fifteen and forty.[12] The results of this epidemic seriously compromise the efforts and investments in matters of public health and social development that have been made with the goals of controlling infant mortality and raising the life expectancy of Venezuela's population.

The cost of violence in Venezuela is incalculable, especially in terms of human pain and suffering. Preliminary estimates show, however, that at least 5 percent of the country's GDP is lost each year because of violence, without counting hospital costs, inhibited economic activity, insurance, and intangibles such as fear.[13]

Among the characteristics of urban violence is its instrumental character, with a remunerative goal, in those cases (around 50 percent) in which an economic gain is sought, such as muggings, robberies, and so on. When violence is an end in itself or its purpose is to injure or eliminate another person in order to resolve an interpersonal conflict, it is considered relational. This type of violence is present in approximately 60 percent of the cases in which causes are known.[14]

Youth violence, for its part, is committed with differentiable intentions. On the one hand, there is instrumental violence, which is used in order to acquire goods or preserve territory. On the other hand, there is violence that has no specific or concrete goal but is charged with symbolic content, carried out to defend the vital spaces of identity that are indispensable for survival in an environment made dangerous by the precariousness of the surrounding order, institutional abandonment, and violence. Territorial wars among youths grow; their objective is the defense of honor, a conflict that is resolved only through the annihilation of opponents or challengers.

To summarize, the violence present in the most important Venezuelan cities and its criminal expression manifest a marked absence of the state in various senses. The first is the state's selectivity in effectively controlling criminal behavior, inasmuch as the principal crimes occurring in areas with fewer resources frequently go unpunished. (In the last ten years, only 40 percent of the total cases reported have been closed by the police, of which scarcely 5 percent led to immediate sentencing; in 1998, 8.5 percent of vehicle robberies were solved, 22.7 percent of robberies, and 22.4 percent of homicides.) Moreover, the high number of violent acts associated with interpersonal conflicts confirms that institutions for pacifying social relations are limited and that the mechanisms for resolving conflicts are inadequate or unavailable to most citizens. Finally, the fact that this kind of violence overwhelmingly occurs and is expanding uncontrollably in the most vulnerable sectors of society demonstrates the state's incapacity for maintaining universal law and order whereby it would provide the poorest with access to citizenship.

Furthermore, the state does not completely fulfill its undelegatable function as the body governing public policy on this matter. This is evident not only in the inadequacy of the mechanisms of social control required by the national situation of social violence, but also in the demonstrated limitation of its capacity to prevent and impede violence. The mechanisms of social control put into practice in recent years have not been directed toward resolving the state's deficiencies in justice or citizen security. On the contrary, institutional efforts and resources have been largely concentrated in a disproportionate increase in security forces and increased incarceration, among other hard measures. Unfortunately, these changes have not reversed the indices of violence and criminality but appear to have increased and consolidated them. With regard to prevention policies, there is an almost complete absence of programs specifically designed to control and reduce violence, especially in peripheral areas with greater vulnerability to and risk of criminality and violence. Among the citizens of the periphery, the multiple problems of a difficult coexistence and an extremely adverse daily reality do not find an adequate institutional or communitarian channel for redress; as a result they burst out as uncontrolled violence.

The Exercise of Citizenship in Venezuela

In a public evaluation of the effectiveness of the justice system, 85 percent of those interviewed revealed that they had little or no confidence in it and 75.5 percent stated that it does not work and should be transformed.[15] The three problems cited as most serious were prison overcrowding, corruption of judges and functionaries, and the slowness of the process. According to 94.5 percent, moreover, justice in Venezuela favors the rich, while 49.9 percent of those interviewed favored taking justice into their own hands. It is clear that the legal machinery to carry out the law has enormous problems of legitimacy, which drastically reduces its effectiveness in regulating social life.

A recent study of the real opportunities for exercising citizenship in Venezuela investigated the juridical background of citizen security in order to establish the ways in which the Venezuelan state regulates social life, to determine whether or not the judicial and legal framework is guided by universal criteria and whether the state of law prevails for the majority.[16]

In the first instance it was determined that the notion of citizen security—and for that matter, its body of laws—does not exist for the Venezuelan state, if citizen security is understood as the minimal conditions that the state should procure for the promotion and protection of rights, public freedoms, and guarantees to which all citizens are entitled, conditions that are consonant with the political regime of democracy. On the contrary, starting with the Constitution (including the Constitution of 1999), the predominant concern is for public order. The notion of public order alludes to a singular social order—for the most part nonexistent, given growing social diversity—that privileges goods over citizens and is related to the security of the state, whose nature, entity, and objectives are widely different from and even antagonistic to those of citizen security. As a political objective, the idea of public order has been surpassed in contemporary democratic legislation, since it corresponds to totalitarian or military political regimes like those that predominated in Latin American throughout much of the twentieth century. Such a notion implies the state's tutelage of its citizens, a relationship that is necessary and almost indispensable, according to this logic, because the citizens are not yet entitled to many of the individual rights consecrated by international law.

With regard to criminal law, the obsolescence of the hundred-year-old penal code has been demonstrated. The regulatory norms of social life are also considerably outdated; specifically, the standards that Caracas police forces use in minor legal transgressions and infractions dates back to 1926. The fact that most of these transgressions go unpunished or underpunished has significant effects on the quality of social coexistence. Ordinary, socially accepted or acceptable behaviors are treated as transgressions or crimes; the police focus their work on repressing social conduct, converting their function into a sort of moral tutelage over citizens rather than the protection of the free exercise of their rights or the ensuring of security in high-risk areas of the city. Because it cannot meet the complexity of contemporary social life, the prevailing norm allows for a broad interpretation of police agents' role, increasing the arbitrariness and discretionary character of the sanctions exercised. According to statistics published in 1996 by the Metropolitan Police of Caracas—the most important of the city's police forces, both in terms of area of influence and number of officers—of the total arrests made only 3.59 percent corresponded to actual crimes such as robberies, thefts, homicides, personal injuries, and the like. The majority of arrests were for drunkenness (10.7 percent), disobedience of authority (5.57), drug addiction (1.16), homosexuality and prostitution (2.65), lack of identifying documents (11.5), and other lesser causes (29.3). It should be pointed out that under current Venezuelan legislation, drug addiction, homosexuality, and prostitution are not categorized as crimes; in this kind of arrest the individual is penalized for "illicit demeanor" (el porte ilícito de cara). In other words, the reason for arrest is a perception of social danger. This is the kind of police behavior that typifies repressive societies rather than democratic ones.

In this way, a variety of social phenomena associated with violence should be considered criminal but cannot be recognized by the penal system and therefore remain without adequate sanction, increasing social violence. It is symptomatic of this problem that different methods of sanction are used in the city of Caracas in each case of what can be considered domestic violence, undoubtedly destroying the element of foreseeability required to legitimate norms and standards in the eyes of citizens.

Regulations on the role of the police show similar characteristics. Not only is police work carried out with the support of a judicial framework that promotes arbitrariness and discretionary judgments on the part of the agents, but also, to make matters worse, the internal regulations they must follow are based on military-style rules that privilege carrying out superiors' orders and loyalty to the institution over respect for citizens and the guaranteeing of free exercise of their rights. Thus—although the country signs the international conventions on human rights—penalizing crimes associated with human rights violations or judicial excesses is virtually impossible, since whenever charges of police abuse or extralegal tactics are raised, the officers attest to having met regulations. As a result of this practice, citizens' defenselessness against police power is almost complete. It is clear that the poor population is much more vulnerable to all of these institutional and juridical failings, given that the middle and upper classes have more resources at their disposition for the exercise of their rights and other mechanisms to guarantee their defense before the state.

The loss-making regulation of social life on the part of the Venezuelan government, the non-universality of its juridical and legal framework, and the lack of validity of the state of law for the majority are due in part to the fact that the legal codes designed to protect the free exercise of individual rights of citizens are misaligned and guided by a principle of moral tutelage that corresponds to other political orders. In that sense, it is striking that a stable democracy, reasonably capable of guaranteeing a series of political rights to Venezuelans, has accumulated such deficits in relation to the guarantee of individual rights necessary to control state power and to facilitate the exercise of true citizenship for all.

Some Preliminary Conclusions

Despite the sharp deterioration of social conditions in Venezuela in the last fifteen years—with its resultant unemployment, poverty, and exclusion—the causes of the exponential increase in social violence must also be sought in a state of law that is deeply flawed, in the lack of an institutional structure that matches the new social differentiation, and in the inadequacy of the juridical framework to provide citizen security, since in practice it renders the poorest sectors of the population defenseless against other sectors as well as the state.

The extreme fragmentation of civil society and the persistent inability to control and prevent the multiple manifestations of violence suggest a dangerous weakness in the Venezuelan state. The reconstruction of the state is an urgent imperative, especially in those areas that show the greatest lack, such as the administration of justice and the distribution of resources and social goods.

Unfortunately, the current political situation, which has brought about a change in the constitutional norm and the transformation of certain institutions, has not been enough to guarantee the improvement of social relations, which continue to show evidence of a high degree of conflict and, at least in the short run, no solution.

Guaranteeing the universalization of laws and making the state of law valid for everyone may well be the most desirable social changes in the spirit of democracy and citizenship. Both of these steps are fundamental to the sustainability of the profound changes that Venezuelan society has sought for years in its institutions and its political regime.

TRANSLATED BY JENNIFER FRENCH

Notes

1. See Garretón, "Situación actual y nuevas cuestiones."
2. Przeworski et al., *Democracia sustentable*.
3. Kymlicka and Norman, "El retorno del ciudadano."
4. O'Donnell, *Contrapuntos*.
5. Sanjuán, "La actual coyuntura venezolana."
6. Sen, *Bienestar, justicia y mercado*; Fitoussi and Rosanvallo, *La nueva era de las desigualdades*.

7. Rubio, *Crimen sin sumario*.

8. Camacho y Guzmán, *La violencia*.

9. CISALVA, *Dimensionamiento de la violencia en Colombia*.

10. Sanjuán, *Notas Técnicas sobre Violencia*.

11. Sanjuán, "La actual coyuntura venezolana."

12. Pan-American Health Organization, "Situación de Salud en las Américas."

13. See IESA (Instituto de Estudios Superiores de Administración)-LACSO (Laboratorio de Ciencias Sociales), *Magnitud y costos de la violencia delictiva en Venezuela*, 1997 (mimeograph); and ESTRATEGIA Social Consultores, *Análisis de los costos de la violencia en Venezuela*, 1999 (mimeograph).

14. In addition to the works cited, see Sanjuán, *La criminalidad en Caracas*.

15. "Diagnóstico sobre la Percepción Social de la Justicia en el Area Metropolitana de Caracas, Encuesta de Opinión Pública, Informe Final," United Nations Development Program, March 1998, Caracas.

16. ESTRATEGIA Social Consultadores, *Marco legal de la seguridad ciudadana en Venezuela*, 1999 (mimeograph).

Youth Crime in São Paulo

SÉRGIO ADORNO

Myths, Images, and Facts

THIS ESSAY EXAMINES THE ROLE of adolescents in urban crime in the city of São Paulo, Brazil, from 1988 to 1996 and is based on recently completed research, the final report of which was published in 1999.[1] I focus my analysis on one specific social problem: the emergence of public and collective concern regarding the role of children and adolescents in the world of crime, particularly that of violent and organized crime. In addition to analyzing the evolution of urban juvenile delinquency in the metropolis of São Paulo, I seek to expose the way in which the relationship between youths, violence, and crime has been problematized within diverse social discourses, particularly those that negotiate public policies of social control and often appear in newspapers and on television.[2] What does it mean to speak of juvenile delinquency today in a city like São Paulo? Will there be a correlation between public concern and the evolution of the condition of delinquency? If so, in what terms and to what extent?

Public Opinion and Juvenile Delinquency:
A Brief History

In Brazil, children working and living in the streets is not as recent a development as one might think. As early as the colonial period, historical registers record daily customs that show adults abandoning poor children, many of whom were orphans, or leaving them with foundling hospitals maintained by benevolent philanthropists, in particular the Santas Casas de Misericordia.[3] The establishment of an independent national society, under the aegis of the empire (1821–1889), does not seem to have changed this custom. During this entire period, there was little concern for the fate of children and adolescents living in charitable institutions. People spoke of vagrancy and begging as "vices" that needed to be corrected, and it was thought that one should avoid the "almost certain" drift from delinquency to crime as much as possible. The end of the monarchical form of government and the advent of the republic coincided with Brazil's entry into what was called the era of economic and social modernization, a process that was accompanied by the introduction of a series of initiatives in the area of social control.[4]

During the first half of the twentieth century, the presence of important foreign (North American and European) missionaries in Brazil, many of whom were religious, was intended to show that impoverished children were a depository of moral virtue. Their goal was to distribute some aid and even a certain amount of social justice to the poor and needy segments of urban populations that were starting to grow in large cities like Rio de Janeiro and São Paulo due to rapid changes in the urban work force.

The local political elite, particularly in sectors that were rapidly becoming modernized, were motivated to invest in an urban-institutional infrastructure that supported industrial development in the southeast region of the country, and in an infrastructure aimed at guaranteeing public peace, security, and the efficient control of common crimes.[5] At the end of the 1920s, at the height of these changes, the treatment of poor youths was modernized. The poor child became a "minor" and was listed in the courts as a protected, impoverished being who depended on the initiatives of philanthropic aid and on social control acting in loco parentis; the publication of the Minor Code (1927) solidified this principle. In addition to repressing activities related to mendacity, vagrancy, and petty crimes, it dealt with rescuing minors so that they might lead dignified adult lives—a place in the social order determined by the working society being built in Brazil. This is not to say that juvenile delinquency containment policies had been completely abandoned. On the contrary, the restriction of freedom was always a recourse available to the authorities willing to use it, even in situations that were less serious or less dangerous to the general public. However, the principle of restricting freedom was now integrated into a system of protection for minors. Removing minors from the streets and from public and free circulation meant subjecting them to a treatment whose main principles rested on schooling and occupational training.

This politico-institutional strategy seems to have produced the desired results. From the end of the 1930s through most of the 1960s, public and collective concern about the problem of minors seems to have diminished. In most cases minors became pertinent problems only for specialists, of little interest to wider audiences. At the end of the 1960s, when Brazilian society was at the height of social change and experiencing institutional ruptures due to the military coup (1964), which was followed by a political dictatorship (1964–1985), the somewhat calm perceptions of the presence of children and adolescents as minors in the world of crime and violence underwent notable changes. This culminated in the founding of a national policy of child welfare in the beginning of the 1970s that established state-run foundations for children (Fundações Estaduais do Menor, FEBEMs) throughout most of the country.

However, since the early 1970s, at least in large Brazilian cities, the presence of children and adolescents roaming the streets, begging, watching over parked cars, and selling candies and sweets at traffic signals in exchange for small sums of money has been seen as a social problem and has been the subject of public debate. Little by little, an enflamed public opinion, most certainly influenced by the impact of the rapid growth in violent urban crime on collective behavior, started to suspect a growing and unyielding involvement of those youths in crime, particularly those who come from the poorest working-class sectors.[6]

How much these images, which circulate in various social discourses, are based on objective fact is the subject of controversy. But right or wrong, the way of perceiving the associations between youths and the world of crime and violence has changed. The images of youth as associated with obedience to dominant moral and social rules gave way in many social groups to images associating youth with social danger, risk, and lack of safety—ideas that inhabit the popular imaginary of multiple social segments, albeit at times more dramatically for some than for others.[7]

The Social Context and the Emergence of Juvenile Delinquency

The emergence of juvenile delinquency in Brazilian public debate and in the realm of collective sensibilities—in other words, its problematization—occurs at the core of a complex and dense social context. Although there is no consensus among the available analyses, one cannot ignore the weight of social authoritarianism or the legacies of the authoritarian regime on the agencies in charge of controlling the general public. Since the mid–1960s, preventive and ostensive policing has been militarized, making arbitrary police inspections in the streets frequent, especially in low-income housing, including such practices as dragging people from bed with no authorized judicial warning.[8] This is in addition to the torture and mistreatment carried out in precincts and police stations of prisoners suspected of committing crimes.

The process of centralizing the control and militarization of public security had at least two institutional consequences. First, it transformed the control of common criminality into an internal security problem, creating, voluntarily or involuntarily, confusion between the civil control of the general public and the control of national security. Second, problems related to the repression of common crime became increasingly linked to police agencies, particularly the military police. Consequently, the militarization of security has grown, and the strategies and tactics of war are seen as more relevant to problems of public security, especially to the suppression of a common enemy, the gangster, that often poorly defined and poorly identified figure. Everything indicates that the reduction of the term "gangster" to poor adolescents in low-income housing (such as the slums carved out in the hills of Rio de Janeiro or the poor outskirts of large metropolitan areas such as São Paulo) was initiated and fomented in Brazilian society during those dark years.

This period also coincides with the rise in violent urban crime and institutional confusion in the field of child welfare policy.[9] The pattern of urban criminality changed and has been changing over the last two decades. First, although nonviolent crimes still make up the greatest proportion of penal code infringements in most Brazilian cities, violent crime has increased rapidly, particularly voluntary homicide. (Nonviolent crime does not involve a serious threat to physical integrity or life; violent crime does.)

Second, one can note a strong change in the pattern of criminality. Organized crime related to international drug trafficking seems to be taking the lead, colonizing both traditional forms of delinquent action (such as the various types of theft) and more contemporary ones (such as weapons contraband and the kidnapping of company officials). In this area, Alba Zaluar's pioneer studies of the development of the lower classes and drug trafficking in the state of Rio de Janeiro are exemplary. They reveal, above all, how children and adolescents are recruited and selected for the business of drugs, thus fomenting fear and worry in the popular imaginary, which associates the rise in crime with the rise in adolescent participation. These youths are younger and younger, on the threshold between childhood and adolescence, highly armed and prepared to kill for hire.

Third, urban crime has become internationalized.[10] Everything indicates a steadily growing link among delinquent groups controlling local drug deals, gangs controlling the movement of these goods throughout the country, and groups headquartered in Colombia, Bolivia, and Mexico that control the production, circulation, and distribution of drugs, particularly cocaine.

Governments and criminal justice systems have proven ineffective in dealing with this complicated and complex situation.[11] This is due primarily to the fact that criminality grew exponentially while institutional responses remained practically fixed at the levels and patterns of the early 1970s. Brazilian penal law became outdated, contributing to an increased perception that crimes were going unpunished to an unprecedented extent.

The repercussions of this situation also emerge in the areas of childhood and adolescence law and the child welfare policies that state governments formulate and implement. Recent changes in child and adolescent protection legislation have stimulated public debate and even polarized opinions regarding solutions for limiting juvenile delinquency. With the 1988 Constitution, a new policy of protecting and caring for children and adolescents has taken shape. Unlike the former one, this policy considers children and adolescents to have rights: the right to a dignified existence, health, education, leisure, work, and above all, legal aid. On July 13, 1990, constitutional precepts were regulated through law number 8069, which revoked the Minor Code (1979) and instituted the Child and Adolescent Statute (ECA).

The ECA has been the subject of a widespread debate since its publication. Some see it as an efficient instrument for social protection and control. Those opposed to it consider the ECA a legal instrument that cannot be applied to Brazilian society. They argue that juvenile criminality has risen because young delinquents are not punished or are punished by socioeducative measures lenient in light of the severity of their crimes, which include robbery, homicide, rape, drug trafficking, and weapons possession.

Government response has been mixed. On the one hand, the government is applauded by public opinion when it imprisons juvenile delinquents. On the other hand, doubt is cast on the efficacy of alternative measures to imprisonment. This doubt leads to the implementation of familiar measures that, while they might not solve the problem, at least do not seem to aggravate it. Justifiably, government invests almost nothing in the institutional infrastructure needed to guarantee the implementation of socioeducational measures called for in the ECA, such as community service involvement, reparation of damages, half-way houses, and foster homes. Thus, the government response ends up, however indirectly, accentuating segregationist aspects of the judicial culture.[12]

This complex social and politico-institutional context not only divides public opinion but contributes to the images of apprehension, fear, danger, and risk related to juvenile delinquents, thus increasing expectations for a situation that is more and more uncontrollable and unsustainable.

The Evolution of Juvenile Delinquency in São Paulo

Among these suspicions, what is myth and what is reality? Has juvenile delinquency really been growing and, if so, in what direction? Do the movement and evolution of this criminality follow more general tendencies found not only in Brazilian society but also in other Western societies, or do they reveal distinctions? These are the questions we aim to answer by presenting and analyzing the results obtained in the research conducted.[13]

In general, the analysis of the presence and participation of adolescents in the urban crime movement in the city of São Paulo from 1993 to 1996 reveals appreciable changes compared to the 1988–1991 period (see table 8.1). If we focus on the type of crimes committed by adolescents, we notice the following tendencies: in the recent period, there is a rise in the percentage of bodily injuries and robberies and a decrease in stolen property. Nevertheless, one cannot say that these differences are significant, since the values for the period between 1993 and 1996 fall within the limits of the margin of error for that period.

Crimes against private property between 1993 and 1996 represent 51.1 percent of all those committed by adolescent violators (in the prior period, 1988–1991, they represented 49.5 percent). Robbery ranked highest among these crimes, a position formerly occupied by theft. Crimes related to drug use and possession represent 4.3 percent, drug trafficking, 2.9 percent. The occurrence of homicides is very low (1.3 percent), although this type of crime has the greatest effect on public opinion and instills fear and worry in the collective imaginary. It is significant that 11.7 percent of all crimes refer to bodily injuries resulting from assaults, a percentage almost three times greater than illegal weapons possession, drug possession, drug use, or drug trafficking.

As the specialized literature in this area indicates, the breakdown of juvenile delinquency follows general tendencies. In the United States in 1993, while 29.35 percent of the total number of infractions committed by youths involved crimes against private property, only 0.16 percent involved homicide. Violent crime remained the same, around 13 percent of all incidents, from 1972 to 1993.[14]

In England, the tendencies are not that different, although they do indicate some peculiarities. Property crimes also predominate. The most frequent crimes, in order, are theft, breaking and entering, and

Table 8.1
Police Incidents Involving Adolescent Violators, City of São Paulo,
1988–1991 and 1993–1996

	1988–1991 %	1993–1996 %
Against Individuals		
Homicide	—	1.30
Attempted homicide	—	0.60
Kidnapping	0.10	0.00
Bodily injury (assault)	6.80	11.70
Against Private Property		
Theft	23.00	18.40
Attempted theft	6.90	7.60
Robbery	15.60	19.00
Robbery followed by death (armed robbery)	0.30	0.50
Attempted robbery	2.30	4.20
Fraud/Attempted	1.40	1.40
Against Public Peace		
Member of gangs or groups	0.20	0.20
Against public safety		
Drug use	—	0.70
Drug possession	—	3.60
Drug trafficking	0.70	2.90
Against Morals		
Rape/Attempted	0.60	0.70
Violent indecent assault	—	1.00
Other sexual acts	—	0.50
Other Incidents		
Weapons possession	6.90	4.40
Driving without a license	9.40	6.50
Others	17.80	14.80
TOTAL	100.00	100.00

Source: "Poder Judicial/Varas Especiais da Infância e da Juventude da Capital"; Convénio
Fundação Sistema Estadual de Análise de Dados–Seade/Núcleo de Estudos da Violência (Violence
Studies Nucleus)/University of São Paulo.
Note: The report includes the total number of adolescents passing through the justice system for
each period.

crimes against individuals, a pattern that seems to have stabilized between 1985 and 1995. Severe criminal offenses are less frequent. From
1979 to 1994, 210 adolescents age seventeen were convicted for intentional homicide and 220 for unintentional homicide. However, there
was a 40 percent rise in violent crimes from 1987 to 1993 and a 40
percent decrease in the number of thefts. Nevertheless, when we

juxtapose both tendencies, we find that violent crime rose at a greater pace and at a higher rate than in the previous decade. There was also a rise in drug use cases starting in 1985.[15]

In France, while crime in general decreased roughly 3 percent in 1996, the rise in juvenile delinquency was around 14 percent. During the period from 1974 to 1995, crimes against private property ranked the highest, and they remained steady. There was a significant rise in crimes involving damage by dangerous means (such as fire), which rose from 23.3 percent in 1974 to 40.7 percent in 1995. Increases were also recorded for violent crimes committed by juveniles (from 19.8 to 30.9 percent), weapons possession (from 8.3 to 14.2 percent), assault and battery (from 7.2 to 12.2 percent), and homicides (from 5.5 to 7.1 percent).[16]

There is little information regarding juvenile delinquency tendencies in Brazil. According to Simone Assis, violent crimes committed by adolescents in Rio de Janeiro went from 2,675 incidents in 1991 to 3,318 incidents in 1996, an increase of roughly 25 percent in five years. During the same period, crimes against private property decreased, but there was a remarkable increase in drug involvement among adolescents, 70 percent of whom have some sort of connection with trafficking. Homicides represent 1.3 percent of all infractions.[17]

A detailed study of juvenile delinquency for the period from 1974 to 1996 in the city of Riberão Preto, in the state of São Paulo, adopted methodology similar to the one used in this study, so comparisons are quite suggestive. The study showed that crimes against private property were the most frequent, representing 40.88 percent of the cases investigated. In 1974, they made up 28.09 percent of all infractions, in 1996, 51.16 percent. Theft increased 1.66 times, though the percentage decreased from the beginning of the study period to the end (31.84 and 20.09 percent, in 1974 and 1996). Robbery and extortion increased 6.07 times; drug use and possession, 4.02 times; drug trafficking, 23.75 times; unintentional bodily injury, 1.38 times.[18] The case for an actual rise in juvenile crime, particularly violent crime, can be seen in the data reported in table 8.2. When one compares the patterns of criminality observed in the general public, one notices a greater rise in violent crime among adolescents. It is even more surprising to note that, in the second period of investigation (1993–1996), the percentage of violent

Table 8.2

Police Incidents Involving Adolescent Criminals by Number of People
Involved, City of São Paulo, 1988–1991 and 1993–1996

	1988–1991	**1993–1996**
	%	%
Acted alone	43	30.5
Acted in conjunction with one or more adolescents	38.0	44.8
Acted in conjunction with one or more adults	11.5	22.3
Acted in conjunction with others unidentified	7.5	2.4
TOTAL	100.0	100.0

Source: "Poder Judicial/Varas Especiais da Infáncia e da Juventude da Capital"; Convénio
Fundação Sistema Estadual de Análise de Dados–Seade/Núcleo de Estudos da Violência (Violence
Studies Nucleus)/University of São Paulo.
Note: The report includes the total number of adolescent criminals passing through the justice
system for each period.

crimes committed by adolescents is greater than that of the general
population.

This tendency is not peculiar to Brazil. In the 1980s in England,
one finds an increase in all types of crimes and juvenile delinquency
tending to outdistance adult delinquency dramatically. Offenses by male
adolescents increased substantially from the mid–1960s to the mid–
1970s. Thereafter, this pattern halted and even tended to drop slightly
until the mid–1980s, when it returned to 1970s levels.[19] In France in
the period from 1974 to 1995, the number of violent crimes committed by adolescents also rose. During this period, all types of robberies
decreased, while crimes against individuals, the public order, and drugs
rose. The rise in adolescent versus adult involvement in violent crime
in the city of São Paulo from 1993 to 1996 thus correlates in large part
with a general trend in the countries studied, regardless of their degree
or level of social-economical development.

Yet one cannot disregard the possible effects of the "youth wave."
Although an analysis of this movement would require more sophisticated technical procedures, one can at least venture hypotheses. Between 1980 and 1996 in the city of São Paulo, population growth
dropped in some districts. However, this drop has not been uniform in
all districts; in some districts, the rate of increase has remained very
high. This development has led to changes in the age profiles throughout the city.[20] The concentration of the youth population in certain

pockets or regions where the rate of increase remains high is astounding. For example, in Jardim Ángela, one of the neighborhoods that has turned out to be a veritable social laboratory due to the characteristics and composition of its population, the annual increase has been 4.4 percent during the 1990s, while the average population increase of the city has been 0.34 percent. In 1995, the city's "Violence Risk Map" indicated that the rate of homicide for those between the ages of fifteen and twenty-four was 222.2 per 100,000 inhabitants.[21] It is no accident that Jardim Ángela, with its higher rate of population growth and its high percentage of young residents, is one of the neediest areas, with the highest rates of fatal violence. (Just how much these two phenomena intersect and how much juvenile delinquency has been influenced by these demographic tendencies is apt material for another research project.)

Finally, an argument can be made for the influence of organized crime, whose presence and significance in connection with urban crime in Brazil has been noted for two decades and documented by research. The data available for analysis for organized juvenile crime from 1988 to 1991 did not clearly confirm either the existence of groups and gangs as an emerging pattern or their being dominated by juvenile delinquents (see table 8.2). On the other hand, the following period shows a decrease in actions committed alone in comparison to those committed in conjunction with one or more adults.

Organized crime and the creation of adolescent groups and gangs in the United States are much studied issues.[22] Mindful of the differences between continents, Brazilian researchers have been paying more and more attention to the phenomena of groups and gangs.[23] According to Zaluar the emergence of organized crime in the lower classes of Rio de Janeiro has to do with the dismantling of traditional juvenile socializing mechanisms and of equally traditional local social networks.[24] In the past, these networks were anchored by relationships in which the rich helped the poor, and more recently through a new type of political clientelism; this help converges in popular lottery games [jogo do bicho] and samba schools. The dismantling of these traditional social networks was accompanied by a growing gap between parents and children; this is a driving force behind the changes in the function of socializing agencies, such as schools and social and political resource centers, which are now invested with the duties formerly reserved for parents.

It is precisely in this process of social transition, a process in which the new socialization agencies have not yet participated, that organized crime, particularly drug trafficking, captures young inhabitants of low-income housing or the slums in the hills of Rio de Janeiro. This attraction is not a reaction to a world of social injustices and moral degradation, or to the shrinking opportunities offered by the formal job market. On the contrary, it is a response to that which is offered by consumer society and the possibilities for affirming a masculine identity associated with honor and virility in an era characterized by the restriction and reduction of the options for personal choice. The result of this process is not, as Zaluar emphasizes, the creation of bonds of solidarity between the poor and outcasts in the realm of drug trafficking, but rather an explosion of individualism that, for young people, translates into appreciating "goods such as guns and dope, money in one's pocket, cool clothes, and the willingness to kill" (102).

Compared to Zaluar's study on Rio de Janeiro, there is little research on juvenile delinquency in the city of São Paulo. Yet, it seems worthwhile to note three aspects of it. First, official statistics take almost no notice of groups or gangs, despite their impact on the media, public opinion, and the popular imaginary. Similarly, the rates of consumption, possession, and use of drugs among juvenile delinquents still do not seem to be substantial, at least not in terms of that which is officially noted by crime control agencies. As a result, it is possible that the relationships between drug trafficking, gangs, and juvenile delinquents in São Paulo have not been established in the same way as in Rio de Janeiro, despite the discursive fabrication to which social images and scenes suggestive of this relationship give rise and that are present in multiple social discourses..

Based on the results of the research, one must be very cautious in examining the role of young people—children and adolescents—in the world of crime. Even though one may suspect a rise in juvenile delinquency, and even though one may feel that some young people have become more and more violent and socialized into the world of crime, indications are that what has changed and continues to change are social concepts of what is or is not violent, of the subjects of violent action, and of the danger in the streets and public spaces, and around residential neighborhoods.

TRANSLATED BY CLÉLIA F. DONOVAN

Notes

1. The research aimed to characterize juvenile crimes in the city of São Paulo: to discover the magnitude of the recent evolution of juvenile crimes, characterize the social profile of the minor violator, and evaluate the application of the socioeducational measures provided for in the Child and Adolescent Statute. The empirical portion of the study consists of police incidents involving adolescents between the ages of twelve and eighteen who were awaiting the opening of an inquiry in the four specialized jurisdictions of youth law. The study was based on a collection of objective data taken from official documents (court cases). See Adorno, Lima, and Bordini, *O adolescente na criminalidade urbana*, 77. Although this essay is based on collaborative research under my direction and co-authored with Renato Sergio de Lima and Eliana Bordini, it is the result of my own interpretation of that research.

2. I am using the word "problematizing" as defined by Michel Foucault (1984); the word refers to the emergence, the eruption, of a social problematic within scientific, institutional, political, and commonsense discourses. Within this context, one examines not only the way in which such a problematic is "set into discourse," but also how it circulates within distinct social spaces as well as power relations and how it emerges into the public sphere of social life.

3. Adorno, "A gestão filantrópica da pobreza urbana."

4. Adorno, "Consolidação democrática e políticas"; Salla, *As prisões em São Paulo.*

5. Adorno, "A gestão filantrópica da pobreza urbana."

6. As is well known, the concept of public opinion is charged with a series of problems and objections, as noted in the literature on the subject. I am using the concept to allude to the group of images, representations, values, ideas, and ideals often transmitted by mass media, and through which certain opinion parameters have been shaped as if they were hegemonic, dominant, and consensual. Throughout the 1970s in Brazil, one can identify some of the parameters that centered around the relationship between urban poverty and juvenile delinquency, urban delinquency and organized crime, debates on the absence of efficient social control policies to deal with the pertinence of the current juridical instruments regulating the protection of children and adolescents in Brazil, the Child and Adolescent Statute (Federal Law No. 8,069, July 13, 1990).

7. Wieviorka, "O novo paradigma da violência"; Martucelli, "Reflexões sobre a violência."

8. See Pinheiro, "Police and Political Crisis."

9. Many Brazilian studies report the statistics on urban crime; see, for example, Adorno, "O gerenciamento público da violência urbana"; Paixão, "Crime, controle social" and "Crimes e criminosos"; Zaluar, "Violência e crime"; Beato, "Determinantes da criminalidade"; Delassoppa, Bercovich, and Arriaga, "Violência, direitos civis e demografia."

10. The Comission Parlamentar de Inquerito (CPI, the Special Police), which is currently an active part of the National Congress and responsible for investigating drug trafficking in Brazil, has astonished Brazilian society with such spec-

tacular discoveries as the extensive and dense network of international drug trafficking connected to politicians, including members of parliament, entrepreneurs, and civil servants. The work of the CPI suggests that the substratum of Brazilian society is as contaminated by this network as it is agitated with respect to recent discoveries.

11. The Brazilian criminal justice system consists of four large segments: the police system, Ministerio Publico, the judiciary, and the penitentiary system. The Brazilian police system operates on federal, state, and municipal levels. The federal level deals with cases of crimes involving the country and the borders between states. The state level police are in charge of common crimes; this level is divided into the military police and the civil police. The military police are in charge of ostensive and repressive policing, constitute the "reserve armed forces," and are organized militarily. The civil police are in charge of judicial functions (criminal investigations). At the local level, we find municipal guards whose function it is to protect public spaces and property. On the federal level, the police system is subordinate to the minister of justice; on the state level, to the state government (executive); on the municipal level, to the prefect.

The Ministerio Publico, an autonomous organ, is in charge of pronouncing indictments in the criminal justice system and holding defendants accountable for crimes committed; it is part of the national executive branch. The criminal justice courts are part of the judiciary, a branch autonomous from the executive and legislative branches. Finally, there is the penitentiary system, which is in charge of carrying out the sentences, particularly the restriction of freedom; it also is dependent on the national executive branch. Although the youth justice system maintains part of this structure and is quite similar to the penitentiary system, it does possess distinct characteristics, some of which stem from legislation currently in process.

12. Actually, our research identified progress in this area. For example, the expansion of halfway houses, which represented 9.2 percent of the measures applied between 1988 and 1991, jumped to 24.2 percent between 1993 and 1996. Community service projects represented 3.2 percent of the judicial sentences in the period from 1993 to 1996. In any case, mistrust remains. The series of rebellions in various FEBEM–São Paulo positions, which even forced the state governor to directly take over the foundation's presidency, suggest that the problems arising from outdated policies still predominate.

13. The "evolution of juvenile delinquency"—the movement, in specific times and spaces, of penal code infractions committed by adolescents (ages twelve to seventeen)—does not refer to just any "evolutionist" concept, in the sense of a progress of present crimes with respect to the relative peaceful life in recent times. Nor could it refer to it, given the theoretical view adopted in this essay, which focuses on the way in which the role young people play in the delinquent world is socially constructed, either as a discursive representation or as a nondiscursive practice. The section that follows is a partial reproduction of chapter 1 of the recently published research I carried out with Lima and Bordini.

14. Apud Donziger, *Crime in the United States* (Washington: U.S. Department of Justice, Federal Bureau of Investigation, 1993), 132.

15. Newburn, "Youth, Crime, and Justice."

16. Aubusson de Cavarlay, "La place des mineurs."

17. Assis, "Situación de la violencia juvenil."

18. Silva, *O jovem no conflito*.

19. Newburn, "Youth, Crime, and Justice."

20. IBGE, 1980, 1991, and 1996. See Fundação Instituto Brasileiro de Geografia e Estatística, *Participação político-social no Brasil, 1988*, and *Anuário Estatístico do Brasil, 1970–1991*.

21. Centro de Estudos de Cultura Conteporânea. *Mapa de risco da violência*.

22. Thrasher, *The Gang*; A. Cohen, *Delinquent Boys*; Yablonsky, *Gangsters*; Short, *Gang Delinquency*; Klein, *Street Gangs and Street Workers*; Miller, "Gangs, Groups"; Jankowski, *Islands in the Street*.

23. Zaluar, *Condomínio do diabo*; Vianna, "O funk como símbolo da violência carioca"; Misse, "As ligações perigosas"; Diógenes, *Cartografias da violência*.

24. Zaluar, "Teleguiados e chefes."

The Stories

A Small Mistake

JOSÉ ROBERTO DUQUE

These events took place in a poor barrio in Caracas, Venezuela, and the story appeared in José Roberto Duque's column "Guerra Nuestra" (Our war). It was originally published in *El Nacional*, a Caracas newspaper, on July 31, 1997, as "Manual práctico para acabar con la justicia" (A practical guide to doing away with justice).

Friday, July 4, 5:00 A.M.

More intense police activity than usual in the Tercer Plan de La Silsa. It is not uncommon to have confrontations of varying importance there, given the perennial problems of drugs, bad habits, and some people's need to act the tough guy. And when these things happen there is sometimes a stray bullet that veers off its path, and then Pow! there goes an innocent. So regardless of the noise and the discomfort of having to interrupt one's dreams so early, sometimes one of those police operations is welcome. No need to speak of police mysticism; that's what they're paid for.

The members of the Rondón family hear the authorities' knock at the door on Ricaurte Alley, at the entrance to their house. Suddenly, they hear an odd noise at their own gate: someone bangs a few times, they hear the sound of the metal giving way and then the crumbling of the wall when the gate that protects the house is yanked out of its hinges. Señor Teófilo Rondón goes out to see where all of this is coming from and finds several uniformed men who politely ask his permission to enter the premises. One of them is holding the entryway grille in his hand, but he abruptly throws it to one side and bursts into the house with the rest of his colleagues without waiting for Rondón's authorization. Such safe conduct with rifles, pistols, and adrenaline flowing through their bodies! Two of them drag someone with them who—how strange!—is hooded. They ask him: "Here?" He responds: "Yes, here."

5:10 A.M.

Several of the men, later identified by the Rondón family as members of the Grupo BAE [*Brigada de Acciones Especiales*, Special Actions Brigade]—by the emblem that each one wore on his shoulder—search two rooms on the first floor of the house and then go to the second, to the room of José Gregorio Rondón, a young man recently discharged from the Military Police. Some of the remaining men guard the room to which the family—father, mother, and daughter, Ana Rose—has been led, and the rest wait in the living room and entryway. A pretty dramatic dialogue is heard from upstairs:

"Ah, you're the rat."

"Here, sir, look at my documents. I'm a reservist."

"Ah, you're a reservist."

And immediately the sounds of punches and kicks, of José Gregorio's screams, are heard. The boy's mother, Señora Margarita, tries to leave the room in order to intervene and one of the agents sends her back to the bed with one of those slaps that really stings, especially at five in the morning when your son is in trouble. The hooded man, the guy that they'd asked a few things before beginning, says: "Listen, put me in the squad car because they're gonna mess with me." Before he can finish his request, the sharp sound of gunfire is heard from above. A hail of bullets in the Rondón house; below, the others continue to keep the family, whose nerves are already in a state of crisis, from leaving. Partly in order to calm them, to relieve the tension and discomfort, one of the agents starts up a conversation with the family members. He begins by asking them a trivial question, you know, nothing important, just to gain their trust:

"Okay, then, how is El Chino behaving?"

"What *chino?*" responds Teófilo Rondón. "We're all black, there's no *chino* here."*

"Fine, but they call your son El Chino, right?"

"No, they don't call him by that name."

Ten seconds of silence. The avengers exchange an icy look.

"Let's take this step by step, sir," the policeman says to Teófilo, changing his tone. "Is this not house number 20, Vuelta del Mocho?"

"No, sir. This is house number 20, but on Ricuarte Alley. La Vuelta del Mocho is about eight blocks up."

"Ah, shit."

One of the officers coughs, another goes pale, one starts to hum a song, and the other bolts out of the room in order to speak to his colleague. He says in a voice that is low, but loud enough to be heard in New York, "All right, let's go. I think we slipped. It's the wrong guy."

The news spreads among the members of the police commission. There is an exchange of murmurs and signs. They're deliberating. The brain, buddy, these guys really make the brain work. They're smart. They make a decision.

"Don't worry, ma'am, we're just going to take your son in for some questioning for a minute. And you, miss," addressing Ana Rosa, "will come with us because we want you to make a statement. It turns out that we have found these weapons and drugs in El Chino's room—I mean, in the young man's room."

Only then do they allow the family to leave the room, just in time to see them throw a package from the terrace roof to the street. Even though dawn hasn't quite come, it's easy to guess that the thing that they throw from up there is José Gregorio's body. There's a rope tied to the left foot. They put it into a Bronco truck and take it away.

8:00 A.M.

Anxiety, anguish, confusion in the Rondón house and throughout the area. José Gregorio's family has gone up to his room and encountered a battle scene: a lot of blood on the bed, bullet holes in the walls. Señor Teófilo had the good sense to write down the numbers of the cars that the police had come in: Squad Car 003, Squad Car 164. They will soon learn that the first belongs to the Western Commission, the second to Ocumare del Tuy.

Shortly thereafter, one of the women in the neighborhood, a nurse at Periférico de Catia hospital, calls Teófilo aside: his son is in the hospital, dead. Upon identifying him, the woman had dared to lift the sheet that covered him and counted four bullet holes in the young man's body.

Then the grueling procession begins. First they go to the hospital, but when they get there they are informed that the body has been transferred to the morgue. They go to the morgue and there it is, yes, but they can't claim it yet, there is an inquiry in progress, etc., etc. Upon returning to the house, news from Ana Rosa, who has already arrived: she was in the Anti-Crime Division of the PTJ [Policía técnica judicial, Judicial Technical Police Unit] with some of the Rondón family's neighbors. They were asked some questions about her brother, the young woman says, but beforehand they were given an introductory talk: When they ask you, you should respond that José Gregorio was a rat, a damned delinquent, a neighborhood bully. If you don't, its fifteen years in prison for withholding evidence.

"Let's see. Who was José Gregorio Rondón?"

"A neighborhood bully, a delinquent."

"Very good. Mr. Secretary, make a note of that. Twenty points for the Ricuarte Alley neighbors."

6:00 P.M.

Everything by the book, everything in order for the return of the body. Teófilo Rondón and his daughter go to La Pompa funeral home so that the body can be turned over. The morgue employee was going to do it, but none of that, my love, not so fast: a unit from the BAE on the ho-

rizon appears, and two officers get out, foaming at the mouths. The order is to leave the boy's body where it is.

"But these are his relatives," argues the guy from the morgue.

"You don't understand, *papi*," says one of the BAE agents. "If you
turn over this body you're going to have yourself one hell of a problem. In other words, don't turn it over."

And the man didn't, of course. Nobody wants to get in trouble,
right?

Saturday, July 5, 8:30 A.M.

Teófilo and his relatives return to the morgue to see if the mood has
changed. And it has: they sign a few documents without a lot of for-
malities and the attendant proceeds to turn over the body of José
Gregorio Rondón so that it can be taken to the funeral home. The family is given a death certificate in which there is one fact that doesn't
fit: "Impact of a bullet in the left intercostal region," and nothing else.
Nothing of the four bullet wounds that their neighbor mentioned, nothing. Anyway, the important thing is that they can have a wake now
and say a last goodbye to the murdered boy. Hey—watch your language!
What do you mean, murdered? We're talking about the BAE. Okay, fine,
the deceased.

Just one small detail: the funeral home employee who was given
the job of preparing the cadaver goes out for a moment and tells Señor
Teófilo: "Sir, they didn't perform an autopsy on your son. That body is
decomposing. I can do it here, but it's going to cost you X amount of
dollars."

An extra race for Teófilo Rondón in search of X amount of dollars. That step taken, let us finish, then, with this painful subject.

The Rondón family goes to the Disciplinary Division of the PTJ
in order to clear up a few grey issues. They speak with Commissioner
Gerardo Quintero, tell him about the coerced statement, the irregular
procedure. The witnesses that made statements visit the head offices
of the PTJ again, and this time they tell the true story. They place a
huge book of photographs in Ana Rosa's hands; in it she identifies a
few faces: some are of the agents that murdered her brother, others are

of those who intervened in the farcical interrogation. The action of justice—true justice—is not far away: the case is now in the hands of Penal Judge 45, Rosa Figuera Medina, and those of Doctor Yadira Rangel at La Fiscalía [the attorney general's office].

TRANSLATED BY KATHERINE GOLDMAN

Translator's Note

* The term *chino* has many meanings in Spanish and is used to demonstrate the family's confusion. It could refer to the racial category (*chino*, as in Chinese), the father's understanding of the term, which explains his response, "We're all black." It could also be a nickname, El Chino, which is the way that the police officer uses the term, mistakenly thinking that Teófilo Rondón's son is a criminal who goes by that name.

Ciudad Bolívar

JOSÉ NAVIA

Brush Strokes against Death

This article was first published in *El Tiempo* on March 22, 1994.
The conditions remain almost unchanged. In the first six months
of 1999, Ciudad Bolívar had the largest number of murders
among the twenty districts of Bogotá.

WHEN THE REST OF THE CITY SLEEPS, a multitude begins to stir in the
narrow, labyrinthine, unpaved alleys of Ciudad Bolívar, in the south of
Bogotá. It is a mass that pursues crowded buses and run-down collective taxis, or that comes down from the hills at a trot, sheathed in pon-
chos and jackets, with the breath of dawn painted on faces puckered
by the cold.

One of those who come down from the hills, squeezed into a
cramped and crowded truck headed for Central de Abastos, is José Rojas.
He is a member of a youth group that has begun to change things little
by little in these hills, which have been stigmatized by death, by means
of cultural activities. Those who form part of this phenomenon live the
same reality. In the mornings, day laborers who are theater people, package deliverymen who are *cumbia* and *mapalé* dancers, and street vendors

who are puppeteers, painters, or rappers come down from the hills. And students who spend their free time dreaming of sets and applause that reaches beyond the limits of their neighborhoods also come.

All of them, artists of stage and *rebusque* (the informal economy), practice in dilapidated rooms and in spaces provided by private and governmental groups. The conditions of their lives are similar to those that exist in Aguablanca, in Cali, or in the slums of Medellín: misery, unemployment, closed doors, intersecting acts of violence, and a stigma that the inhabitants carry like a heavy cross before the rest of the city.

Perhaps it is for this reason that life acquires more value in these hills inhabited by migrant peasants and their descendants, children of *rebusque*, of video games and violence, sneakers and brand-name clothes. In this world, cultural activities have become a refuge for dozens of children and adolescents in Ciudad Bolívar.

"It is the time for happiness, for rumba, for the multitude. It is the hour of youths on their feet, united, demanding a future, building a life," reads one of the six murals that some twenty young people painted in the Meissen, San Francisco, Compartir, and Juan Pablo II barrios three months ago.

Until now, walls and small neighborhood newspapers published by the skin of their teeth were the only modes of expression for the one million people, almost all of them undocumented, who live in 240 different barrios.

"The journalists only go up to the hills when there are deaths," says a young man from the Creative Seeds Community Library.

Now, from speakers used to broadcast town meetings—tied with wire to *guadua* trees and light posts—one hears a cassette recording of the first radio program made by ten young men who received financial support from the president. They speak of *cocinol*, of legalizing the barrios, and they invite life to be created in the place of death.[*]

Rebusque *Is Key*

Another group from the Jerusalén barrio has been creating video clips and documentaries funded by the president and a private corporation since last year. Fifteen days ago the young people mounted a screen above the steep streets with cords and projected one of their clips for the first time, holding a gathering with their assistants. Peasant migration, public transportation, consumerism, and rap are a few of their themes.

José Rojas, the young man who comes down each morning to deliver packages in Corabastos, is one of the seven founding members of the group, which was baptized Proyvisión. Helver Pira, another of the collective's members, explains its objectives: "[We want] to create the basis for youth culture in the barrio. We also try to show another side of Ciudad Bolívar, and to create a network of videos and other forms of communication with other barrios in Bogotá."

Up until a year ago, a newspaper called *Hola* circulated in one barrio for four years. In Ciudad Bolívar, *El Gritón del Barrio* and *Juventud Pilosa* still survive, guaranteed future editions by official financial support. Dance, music, theater, and puppet groups exist in almost every barrio. There is also a cultural center that has been operating for ten years and a cooperative cultural group that is currently in search of legal status.

But in Ciudad Bolívar, as in all of the marginal urban sectors, the groups appear and evaporate with unusual frequency. The explanation? The existence of these groups is directly proportional to their participants' capacity for *rebusque*. They practice and practice, and after a while they slam up against their inability to scrape up costumes or instruments. Or, quite simply, the need to survive forces them to either abandon their activities or restrict them to a few hours of entertainment.

This is what happens to John Darío Arce, a youth from Juan Pablo II who crosses himself before an image of the Virgin of Carmen every morning and then leaves the run-down house where he lives with his mother to wait for the bus that comes from Villa Gloria. By day he is an assistant in a store in the San Francisco barrio, and he practices *cumbia* steps two evenings a week in the offices of the Pancandé folkloric group in Juan Pablo II.

The group is four years old and "we haven't stopped practicing," says Francisco Galán, its director, "not even during the massacres." Five hundred young people died violent deaths between 1990 and 1992 in Ciudad Bolívar. Nevertheless, it is in the most critical moments that the inhabitants of these hills populated by half-built houses feel the greatest need to live.

This is how the Kitaro Theater, a collective of thirty students from Vasco Núñez Balboa High School in the México barrio, was born. "Kitaro is the offspring of violence," says its director, Hernando Villamor, "because the state arrived with financial support for cultural activities only after the second massacre in Juan Pablo II, in July of 1992. We presented the project and they funded it." Its objective is to offer youths options other than the ones found on the street.

Painters and Rappers

The children who join Kitaro Teatro are convinced that painters, poets, athletes, and musicians hide beneath the tough skin of the many gang members who had no path to follow besides that of weapons. Fortunately, not all of them were dragged down by that avalanche. This is the case for Harold Bustos and Carlos María Moreno, two young painters from Juan Pablo II who dream of studying fine arts at the National University.

Carlos María Moreno walks around with his paintings under his arm, uphill and down, until he gets tired and gives them away. And Harold Bustos pays two million pesos for a narrow room with wooden walls and a zinc roof, miraculously constructed on the steep terrain. He calls it his "studio." He spends his time there painting vague, abstract figures in which one can see "the things that happen here": drawn faces with eyes bulging from the horror of the massacres, revolvers amid formless images, policemen who share secrets with delinquents, flowers born of death, and arid, ocher landscapes with a few stains of green. There are many young people like him, but no one knows just how many because there is no census of the groups formed by young people who have rebelled against death.

Many women also form part of this movement. Ten of them, between the ages of ten and twenty, began a puppeteering group in Huitaca two years ago. It is supported by a private foundation and its themes include machismo, family violence, and other phenomena that directly affect its members.

These problems are also present in a musical movement that becomes more popular among the region's youth every day: rap. Bhoery Rap, Amigos del Rap, and Peligro Social are some of the groups that come together to sing about their everyday lives. Their compositions are heard in marches for life, in *parche* festivals, and in the community protest that was held last November. Because of this, the five members of Bhoery Rap offer up their lyrics any night of the week from one of the narrow alleyways in which life and death intermingle:

> Five cops
> Want to trap me
> But I could take them out
> with my left hand!
> One of them
> Looked at my pants,
> Thinking I was
> Sylvester Stallone.
> Another one
> Looked at my shoes,
> Thinking I was
> The king of the gangs!

TRANSLATED BY KATHERINE GOLDMAN

Translator's Note

* Cocinol is a gas used for cooking, usually in poor areas where natural gas is not available. Highly flammable, its use has led to many accidents in which children and adults were badly burned. This brings up issues involving equal distribution of resources and the ways in which localities such as Ciudad Bolívar are marginalized, which are currently significant political issues in and around Bogotá.

The Drive-by Victim

ALBERTO SALCEDO RAMOS

I TOOK A TAXI FROM DOWNTOWN at nine o'clock at night. Excessive trust—without a doubt a holdover from my rural upbringing, removed from paranoia—did not allow me to see this as an indiscretion. When I gave him the name of the barrio to which he should drive me, the driver asked me which way we should go and I told him to take Thirtieth Street.

"Where do you want me to pick up Thirtieth?" he inquired in a friendly tone.

I responded that we should take Twenty-sixth, and it didn't make me uncomfortable that he spoke without looking at me, or that his car was so rundown. As I write, I think that hailing a taxi on a Bogotá street at night—or even during the day—turns us into Russian roulette players: that the only defensive maneuver we have left is hoping, sometimes with ingenuousness, sometimes with arrogance, that the fatal shot doesn't hit *us*. The many decent and honorable taxi drivers still left, who also risk their lives without any armor besides the need to earn some money and a picture of the Virgin, must think something similar.

None of this passed through my mind as the old car moved forward. The driver only opened his mouth to ask questions directly related to the route: "Right or left?" When I responded, he threw out phrases like "Very good, sir," or "At your service." Six blocks from my house, on a narrow street where a military officer lives, the guy asked me a very strange question, but not even this activated my precarious alarms.

"So, what . . . Should I turn around?"

"No, keep going straight."

"Ah, I thought I had to turn around." This last sentence was even stranger, and only now do I perceive that it was pronounced with anxiety. I had always seen the street where the soldier lives closely monitored, but this time it was empty. At the end of the block, in front of a dark square with pretensions of being a park, there was a reduction in speed, the kind that we refer to in Colombia as "sleeping cops." The driver stopped there, simulating that the car had stalled on him. In that instant I clearly saw what was approaching, but it was already too late. Two burly men rushed toward the back doors of the car and were inside before I could recover from my surprise

Breast Beating

The first thing that the man who seated himself to my left did was give me a slap in the center of my face that still burns. The other grabbed my hands and ordered me to slide over on the seat. The taxi driver turned his face to me for the first time, and what I saw seemed vulgar: the man was chewing gum with a self-assurance that wasn't theatrical, calculated to intimidate, but absolutely spontaneous.

The yell that I let out was also spontaneous, a loud moan that aggravated my neighbor to the left. With a new slap on the neck that made my eyeglasses fly through the air, he indicated how he wanted me to behave from that moment forward: no revealing noise, no giving myself over to sharp, loud crying so that someone would hear me. But since my weeping had nothing to do with strategies and came instead from physical terror, there was no way to control it, not even with the brutal pedagogy of slaps across the face. The man on the right, chubbier than the others, crushed his rough hand to my mouth and told me he'd had enough child's play. If I kept crying, he said, they wouldn't hit me anymore: they would be forced to kill me.

"Okay, you son of a bitch"—intervened the ruder one—"I want you to close your eyes. I'll kill you if you open them."

"The thing is that these *gonorreas*"—said the fat one, with a tone of visceral hatred—"come here to snoop around and aren't even good at that."*

"Not even good at that," repeated the driver, as if he were approving the greatest statement he'd heard in his life.

I understand very well what they were saying by calling me "snoop": I had not only defied their empire by taking a taxi on the street on a Friday night—I had also done it in the most ostentatious manner possible. I was wearing a leather jacket that any designer would have rejected at a glance, but that in their eyes must have lent me the bearing of a magnate's heir who had gotten separated from his bodyguard. It would have been pointless to explain to them that I had bought the jacket on sale, that the watch, like every watch I have had in my entire life, had been a gift, and that I don't make cell phones but only use them for work. The pen, a lustrous Mont Blanc, was another story, although I'd also received it as a gift. It made me seem, and not without reason, someone who exhibits himself cruelly with his useless but expensive trinkets in front of a gallery of humiliated people.

So it was my fault. Did I think that I could trick them by acting like I had old-lady syndrome? The only thing that mattered was that I was there, in that dilapidated taxi, looking like a presumptuous animal that didn't know the laws of the jungle. If I wasn't rich but merely a poor copy, all the worse for me, not for them. Bad luck for me if I came to snoop around and am not even good at that, because, as can be deduced from his bitter reproach, a snoop should have at least a pistol to defend himself, instead of crying like a girl.

Let's Be Clear: This Is a Robbery

Before informing me that it was a robbery, they asked my name and profession. The taxi driver took in the information with a triumphant exclamation: "Those reporters make money!"

The fat one then asked me if I had a savings account and, when I said yes, he told me that if I gave them the code and behaved myself, nothing bad would happen to me. The neighbor on the left seemed to judge the consoling tone of his friend's advice as inconvenient: "What do you mean nothing bad will happen?" he thundered, spattering my face with his stench of *aguardiente*. "This son of a bitch is going to die! I'll kill him myself if he doesn't cooperate!"

I told them they could relax if the only reason to kill me was if I didn't cooperate. I whimpered, I mentioned God, I invoked my children, and in the darkness I was surprised that that voice, my own voice, didn't sound so weak, as if it came from a mouth less frightened than my own, that it would try to save me at the last minute, organizing the pieces of my sentimental arguments and letting them tumble out. The vile exclamation that the driver let out after my speech reminded me that none of them planned to be moved: "Bingo! He's got kids!"

"And what are their names?" asked the one on the right.

"What?"

"Your kids. Didn't you just say you had kids?"

I said the first names that came to mind without hesitation.

"Oh, man," responded the fat one, "sometimes really bad things happen to kids. Especially to the girls. That's why good daddies stay out of trouble."

A new blow from the left smashed against my face. It didn't take me long to discover the motive.

"Close your eyes, you son of a bitch!"

The neighbor on the right also became impatient and punched my shoulder. "What are you doing, you, bastard? Are you thinking of spying on us, or what? Open your eyes again and you die."

While they lifted me off the seat to take my wallet from one side, a voice seeking the exact address of my house came from the other. When I gave him the information, one of them said: "Okay, we're going to make a note of that."

"And the phone number?" asked the driver.

Once again, the information was provided, and I heard the syllable-by-syllable repetition of what he was apparently writing down. Then the fat one spoke. He did it in a reflexive, intimate tone, as if he were alone in the car. "This guy isn't wearing any jewelry at all."

"You don't like gold?" asked the driver.

I said no and then begged them to go to the automatic teller soon so that they could let me go. The guy on the right spat out a compassionate answer, with a little laugh that seemed more than ironic and didactic to me. "This guy doesn't want to understand that this is a robbery. He's wondering why we don't do things when he says to!"

A Manual for the Unarmed

Suddenly, the guy on the left took me by the shoulders and sunk me into the seat, speaking to the driver. "Drive, boy, hit the gas hard! Harder!"

Four hands pulled my jacket by the neck and covered my face with it. I felt like they were snapping my head off instead of just covering it. I felt drowned, reduced. I felt that even death itself couldn't be worse than that overwhelming asphyxiation. And they kept pulling on the jacket. Their voices sounded anguished.

"Quick, dumbass!"

"You move, you die!"

"Don't open your eyes!

"If there's a shoot-out, the police won't suffer. You'll be the first to take a bullet."

"Faster!"

"Okay, man, don't hound me so much! That taxi's one of ours."

"Are you sure?"

"Can't you see it?"

"Yes, yes, that's El Indio."

"And we were so scared we almost suffocated the poor guy."

"Okay, let's lower the jacket so he can breathe."

When they finally took the jacket away, the air came back. I breathed it in with urgency, with gratitude, and I told myself that as long as I had air to breathe, being alive wasn't so bad.

"It's just that there are lots of nosy drivers around and you have to be careful," noted the fat one, once again assuming his role as intellectual spokesman for the group.

"They think they're the law, damned *gonorreas*."

The less talkative of the three, my neighbor on the left, then removed from his sleeve a poisoned ace on whose presence I hadn't been counting.

"Well, friends, let's see if he'll repeat his address."

"But there's nothing in the house that could be of any use to you!" I exclaimed, terrified.

"We're not interested in going there," explained the other. "We're doing this in case you suddenly turn on us and squeal to the cops."

"What do you mean we're not going to go?" intervened the more violent one. "We'll go there and kill every one of the sons of bitches. Wait and see."

I said they could do whatever they wanted to me and pleaded that they not involve my family. I added that I was so ready to cooperate with them that I had given them my address.

"Yeah, and we wrote it down," observed the driver. "But we want to be sure."

"Repeat it, asshole!" screeched the guy on the left.

Since the address that I gave them at that point didn't coincide with the one I'd given them earlier, they unleashed their most varied repertoire of punches.

"Ah, no, man," said the one on the left, irritated as usual, "this guy's screwing with us."

"We're going to have to kill this son of a bitch."

"Ah, and on top of everything else, the *gonorrea* is looking at me!"

Using one of his fingers as a dagger, the man gave me a brutal blow. He didn't hit the open eye, as he had tried to, but he left me with a scratch on the left eyebrow. And he hurled the nth threat, his breath smelling like distilled alcohol in the sewers: "Next time I'll take it out, bastard."

The most painful part of the drive is the darkness that weighs on your eyes and makes you feel humiliated. When you close your eyes, the executioner shatters your chance of calibrating his intentions, of trying to manipulate him. With diminished strength and your arms tied down, they have you at their mercy. They only leave you a pair of ears that, as you can imagine, are not a weapon against them but against yourself, because they magnify the horror of every word that you hear in the shadows. The option of using your own words to defend yourself remains. Sometimes instinct will speak for you. Sometimes the brain

will. In any case, it is worth clarifying that you have no interest in identifying or turning in anyone, nor impeding the robbery, but only in living. If you're a convincing stiff, it's possible that when your eyelids come
apart in panic, you'll only be left with an ugly line across your eyebrow
rather than a missing eye.

The Last Option

When I gave them the address and phone number again, I had already
learned the lesson: I had to memorize the details so that I wouldn't make
another mistake. The man on the left got out of the car to happily help
himself to my card at an automatic teller. The fat one warned me that
if I tried to escape he would blow my brains out, since he had stayed
alone with me in the back of the car. I didn't sense that they were
armed—not then, not before, not afterward. But I am absolutely certain that they didn't need to be. The relief I had felt when the most
hostile behavior ended had already vanished. When the other two
started to drive me around, I understood that once they had the card
and the code, my life was no longer worth a nickel to them. If they let
me live, I thought and said in a low voice, it would be a favor for which
God would reward them. I asked them why they were keeping me in
the car if their partner had already gotten out.

"Because we aren't assholes," responded the driver. I cried, said I
wanted to die, that if I was saved from this I might end up hanging
myself. The driver spoke again. "No, old man, it's not like that either.
That's the problem with people like you. You start complaining before
you even know what abuse really is. You haven't seen anything, son."

"We're thieves, man, not killers," said the fat one, in a tone of offended dignity. "The only ones who die are the ones who don't cooperate, and you've behaved well."

"We're almost finished," observed the driver. "Don't cause any problems at the last minute and you'll see that nothing will happen."

"But if you're finishing up, where are you taking me?"

"Look, man, are you trying to piss me off?"

"We have to leave you in the middle of nowhere. What if we take
you to a neighborhood full of people and you turn on us or start to
scream?"

I think that if the lunatic on the left hadn't gotten out of the car, his two accomplices wouldn't have used their consoling tone, which offered me some kind of comfort.

"Do you know why we are doing this?" asked the driver. "Because they hurt one of the guys in the gang and we have to get together three million pesos tonight."

"We're all unemployed!" said the other.

That was the most dramatic moment of the evening. But it was also the most cynical. That cynicism became evident when the fat guy put his hand in my shirt pocket and told me to take ten thousand pesos so that I could take a taxi home. I told him I was afraid that the next taxi driver would rob me as well, and his answer, which was supposed to be tender, turned into a legitimate jewel of black comedy, even though he didn't want it to be:

"Nooooo, how can you even think that? We're gonna write down the son of a bitch's license plate number!"

Then he placed a cold object in my right hand.

"What's that?"

"Your glasses, asshole. Had you already forgotten that you wore glasses?"

Taking advantage of such camaraderie, I asked them to leave me the pack of cigarettes, as I remembered that I had three left.

"Ah, no, not that. We can't lose even one. We smoke, too."

I should state with absolute frankness that I don't ask for any pity for them today. But when they let me go, on Thirtieth Street, toward the south side of the city, I felt a great gratitude toward them. If I didn't shake their hands and invite them to breakfast the next day, it was because I wasn't brave enough. Standing on that lonely street, unhappy and cramped, I knew very well that it wouldn't be prudent to declare victory. I cried again. It didn't occur to me to look at the moon. And I thought that we are so screwed in this country that the only option left to us in the end is thanking the thieves.

TRANSLATED BY KATHERINE GOLDMAN

Translator's Note

* *Gonorrea* (literally, gonorrhea, the disease) is generally a pejorative term, used among men as a type of informal address.

The Attitudes

State Violence in Brazil

MARTHA K. HUGGINS

The Professional Morality of Torturers

Sᴇʀɢɪᴏ, ɴᴏ ʟᴏɴɢᴇʀ ᴀ São Paulo State Political Police (DOPS) official, had entered the São Paulo State Civil Police in 1956; he quickly became an important intelligence operative for the state's governor. Without any particular training for secret service work, Sergio began an intense all-consuming life in intelligence, spending days and nights tapping phones, installing surveillance microphones, and infiltrating unions and leftist political parties. This almost immediately isolated Sergio from family and nonpolice friends.

Eight years later, on the eve of Brazil's 1964 military coup, Sergio found himself "worn out" from years of intelligence and operations. "Fed up," he delivered his resignation to the governor. Rejecting Sergio's proposal, the governor promoted his close friend to POLINTER intelligence, the São Paulo Police Interstate Intelligence Division, claiming that he needed Sergio too much to let him leave this work. In POLINTER, Sergio supplied information to the governor to help engineer the 1964 military *golpe*.

By the end of the 1960s, feeling isolated and exhausted, Sergio tried again to leave police work. Rejecting Sergio's resignation, the governor appointed Sergio director of DOPS. He was in charge of all political police intelligence in Brazil's most populous and politically important state. Working twenty-four hours a day—directing and often even carrying out police operations himself—Sergio remembers his work as "intense and permanent." Recalling that there were labor and student "strike[s] every two, three days, [often with] vandalism," Sergio had to predict and effectively quash such strife. Feeling unable to delegate much of this work, Sergio himself ended up in all-important operations, "infiltrat[ing] literally everywhere, every movement, [especially] the [Communist] Party." Sergio had to "pick up on everything," since he was not able to assign much work to his subordinates.

Feeling "lost in the midst of [that] shit, [knowing that] tomorrow anything could happen," and considering himself impotent to effectively control his own future—sometimes even finding himself under death threat from the officials the governor had sent him to investigate—Sergio pleaded with the governor to let him resign. This time, the state's highest official transferred Sergio to the DEIC, the Civil Police robberies and thefts division. Known for its liberal use of torture, the DEIC tried to get its job done quickly and efficiently. Increasingly finding DEIC's normal investigation strategies deficient, Sergio set up a secret death squad inside his directorate. It could accomplish what regular police were reluctant to do.

By 1971, Sergio was totally drained from a decade and a half in intelligence and operations. Reeling from the pressures of DEIC's robbery division and the additional demands of his own "off-duty" death squad, Sergio was "unable to think or sleep; totally absorbed by [work-associated] problems." At this point, Sergio finally insisted on retiring from civil policing.

Interviewed in 1993 in his lavishly decorated apartment in São Paulo City's exclusive Jardims district, Sergio—severely debilitated from two heart attacks and a mild stroke—presented the most complex moralizing about torture and murder of any violence worker I interviewed in Brazil. Perhaps because Sergio's moral system is rich and varied, a tightly woven labyrinth of explanations for violence—sometimes congruent and sometimes contradictory—his justifications for police torture cover the entire range of moralities that emerge in the discourse of the other thirteen violence workers interviewed.

A Moral Universe

Sergio emphatically denies having personally carried out torture, citing his opposition to the violence that was routinely "used by OBAN and DOI/CODI" (Operação Banderiantes and Departamento de Operaçãos Internas/Centro de Operaçãos Defensa Interna), the military period's most notorious torture and murder organizations. In effect, Sergio "diffused" responsibility for torture into organizational entities that he claims not to have been in. Further validating his argument, Sergio maintains that he "didn't work th[e] way" OBAN and DOI/CODI agents did, adding that if he had, he "would have been revolted" by their practices. Yet Sergio apparently sees no contradiction in his calling the men transferred from his command into OBAN and then into DOI/CODI "close friends." He offers an explanation for these agents' violence that places an onus on them as individuals, explaining that the kinds of men invited or "funneled into" these internal security organizations were already "very hard-nosed" (i.e., physically and emotionally tough); the extreme violence they meted out further "bestialized" them. Sergio, in effect, excuses their violence as simultaneously part of their "nature" and as being shaped by forces, including his own, beyond their control.

Sergio recalls regulating his subordinates' violence by saying, "OK, slow down," implying that if bad behavior can be controlled by good and rational police officials, then it is not really so bad after all—a justification of professionalism for police violence. Indeed, Sergio believes that much "excess" police violence during Brazil's military period could have been avoided if there had been more police training, overlooking the fact that he, who considers himself a professional, had knowingly allowed torture under his command. In any case, Sergio seems to justify such torture as skillfully regulated by himself, a self-defined competent and "professional" police official.

Sergio grants limited acceptance for the torturing he himself did if there is a "just cause," arguing hypothetically that "if a little girl's life were at stake, and if by torturing someone he could save her life," Sergio would "torture—or order his men to do so." However, Sergio considers it wrong to torture a person who has "a political ideal": "I never used violence against anyone in the Communist Party. . . . I always respected their ideals." Yet Sergio almost beat a student to death for denying that he was in the Communist Party. The student was "so cynical . . . , if he had said, 'I took the [guerrilla] course' . . . but he was uppity, [so] I lost [my] head."

Whether these accounts represent Sergio's complex moral assumptions about the extent of violence permissible in different situations of violence (torture, beatings, or generalized infliction of harm); or illustrate the slipperiness of his discourse about torture (seldom using the "T" word, usually waltzing around or mislabeling it with euphemisms); or simply point to irreconcilable contradictions within Sergio's moral universe (Sergio would not torture, yet does, albeit under a different label), this policeman's narrative about violence reveals the complicated richness of torturers' moralizing about such violence.

Finding Torturers and Murders

During four months in 1993, I interviewed twenty-seven police in four large Brazilian cities and Brasilia.[1] Within this group, fourteen had either tortured or murdered during Brazil's military period (1964–1985).[2] While recognizing that a terror complex functions through a variety of violent actors—for instance, those who deliver victims to torturers; doctors who demonstrate techniques of torture and monitor their use, so that prisoners do not die before their torturers have extracted the information they want; notaries who certify that a victim has not been tortured—this study focuses on those violence workers who most directly tortured, murdered, or both.

Having police contacts in São Paulo and Rio de Janeiro, I began seeking interviewees there, asking each policeman interviewed to suggest a colleague I might also interview. I particularly sought those who had been in police units known to have carried out extreme violence: shock units and SWAT teams, the DOPS political police, São Paulo State's OBAN, and the national DOI/CODI. According to Holocaust scholar Robert J. Lifton, such organizations—functioning primarily to carry out violence—create and encourage atrocity; a member cannot avoid committing brutality, whether directly or indirectly.[3]

The analysis of the interview narratives of the twenty-seven police interviewees secured through these strategies uncovered fourteen who had engaged in torture, murder, or both during Brazil's military period. These men are the focus of this article.

Discourse of the Violent

The fourteen violence workers offered one or more of four inclusive accounts of the torture or murder they carried out: one diffused responsibility into sociocultural or organizational contexts; another blamed individuals—victims or perpetrators; a third cited just causes for violence; the fourth identified professional imperatives and pressures for torturing and murdering.

The first explanation, diffusing responsibility, involves assigning the cause of violence either to other police, to some other internal security agency, or to a broad sociocultural context:

> It was shocking . . . the first time to see someone hanging on the Parrot's Perch with a water hose in his mouth. I didn't agree with that, but I was inside the room and the guys were [torturing him].

> I took my gun and shot. . . . Some guys died, but I don't know who killed them. There were many guys shooting. . . . I don't know who hit the guy and who [didn't]. You just know that people died. Fortunately it was the other side.

> Brazil is a Catholic country. In Brazil they are used to this kind of behavior—like torture, for example—because Catholic churches tortured people for years and years, centuries and centuries.

Blaming individuals, as victims or perpetrators, the second explanation, locates the roots of police violence in either bad victims or bad perpetrators.

> They were tortured because they were stupid. . . . [We said,] "You had the opportunity to talk without being tortured, but you preferred not to talk." If she confessed, she would remain a prisoner but without any torture.

> There [were] certain men in the police, on my team—I knew one—who got pleasure out of killing [crooks]. It wasn't in self-

defense and we couldn't even say, "Let's get rid of this guy, he's bad." No, he really wanted to kill—when one or two bullets was enough to kill someone, he'd wind up taking five rounds—pow, pow, pow. . . . [He'd] kill people as coldly as you'd kill a chicken.

Citing just cause for torture or murder, the third explanation, asserts that violent police were responding to a generalized but declared war, state of siege, internal war, war on drugs, war on crime, or a dangerous situation where a good citizen's life was in peril.

If I arrest someone who has kidnapped a little girl who might be killed in four hours, I'm not going to waste time questioning him for two or three days just to wear him down. So . . . I'll hang that guy up [on the Parrot's Perch], work him over, and he'll tell me in five minutes.

We were proud of what we did . . . working in DOPS . . . that pride of ridding the country of a threat of a Communist regime. . . . [We were] people doing a patriotic job, a big job, an important job. . . . We were a religious people, a Christian people.

"Professionalism," the fourth justification, points to professional mandates and pressures that allow "acceptable" torture, murder, or both:

To kill properly, you can't [just] react; you have to act with reason. Police work is being intelligent, it's reasoning, technique, information. . . . You only kill when there's no other way, when either you kill or someone else dies. Beyond that, you don't kill, in my opinion. Torture is zealousness in trying to discover, unravel a crime. [The police] handle a lot of work. We don't have the resources to work on an investigation. . . . The shortest route is by torturing.

Moral Reckoning by Torturers

The four explanations for torture, murder, or both represent different implicit ways of incorporating body and mind into discourse about this violence. The first three—diffusion of responsibility, individual weakness, and just cause—embody violence by referring to a victim's body

Table 12.1
Torturers' Moral Reckoning

Acceptable	Not wholly acceptable, but understandable	Unacceptable
Perpetrator is professionally trained and controlled.	Perpetrator is youthful, stupid, ignorant; lacks training; temporarily out of control.	Perpetrator is deliberately sadistic, cruel, cold-bloodedly vicious.
Perpetrator uses coercive psychological cunning and intelligence.	Perpetrator is cold, aggressive, and purposely used by superiors; under "bad" orders.	Perpetrator is irrational, permanently out of control (character disorder); judgment is impaired from drugs or alcohol.
To get needed information for a "just cause" where only violence will succeed, or because victim does not cooperate.	In brutalizing social conditions or where perpetrator is actively present but not participating in violence.	For personal satisfaction and/ or economic gain.

or to someone or something that explicitly acts on that body or to both. By specifically linking violence to human physicality, these accounts make torture and murder more visible and less morally acceptable.

In contrast, professionalism disembodies violence by eliminating or obscuring human agency and substituting nonhuman organizational imperatives. By allocating acceptable physical violence to a calculus of the mind, the agents of violence—and its human impacts—are rendered less visible and more morally acceptable. In other words, each in its own way, negative physicality or mental rationality renders police violence morally unacceptable or acceptable.

In the process of interweaving the relationship of violence to physicality, interviewees implicitly constructed a hierarchy of morality that assigned torturing or murdering to one of three moral categories: acceptable, excusable but not wholly acceptable, or unacceptable, depending on the degree of physical involvement and situational context (see table 12.1). A foundation for most interviewees' moral calculus was that, in their minds, torture had to be kept operationally distinct from murder. Torturers who did their jobs properly should not kill: to do so would either represent a loss of self-control (for example, inappropriate physicality) or take the violence worker outside his appropriate jurisdiction (for example, operational "irrationality"). Likewise, killers should not engage in torture: an inappropriate psychophysical (for example, "irrational") interaction or attachment to a victim. As Jorge, a former murder operative for DOI/CODI explained, "It was much easier to kill, because the torturer had to have a commitment to his victim. The killer had no [such] commitment to his victim."

The tendency for violence workers to operationally separate torture from murder led to focusing this part of the analysis exclusively on their assertions about torture.[4] The interviewees suggested that good police torturers were trained and "rational"; they had a clear knowledge of the limits on their behavior or were directed by a rational superior, or both. Under such circumstances, torture was legitimate for furthering a just cause and for professionally interrogating bad suspects. Good torturers' violence was disembodied, justified by organizational or ideological necessity or guided by a rational mind.

On the other hand, bad police torturers either used violence for pleasure, permanently lacked self-control, tortured under the temporary influence of drugs or alcohol, or used torture for dishonest economic ends. Such "unacceptable" torture was embodied—the result of irrational human physicality.

Torturers in the moral middle ground—where torture was understandable but not wholly acceptable—were described by mixed discourse. Torture could excusably result from a temporary loss of emotional control or from the system's selection of an overly aggressive policeman to carry out its violence. In this moral middle ground, torturers were embodied as victimized, physically driven perpetrators whose own biological makeup, or social pressures, had led them to behave improperly.

Changing Accounts:
Explaining the Past Through the Present

Discussing the relationship of discursive content to societal conditions and change, Foucault suggests that to be taken seriously, motivational accounts must now be grounded in a modern contemporary will to truth that has its bases in a corpus of scientifically grounded writing that includes the rules, techniques, and instruments for establishing truth. In other words, with the cultural-historical shift in ideological hegemony from religion to secularism, explanations that rely on religion and the sacred do not have the credibility of those based on science and secularism.[5] According to C. Wright Mills, in a society in which religious motives have been debunked on a rather wide scale, certain thinkers are skeptical of those who ubiquitously proclaim them. Cohen further argues that built into an individual's accounts is the knowledge that certain ones will be more readily accepted and will be honored by the legal system and the wider public.[6]

Much research on Brazil's military period demonstrates that, at that time, the cold war was commonly invoked as justification for state repression.[7] This national security ideology divided Brazil's population into subversives and good citizens, with security forces in an all-out just war against subversion.[8] Since the interviewed violence workers were expected to advance such a justification, it was surprising when only four of the fourteen actually cited national security needs for torture, murder, or both. In contrast, all fourteen interviewees advanced one or more professionalism accounts.

Such discourse seems to reflect a reduction in the cultural and political legitimacy of national security just-war excuses for violence, and an increase in the cultural resonance of professionalism for explaining acceptable police abuse. As has been argued, this may point to a deeper cultural change in the industrializing world, where ideologies rooted in rationality, instrumentalism, and science (e.g., professionalism) have replaced ones appealing to passion and emotion (e.g., a just war). That is, accounts that appeal dispassionately to instrumental values may now be culturally more acceptable than those suggesting a deep emotional commitment to an ultimate expressive value. But what are the consequences of reliance on disembodied professionalism for police training and police conduct, and for evaluating and legitimizing police violence today?

Professionalizing Police Violence

Equated with rational, scientifically guided action, professionalism is understood to include specialized training in a particular body of knowledge, a rigid division of labor, hierarchy of decision making, self-imposed occupational standards, and impersonal and universal rules for appointment, promotion, demotion, and remuneration.[9] For policing in Brazil, professionalism has been operationalized in crime control ideologies and technical militarization.[10] Militarized professionalism, in turn, justifies creating an ever more hierarchical police, fortified by technical crime-fighting squads and the militarized materiel to combat a generalized enemy. By dividing the population into good citizens and criminals, the militarized crime control orientation retains the Brazilian military's older Manichean division of the population: citizens defined as criminals are transformed into rule-violating outsiders to be managed through heavy, generalized police repression.

Seen as the opposite of unreason and unpredictability, professionalism is thought to reduce police violence by increasing rational police action. In fact, however, militarized professionalism both increases police violence and disguises it.[11] The assumption that rational-legal professional methods guide police behavior ipso facto rules out the possibility that true professionals could act inappropriately violent—implying that some controlled police violence is acceptable. Police who violate professional standards are relegated to the status of the exceptional. They are bad apples in an otherwise conforming, right-thinking, professional police institution.

Legacies of Military Rule: Authoritarianism in Democratic Transitions

Writing about the causes of torture, Crelinstein argues that its routine, systematic use is only possible within a closed world imbued with an alternate reality separated from that of conventional morality.[12] While Crelinstein is correct that torture occurs within, and is fostered by, isolation, it would be misleading to view torture as outside conventional morality. One such conventional morality—professionalism—is a modern, secular ethos that includes principles about right and wrong and that sees science and reason as appropriate guides for moral conduct. The ethos of professionalism allows relatively autonomous police professionals to decide on the acceptability, excusability, or inappropriateness of gross human rights violations. If carried out by professional police acting professionally, police violence is considered acceptable. Seen as a scientifically based standard for assessing the appropriateness of torture or murder, the tautological, secularized morality of professionalism provides a legitimate justification for police violence. Or, as Armando, a retired chief of Rios Municipal Police explained, "I don't use . . . violence outside the standard of my conscience as a human being. I'm a conscientious professional. I know what to do and when to do it."

Notes

1. Of the twenty-seven interviews, three were done by Mika Haritos-Fatouros and Philip Zimbardo through a translator, the other twenty-four by Huggins. Huggins wrote this essay without the direct collaboration of Haritos-Fatouros and Zimbardo.
2. For a description of the sampling procedures and the strategies for discovering torturers and murderers, see Huggins, "Reconstructing Atrocity."
3. Lifton, *The Nazi Doctors*.
4. While not all interviewees included all three categories of moral judgment in their discourse about violence, all discourse shared several features in common. Interviewees had a clear notion of when violence was acceptable and when it was not. All had remarkably similar criteria for assigning past violence to one or another moral category; each interviewee's moral calculus was sufficiently flexible to make violence acceptable in some situations, excusable in others, and totally unacceptable in a third set—with the status of perpetrator, victim, or hero shifting according to the sociopolitical context constructed. Only subtle nuances in Portuguese separated one moral classification from another.
5. See Sheridan, *Michel Foucault*.
6. Mills, "Situated Actions," 910; S. Cohen, "Human Rights," 108.
7. Huggins, *Political Policing*; Langguth, *Hidden Terrors*; Lernoux, *Cry of the People*; the research of Pinheiro.
8. Alves, *State and Opposition*; BNM Archdioceses of São Paulo, *Torture in Brazil*; Skidmore, *Politics of Military Rule*; Weschler, *A Miracle*.
9. Bledstein, *Culture of Professionalism*.
10. See Chevigny, *Edge of the Knife*; Huggins, "Violencia Institucionalizada e Democracia"; for the United States, see Skolnick and Fyfe, *Above the Law*.
11. On increasing, see Chevigny, *Edge of the Knife*; Skolnick and Fyfe, *Above the Law*; on disguising, see Huggins, "Violencia Institucionalizada e Democracia."
12. Ronald Crelinstein, "The World of Torture: A Constructed Reality" typescript, author's files, 1993), 5.

The Impact of Exposure to Violence in São Paulo

NANCY CÁRDIA

Accepting Violence or Continuing Horror?

URBAN VIOLENCE, PARTICULARLY FATAL VIOLENCE, has been on the rise in Brazilian urban centers, and this is especially true in the metropolitan regions of Rio de Janeiro and São Paulo. In 1997, the number of homicides in Brazil reached over forty thousand, 38.8 percent of which occurred in the two metropolitan regions of Rio de Janeiro and São Paulo.[1] The rise in this type of violence occurs in a heterogeneous manner in some metropolitan regions, as is the case in Vitoria and Recife.

The breakdown of homicides differs among urban centers, and especially within those centers, but homicides are concentrated in several areas and, within them, in a few neighborhoods. This pattern has been identified in other countries that have experienced a sharp rise in violence in recent decades (the United States, Colombia, Venezuela, Mexico). The number of cities involved in the United States is greater than in Latin America, where homicides tend to be concentrated in regions that have very specific problems. In Mexico this occurs in the capital and in cities that border the United States because of drug trafficking; in Colombia many cities and even some rural areas (due to drug trafficking, the guerrillas, the paramilitary, and the Colombian army) are affected; in Venezuela the main focus of the rise in violence is found in Caracas and is linked to the country's severe economic crisis. Given that there are more large urban centers in Brazil, one expects this problem to be greater. However, the concentration of homicides in four metropolitan regions suggests that there are specific problems in these regions that contribute to the rise in violence.

The information reported in this essay is based on a survey of attitudes, values, cultural norms, and behavior with respect to violence that focused on one of the many causes of violence: its normalization, or the existence of a "culture of violence" stemming from continual exposure to violence.[2] Part of the justification for this approach resides in the existence of reports claiming that certain forms of violence provoke less indignation than would be expected. One finds that there is more indignation about the rise in violent crime against property than toward the rise in crime against life committed mostly by young men from the poorest neighborhoods. This lack of indignation may be the result of various factors: it may indicate the existence of a normalization or acceptance of interpersonal violence when it is committed against those who are thought to be certain "types of people," or in order to resolve certain types of arguments such as drug trafficking.

This study argues that violence cannot be explained by the mere presence of varying structures such as poverty, unemployment, various levels of need, a poorly run criminal justice system, and the presence of alcohol or drugs in the society, and that a set of values and norms that allow violent behavior must be taken into account. Thus, violence has multiple causes, since the values and norms shared within a society are part of this mode of causality.

Creating the survey questionnaire required us to carefully review the literature on the role of cultural attitudes, norms, and values with respect to violent behavior.[3] We also used 1997 ACTIVA (Cultural Norms and Attitudes Toward Violence in Selected Cities of Latin America and Spain) research data published by the Pan-American Health Organization, which studied eight Latin American cities with respect to norms and values regarding violence. The remainder of this essay reports our survey results and our conclusions.

The Perception of Violence

Violence is perceived as a relevant and salient problem and as a growing phenomenon in all of the cities studied and throughout all age groups. Of those interviewed, 95 percent see violence as growing in recent times. In São Paulo, the sentiments of the interviewees and the official statistics converge. Violence in the form of violent crimes has not stopped growing since the mid–1970s. This explains why older people unanimously state that violence has only risen (99 percent). This rising violence mainly affects city life (52 percent agree). In general, people find that family and neighborhood life are less affected by violence. Violence most affects cities' impersonal and anonymous common public living spaces. Young people tend to feel the impact of neighborhood violence the most, while the elderly seem to be more sensitive to its impact on the family. Therefore, despite the almost unanimous perception of a rise in violence, the consequences of this rise, in terms of impact, are not evaluated in the same manner by all.

Exposure to Violence

Measuring exposure to violence is essential to our understanding of which behavioral factors underpin violent measures and criminal acts in the long run so that we may curb violence. Exposure to violence is defined as the experience of direct or indirect victimization. Indirect victimization refers to violence that one witnesses, or cases of violence that a victim's parents or close friends hear about. Being more or less exposed to violence is not a neutral event in people's lives and represents not only differences in the quality of living standards but also new risks for victimization. The literature has shown that the risk of victimization is not evenly distributed within the city, but that certain areas are more affected and that within these areas some people are more victimized than others. The literature also reveals that violence that is done closest to people, either to them directly or to their relatives and friends, has the most impact.

Direct Victimization

The interviewees' exposure to violence was measured in three contexts: close to home (the neighborhood), in the workplace (for those who

Table 13.1
Victimization in the Last Twelve Months by Age Group

Please think of what has happened in the last twelve months in order to answer these questions, and tell me whether or not each of these things happened to you during that period of time.

São Paulo	Ages				
Questions	50 and above	35–49	25–34	16–24	Total
			%		
1. Someone insulted you with swear words	20	30	19	19	11
2. Someone threatened to rob you with a gun	7	8	7	6	8
3. You suffered some type of physical aggression	4	8	4	2	1
4. Someone threatened to rob you with a knife	3	4	3	2	2
5. You were wounded by a firearm, such as a revolver	0	2	0	0	0
6. You were offered drugs	7	17	5	6	0
7. Someone asked you to supply drugs	3	12	2	1	0
8. You felt the need to carry a weapon	4	8	2	6	0
9. You moved in order to avoid fear or a threat	3	4	4	2	1
10. You suffered some kind of police violence or mistreatment	3	8	2	1	0
11. A police officer solicited a bribe from you	2	3	4	1	1
12. Your life or that of someone close to you was threatened	10	19	9	7	3
13. A close relative was murdered	4	8	4	2	1
14. A close relative was wounded by a firearm or knife	3	7	3	1	1
15. A close relative was kidnaped	1	1	1	0	1

N= 500

Source: Núcleo de Estudos da Violência (Violence Studies Nucleus)/Ministerio da justicia (Ministry of Justice), 1999

work), and in school (for students). We attempted to determine if violence involved the interviewee or a relative and, in the case of young people, if they knew other young people, friends, or acquaintances who had had those experiences. Those who answered yes were asked whether their role was that of victim or perpetrator.

The majority of the interviewees had suffered some form of violence in the last twelve months or had watched or heard of someone close to them who had witnessed those events. The degree of severity of the violence varies, but there are two recurring patterns: young people are the most victimized, either directly or indirectly, and the most serious and most frequent violence tends to occur in the vicinity of one's house (see table 13.1).

At least 10 percent of those interviewed in São Paulo were robbery victims (threatened with firearms or knives), 4 percent were victims of bodily injury, 3 percent had a relative wounded, 4 percent had
a relative murdered, and 1 percent a relative kidnapped. The youngest
were the most victimized in all of the categories, sometimes representing twice the level of victimization of the other age groups: 12 percent
had been robbed (either with a firearm or a knife), 8 percent suffered
bodily injury, 7 percent had a relative wounded by a gun or knife, and
8 percent had a parent murdered. The young are also most frequently
exposed to verbal insults, 30 percent, 20 percent of this type of aggression, and are exposed twice as much to drugs as the other age groups;
17 percent have been offered drugs (compared to 8 percent of the total) and 12 percent have been approached by people wanting to buy
drugs (compared to 3 percent of the total). This is the group that most
frequently reports negative experiences with the police in the last twelve
months: 8 percent report having been mistreated by the police, and 3
percent report being the victims of police extortion. Since they are victimized the most, it is no surprise that they are the group who most
strongly felt the need to carry a weapon (8 percent).

When we compare these results to the ACTIVA study (1997), we
notice slight variations: the ACTIVA data refer to Rio de Janeiro and
match what we have noted here in general terms. Among the ACTIVA
interviewees, 6.4 percent have been robbery victims, 4.5 percent have
had a relative murdered, and 1.1 percent have been wounded by a knife
or firearm. These numbers are less than those collected in Cali, Caracas,
Medellín, and San Salvador, but the pattern of victimization reported
by the youngest people is the same.

The type of victimization identified in the survey also matches the
U.S. pattern with respect to where victimization takes place. U.S. research shows that the majority of people who were victimized were victims of robberies and thefts near their place of residence. These studies
also show that living in high-crime areas raises the risk of victimization.[4] Direct victimization of those interviewed for the survey also seems
to match the pattern identified in other studies, particularly in the type
of violence suffered and the greater frequency of cases involving young
people.

A longitudinal study financed by the National Institute of Justice conducted in various Chicago neighborhoods also shows that the majority of assaults occur in neighborhoods (in general, outnumbering those committed in schools), and that of those interviewed, 31 percent have suffered physical assault, 15 percent have been robbed, 14 percent have suffered sexual assault, and 8 percent have had gunshot wounds. In their study of youth exposure to violence in schools, near homes, and in homes in Denver and Cleveland, Singer and colleagues verified that young males have suffered more physical violence and that young females have suffered more sexual violence. The house is the most dangerous place for young people in general, while schools are the most dangerous places for boys, followed by neighborhoods. Between 37.5 percent and 42.9 percent have been threatened at school, between 30.5 percent and 40.9 percent have been beaten up at school, and between 9 percent and 10 percent have been robbed at school. Furthermore, between 16 percent and 14 percent have been attacked with a knife and a surprising number had been shot at: 28.3 percent in Denver and 33.4 percent in Cleveland.[5]

This type of victimization would seem to justify the interviewees' perception that violence has an impact on their neighborhoods, cities, and families, and their feeling a greater need to take steps to increase their sense of security. But this is not what seems to happen. The findings suggest that the sense of security or insecurity stems not only from objective experience, but also from the intervention of other factors, such as the type of violence they witness and then relate to their friends, according to the Pan-American Health Organization.

Indirect Victimization

As expected, there is more indirect than direct victimization. The majority of interviewees had seen some type of criminal or violent behavior in the last twelve months, most frequently some form of drug use. The pattern of witnessing violence is similar to the pattern of violence that victimizes. The most violent crimes witnessed are also those that were the most frequently committed. As in the case of direct victimization, the youngest people most frequently report having witnessed all types of crime or violence, in general twice as many as in the group of oldest people. The most commonly witnessed incidents were physical assault (35 percent), armed robbery (21 percent), someone pulling a gun on someone else (21 percent), and someone getting shot (14 percent). Furthermore, 13 percent have witnessed a murder, 11 percent have seen a murder victim's corpse, and 7 percent have seen someone get knifed.

The two crimes that young people have most often witnessed are drug use and drug peddling: 72 percent of the interviewees have seen someone use drugs in the last twelve months and 46 percent have watched a drug sale. Young people are also those who have most often been in prison (21 percent). We have yet to learn if those prisons strictly obey the law or if arbitrary acts were committed throughout the legal process. In other words, we still do not know if being in prison represents the opportunity for the young people to witness the law being applied or if it is an experience that reinforces a sense of ambiguity with respect to the law.

Exposure to violence also occurs through knowing that someone to whom one is close has witnessed such episodes. This type of exposure is less frequent but is nonetheless important since it serves to confirm for the victim or for the witness that such events are not that random. Once again, it is the youngest people who most often report knowing someone who has been the victim of violence. Violent crimes that involve people and property and also involve acquaintances are most frequently mentioned. These crimes tend to be the subject of conversation because they caused the most fear in people.

The exposure to crime by people under twenty was also evaluated through the use of specific questions regarding whether the respondents knew other young people like themselves who had been victims of violent crime in the last twelve months. The responses to this question reaffirm what we have seen up until now: young people are falling victim to violence in their neighborhoods and near their homes. Violence near schools or in the workplace occurs at a much lower rate than near one's home.

Not only do young people know someone like themselves who was the victim of this violence, but they also know the aggressors. As emphasized in U.S. studies, knowing either the perpetrator or the victim increases the intensity of the exposure, and this increases the probability that the events will scar the witness or the person who hears about

Table 13.2
Exposure to Violence: People Under Twenty Who Know Victims and/or Aggressors

Do you have a friend who:

São Paulo	**Yes**
Options	**Percentages**
1. Has attacked or hit a friend	53
2. Belongs to gangs	33
3. Carries a weapon	32
4. Has robbed someone	27
5. Has threatened a teacher	15
6. Has killed someone	12
7. Threatened a teacher with a knife or pocketknife	5
8. Has been wounded by a firearm	24
9. Has been robbed	39
10. Has had their life threatened	35
11. Has been wounded with a knife	14
12. Was murdered	14
13. Has been raped	11

N= 66

Source: Núcleo de Estudos da Violência (Violence Studies Nucleus)/Ministerio da justicia (Ministry of Justice), 1999

what happened.[6] Those episodes become a sort of co-victimization, one of the effects of which is post-traumatic stress syndrome, also known as "survivor's stress syndrome."[7] The symptoms of this syndrome are anger, depression, high anxiety, sleeplessness, memory lapses, lack of concentration, and the desire to escape reality (see table 13.2).

The young people interviewed fall victim to more violence, watch and hear more about violence and often know the aggressors; this is true for both boys and girls. The percentage of young people who know another young person who has been a rape victim is remarkable: 11 percent. The same can be said for the percentage of young people who know someone like themselves who has killed someone (12 percent), who has been killed (14 percent), or who carries a weapon (32 percent).

Thus, the interviewees' responses confirm the official statistics: this group is the most vulnerable and most victimized, either directly or indirectly. They have been the most frequent victims of violence, have witnessed the largest number of cases, and know the greatest number of victims and aggressors. This means that they are exposed to a number of elements that encourage the acceptance of a series of actions in which violence is not an uncommon element.

Could high exposure to violence on the part of young people affect their life expectancy? In order to answer this question, we asked the interviewees twenty and under to estimate the probability of their living to the age of twenty-five. The majority (25 percent) seem to be relatively certain that they will be alive at twenty-five. The violence they have witnessed does not seem to affect their life expectancy, and this signals the presence of a degree of resiliency, or of elements that counterbalance the negative effects of those experiences.

Comparisons of data from other countries allow us to understand the extent of witnessing exposure to violence. Data from the National Institute of Justice show that in Chicago between 23 percent and 30 percent of the inhabitants have already seen a murder or seen someone get shot, 24 percent have seen a murder victim, and 66 percent have heard gunshots.[8] There are also considerable differences among cities in the United States. In Baltimore, studies published in 1988 showed that among young people 60 percent have witnessed serious assault; 51 percent, robberies; 42 percent, gunshots; 24 percent, murders; and 14 percent, rape. Research reported in 1995 shows that in Denver and Cleveland not only are schools and neighborhoods the places where direct victimization takes place for young people, but also they are the places where most violence is witnessed. Furthermore, this research showed that gender plays no role when it comes to witnessing violence: girls and boys have equally witnessed violence, and this experience seems to be more frequent than in the pattern observed in the ten Brazilian cities. In Denver and Cleveland, between 73 percent and 78 percent had seen assaults, between 30 percent and 46 percent had seen someone get knifed, between 37 percent and 62 percent had seen someone get shot, and between 16 percent and 21 percent had seen some sort of sexual abuse. These high percentages are repeated in other research done in the United States.[9]

One explanation for this higher exposure to violence in the United States, where these police incidents are less frequent than in Brazil, could be due to the differences in the groups studied. The Brazilian survey sought a representative sample of the population in the cities studied, whereas in the United States the research sampled young people in a few schools, generally in high crime areas; the only exception to this was a National Institute of Justice study that looked at the entire city of Chicago. The studies limited to young people tend to produce much higher numbers than those limited to adults, as evidenced by the survey; this is due in part to the fact that young people live in areas of greater conflict. This also increases the exposure to violence, as demonstrated in the Chicago study, which showed that exposure to violence is greater in neighborhoods with the higher numbers of police incidents: 35 percent of young people living in the most violent neighborhoods have witnessed shootings, whereas only 2 percent of the young people have had that experience in neighborhoods where the incidence is lower.

It is possible that the violence that they witness and of which they are sometimes victims is not the worst violence. When asked which crimes they consider the most serious and which should always be punished, we found that they were the crimes that either most affect or provoke the most fear in young people: rape, homicide, kidnapping, armed robbery, and robbery. They are life-threatening, violent crimes committed against the person: rape (70 percent), kidnapping (48 percent), and homicide (46 percent).

Whereas young people feel that life-threatening crimes should receive the greatest punishment, the type of violence that they find the most upsetting is violence brought about by the action of "thugs," followed by interpersonal and police violence. Police violence is more important to young people since, as noted, they are the group that is most exposed to negative experiences with the police. Violence in the family, against motorists, and in schools and neighborhoods seems to be less important in terms of causing uneasiness. Violence against motorists troubles the elderly but not the young. Family violence, which literature on the subject often names as one of the factors responsible for violence outside the family, seems to be of little importance to the interviewees, as is the case for violence in the neighborhood, the principal site for exposure to violence. Thus, the most troublesome violence seems to be that which is instigated by someone who is not a family member or neighbor, whether known or unknown to those around them (see table 13.3).

Table 13.3
The Most Troubling Violence According to Age Group

Here are a few types of violence that occur on a daily basis. Which ones, in your opinion, are most troubling to people?

São Paulo	Ages				
Options	50 +	35–49	25–34	16–24	Total
1. Gang violence	42%	36%	44 %	41%	47%
2. Police violence	17	28	19	12	11
3. Interpersonal violence	15	17	16	21	7
4. Traffic violence	9	6	7	9	13
5. Violence in schools	7	6	3	8	10
6. Intrafamilial violence	5	3	7	4	5
7. Violence in the neighborhood	4	5	3	4	4
8. Other/ None of the above	1	0	0	1	1

N= 500
Source: Núcleo de Estudos da Violência (Violence Studies Nucleus)/Ministerio da justicia (Ministry of Justice), 1999

The Consequences of Neighborhood Violence

Although the greatest exposure to violence happens within one's neighborhood or near one's home, the interviewees seem to ignore this fact. According to the literature on violence, neighborhood violence has various impacts on the inhabitant population and even on those who provide services to that population, but this is not so for young people and children. Young people in high-risk situations who witness violence and who are victims of it can, depending on their family situation, become victimizers. Resistance to this violence will depend on the type of support young people have within their families and community, on their own personal competency,[10] and on the degree of the family's integration into the community. If young people are well-integrated into community life, their sense of protection increases, thus reducing the fear of risk despite the actual threat.[11]

It is to be expected that in areas of chronic violence, where people are subjected to real wars between drug trafficking gangs, or between the police and drug traffickers, and where families are forced to lock themselves in their homes for days until the conflicts cease, part of the population presents post-traumatic stress symptoms. When violence is chronic, these effects are amplified and difficult to treat, since the conflict is never ending: peace does not prevail, and people do not have the opportunity to recover from the conflict. In these contexts, it is possible to find periodic surges of increased support for hard-line policies (death penalty, violent police action, etc.) or for attempts to attain public safety by giving private sectors more power.[12] Hence, violence has social, psychological, and economic repercussions.

Violent crimes are associated with contexts that lack social organization, which is understood as locales with low participation in collective activities, little church affiliation, a great deal of mobility among the population, unemployment, and high population density, and urban centers.[13] These areas experience a series of problems. For example, families move to look for better economic situations; there is a sense of dejection in the neighborhood, a lack of connection to one's place, an inferior sense of community, of identification with others, little disposition for collective actions and cooperation. The more fear and mistrust there is between people, the lower the potential for collective organization. In these conditions, there is also less social control, since the more violent a neighborhood is, the greater the mistrust between strangers, the greater the tendency to avoid areas where people live, work, circulate, or spend their free time.[14]

As fear rises, people develop survival strategies that restrict interpersonal contact. Families who do not have the means to leave isolate themselves, limit their contacts with the community, remove themselves from collective life, and confine themselves to their homes. The less contact there is between people, the greater the probability of distrust. This affects collective participation, and the probability of social capital development is lower.[15] Without participation in the search for solutions to the community's problems, the decline of the community accelerates. The literature contends that another effect of the impossibility of being able to leave a violent area might be desensitization with respect to violence or even acceptance of it as a normal occurrence; violence becomes perceived as a fact of life.[16]

Fear could lead people to adopt protection strategies that further impoverish collective life. People change their routines, avoid circulating in certain places, begin using personal security equipment. Their lifestyle also changes: they avoid using public transportation, remove themselves from collective life, lower their participation in collective activities. Fear still reinforces prejudices and stereotypes. People further mistrust young people, strangers, and the poor.

The flight of families toward better economic and social conditions has the brutal effect of reducing the numbers of models of relationships between people, both in the family and socially, of professional profiles, of social ascension, thus reducing the diversity of values to which inhabitants who remain in a given place are exposed or with which they have contact. This would mainly affect younger groups by limiting the availability of models of successful careers within the system of legitimate opportunities; the availability of successful models of the system of illegal careers limits young people's willingness to pursue legitimate opportunities.

Since violence may influence solidarity and relationships among community members, or even the possibility of having a sense of community, the survey investigated what people perceive as strategies for self-protection in relation to violence. What would change in people's behavior as a result of exposure to violence? The data show that what most frequently changes due to violence is "going out at night." The oldest people interviewed are most likely to give up going out at night. The youngest interviewed would do the following: "avoid going out at night" (41 percent), "avoid certain areas/streets of the city" (33 percent), and "change one's route" (23 percent).

The literature on violence predicts that the greater the violence in a neighborhood, the fewer inhabitants will identify with that neighborhood, and the less the sense of belonging to a collectivity, emotional involvement, and commitment to the place; this would hamper the development of social capital. The data from the survey do not corroborate this prediction. Contrary to what was expected, the interviewees claim to be integrated into their neighborhoods, express an appreciation for their neighborhoods, and find their neighbors to be cooperative, brotherly, and trustworthy. This positive affiliation with the neighborhood seems to grow with age: there is more consensus among the older interviewees than the younger ones. Since young people comprise the group that is most touched by violence, the data suggest that neighborhood violence might not have an identical impact on the inhabitants; rather, the impact might be mediated by one's proximity to the violence. In this case, the greater the exposure to violence, the

Table 13.4
Perceptions of One's Neighborhood by Age Group

I will name a series of phrases and for each of them, I would like you to state whether you agree, disagree, or have no opinion.

São Paulo	Ages				
	50+	35–49	25–34	16–24	Total
Statements			Totally disagree		
1. I feel proud of my neighborhood.	67%	54%	60%	68%	86%
2. The government can count on my neighbors to fight violence.	62	57	57	61	74
3. I am in the habit of saying that I live in a good place.	61	47	53	64	82
4. I consider various people in my neighborhood to be close friends of mine.	60	47	57	58	81
5. If I need help, I can count on my neighbors.	60	50	53	64	73

Source: Núcleo de Estudos da Violência (Violence Studies Nucleus)/Ministerio da justicia (Ministry of Justice), 1999

greater the effect on the links to the neighborhood. If this is true, the great violence that young people experience would affect their affiliation to the neighborhood, and this in turn would diminish the neighborhood's potential for being an element of protection against the effects of violence (see table 13.4).

Exposure to violence and the fear it provokes can lead people to support radical self-defense measures. They can, for example, encourage people to uphold extreme measures, making them less tolerant of differences and leading them to favor strict controls or summary punishments, thus fomenting even more suspicion toward those who are different. One way of investigating this hypothesis was to ask the interviewees what preventative measures could be applied to a neighborhood. The answers show that one's tolerance to difference does not appear to be affected. Interviewees of all ages upheld that the makeup of the neighborhood must be heterogeneous in terms of social class, religion, political ideas, race, and color. This notion of upholding heterogeneity was strongest among those who are middle-aged, suggesting that younger generations have been cultivating this tolerance for diversity.

Exposure to Corporal Punishment

The literature points to another type of exposure to and cause of violence: that which occurs within the family, either between the parents
themselves or between parents and children. The survey examined one
of the aspects of this private violence: the interviewees' experience with
corporal punishment. The literature reveals that the use of corporal punishment propagates a type of social conditioning defined as "cycles of
abuse."[17] Children theoretically learn a slate of aggressive actions as a result of suffering physical punishment. Thus, parents who were punished
physically as children would tend to punish their children physically.

Fry also reached this conclusion in a study comparing the child discipline practices used in two Zapotec communities in Mexico that are
characterized as having presented distinct patterns of aggression. The
differences between the two tribes occurred in disciplinary practices and
the manner in which adults related to one another. The children learned
ways to behave not only through what their parents did with them, but
also through the interadult relationships that they observed. Thus the
children imitated their parents' behavior. That which was deemed acceptable behavior for adults ended up being among the ways in which
children behaved. If verbal and physical abuse were the standards
of acceptable behavior in the family, the child would adopt the same
standards.[18]

The experience of punishment is not a neutral factor. The research
demonstrates that there is a relationship between being a victim of corporal punishment during childhood and future aggression. The consequences are intense and long lasting and affect more than one
generation. The literature indicates that this type of punishment most
often occurs in certain contexts, particularly in families where there are
episodes of violence between the parents, in single-parent families, and
when the mother works outside the home. In families where there is
violence between parents, there is also a greater relationship problem
between parents and children, the brothers and sisters talk to one another less and play with one another less, and there is little familial
recreation. It is no surprise, then, that Assis observed that the greatest
domestic violence is present in those families where the relationship
between the members is the worst.[19]

Violent homes are homes where child protection and safety needs are not met.[20] This affects children's emotional development, their participation in society and the relationships they establish at school. These factors aggravate the youths' instability and increase their anxiety and stress, diminish their social competence, and affect how they resolve conflicts.[21] In these homes, mothers tend to have less psychological capacity for controlling rage or depression. These emotions will encourage the children's aggression or submission and will have repercussions in their conduct at school.[22] This will harm the way that they adapt at school[23] particularly their integration and interaction with schoolmates, thus affecting their participation, such as their ability to concentrate.[24] This is in part because children of violent families are tense and stressed. For some authors, familial violence has more impact on children and teenagers than neighborhood violence, since it compromises not only their emotional and cognitive development, but also their participation in school and their futures; it will also define the standards for familial relationships that they will have.[25]

One cannot overlook the consequences of the use of violence as a form of punishment within the family. The parents' relationship with their children is important for the question of violence, with respect not only to crimes but also to interpersonal relationships: this relationship may impede or encourage juvenile delinquency. Parents who have a good relationship with their children, take part in their lives, know their friends, supervise how and with whom their children spend their free time, and have strong ties to their children tend to have fewer problems with their children in terms of juvenile delinquency or gangs. It is not enough for parents to merely supervise their children's activities. This supervision must be part of a good relationship. According to Emler and Reicher (1995), it is this bond with parents, based on affection, care, and mutual respect, that gives young people a sense of good behavior. Young people who do not get involved in gangs or in violent behavior are less likely to upset their parents because they feel a commitment and a responsibility toward them. A good bond with parents is thought to be a strong deterrent to criminal acts. But this commitment is achieved through mutual respect, something that excludes the presence of family violence.[26]

Domestic violence is not, in general, named as a problem by the young people who are its victims. On the contrary, international literature shows that this violence is normalized as part of the familial language. The first consequence of familial violence is that it affects these young people's vision of the world, their moral development and social map, especially when this violence is accompanied by separation, poverty, and discrimination.[27] Domestic violence affects the moral reasoning of children who fall victim to it; those who are victims and who are violent have a slanted perception: their judgment of what is right and what is violent is influenced by the experience itself. Provocative situations are seen as immoral and justify being "paid back" with violence; this will affect interpersonal relationships.

Thus, the experience of being victims of violence makes young people more susceptible to perceiving different situations as provocations to which they must respond in a violent manner.[28] Hammond and Yung, in reviewing the literature on the roots of violence, associate it with self-affirmation among young blacks in the United States: the greater the teenagers' aggressiveness, the greater their rejection by other groups.[29] Violent young people respond to this rejection with even more anti-social behavior in an attempt to recuperate the self-esteem that was wounded by rejection. Teen victims and victimizers frequently tend to have a low self-esteem and a greater need to preserve their self-image: many fights and homicides are the result of disputes that stem from futile attempts to maintain others' respect.

In their study on homicide, Wilson and Daly state that 46 percent of these disputes were caused by retaliations, discussions, or fights; 16 percent by exacerbated rivalry; and 12 percent by jealousy. Thus, preserving one's self-image in front of one's reference group is a powerful stimulus for fatal violence. These young people's perception is also slanted with regard to how they evaluate specific crimes: as individuals who defend their families' or friends' honor, aggressors are seen as deserving respect, not as dealers and murderers.[30]

This is facilitated by how these more aggressive individuals perceive their victims and other aggressors: the victims are not seen as suffering and the aggressors are seen as strangers (unknowns), and both the police and the violent youths underestimate the damage that violence causes in its victims and ignore the fact that most assaults occur between people who know each other. They also are more likely to believe that owning a weapon provides more safety. A greater exposure

Table 13.5
What Were You Hit with When You Were a Child (By Age Group)

What were you usually hit with when you were a child?

São Paulo	Ages				
Object	50+	35–49	25–34	16–24	Total
1. Hand	44%	52%	42%	37%	47%
2. Slipper	43	49	49	38	34
3. Switch or belt	50	37	52	58	52
4. Stick or other hard object	11	11	14	10	9

Source: Núcleo de Estudos da Violência (Violence Studies Nucleus)/Ministerio da justicia (Ministry of Justice), 1999

to violence within the family will aggravate the situation just described, since it increases the youths' anxiety and impulsivity. When parents have a lower education level, these erroneous beliefs about violence and safety have more impact.

The survey showed that physical punishment seems to have been a common experience among those interviewed: on the average, 76 percent had been hit as a child, 15 percent of whom endured punishment almost every day. One-third of those interviewed received regular physical punishment (almost every day, once a week, or once a month). In order to understand the nature of these punishments, one must know how they were applied: in general, a slap has less potential to harm than hard objects, which are capable of causing more injury to the child. The use of potentially harmful objects seems to increase with the age of the interviewee, suggesting that this is perhaps a practice that is falling out of use, but that when it happened it may have been a matter of not only "spanking" but of "whipping," which borders on physical abuse (see table 13.5)

The fact that certain physical punishments resemble types of abuse and extreme violence in some situations suggests that some of the interviewees may have suffered types of violent domestic discipline and incorporated the use of physical violence as an acceptable response to resolving conflicts or disciplining others. As noted, the use of physical punishment influences the future behavior of those who fall victim to it. We examined how the interviewees react to their children's use of

Table 13.6
Retaliate or Avoid Aggression by Age

Your child is provoked in school by his peers and comes home with a bloody nose. What do you expect him or her to do?

São Paulo	Ages				
Actions	50+	35–49	25–34	16–24	Total
1. Look for an authority figure	40%	34%	38%	44%	43%
2. Avoid new fights	39	33	43	40	41
3. Avoid fights, but respond to aggression if provoked	15	23	16	9	12
4. Go back to school to fight with the student who hit him/her	4	8	2	3	2
5. None of the above	2	1	2	4	3
6. Don't know/ No opinion	1	1	0	1	0

Source: Núcleo de Estudos da Violência (Violence Studies Nucleus)/Ministerio da justicia (Ministry of Justice), 1999

violence as well as which punishment they would use on their children if their children presented changes in behavior.

The use of corporal punishment in order to obtain children's "good behavior" is amply rejected: 81 percent disagree with the use of corporal punishment, even for disobedient children. This rejection is much higher than that expressed by interviewees in studies conducted in the United States. Cohen and Nisbett compare the reaction of inhabitants in two regions of the United States: the South and the non-South. They show that 36 percent of those interviewed in the South fully agree with the phrase "disobedient children must be spanked often." This percentage is significantly higher than in other states (25 percent). This led the authors to examine the hypothesis that in the southern United States, there is a culture that favors the use of physical violence as a form of social control.[31]

If violence is rejected as a form of disciplining children, what would happen in a specific context, such as when students behave badly in school? Neither parents nor especially teachers (98 percent think it wrong) are allowed to hit students who destroy school equipment (95 percent think it wrong). Even if a student hits a teacher, 78 percent think it wrong for the teacher to retaliate.

Expectations of Children

What do parents expect from children when they are victims in peer conflicts? Do they expect the children to retaliate against or retreat from physical aggression? Those interviewed are divided between two positions: "seek out an authority figure" (40 percent) and retreat (39 percent). The majority of those interviewed reject retaliating to an act of aggression (19 percent support this alternative). The youngest people interviewed favor retaliation, with one-third in support of children retaliating. We have yet to discover whether the young people who are in favor of retaliation are also those who have received the most physical punishment, and if there is a relationship between these variables and a higher exposure to violence (see table 13.6).

Research conducted in the United States shows that in the South, a region that differs from the rest of the country in its high rates of interpersonal violence and greater use of the death penalty (which has led U.S. researchers to try to identify the cultural variables that might explain these differences) and where a culture of legitimate defense predominates, 38 percent of the interviewees favor retaliation and 68 percent favor avoiding new fights. In the northern states, these numbers are even more significant: 24 percent favor retaliation and 76 percent favor avoiding new fights.[32]

One expects people to give different answers depending on the degree of contextualization of the question. For example, in the case of using physical punishment, one would not be surprised to find that there were changes in response patterns when the question asks someone to define how they would act in specific situations. When we asked parents how they would react to a series of behavioral problems with their children, we noted that the answer most frequently given was "talk to them a lot." The second alternative was to seek professional help for those types of deviant behavior that they feel are the most threatening: drug use, stealing, lying, and tagging (graffiti). Nevertheless, a surprising number responded "hit a lot" or even "call the police." One would not expect "hit a lot" to be as high an alternative as it was when we asked interviewees about the use of hitting "to correct a disobedient child."

Three situations seem to provoke physical punishment: tagging, petty theft, and drug use. These are also the situations that would most prompt parents to seek professional help or even the police. There are some differences in the interviewees' answers according to their age and where they live. The most frequent answer among the youngest group was "not allow watching television or being with friends," probably because they identify these interdictions as being more punitive than the older groups do.

Shoplifting and marijuana use seem to be interpreted more as physical adjustment problems than as indicators of problems with the authorities or the law. These problems seem to be perceived as escaping the parents' control and competency; hence the high percentage of those who responded that they would seek professional help. Tagging, on the other hand, seems to be interpreted as a behavioral problem that could not be corrected just by talking but may require hitting, for example. Prohibiting or restricting television use and seeing friends are less frequent forms of discipline and are adopted as punishment for bad behavior at school.

The Brazilian survey interviewees admitted to using physical punishment less than those in the United States. Cohen and Nisbett's data show that 67 percent of the interviewees from the southern United States and 45 percent from the other states answer that "they would hit their child a lot" if he or she were caught shoplifting.[33] So it would appear that violence would be more acceptable as a form of punishment in the United States than in Brazil. This suggests that the United States is a more punitive society than Brazil. How can we reconcile these differences in the approval of violence as a form of punishment with the levels of violence indicated by violent crime rates? There are two areas to examine in this survey: the values and norms relating to violence, and the causes attributed to violence.

The Values and the Norms Relating to Violence/Aggression

Is the use of force considered acceptable by the interviewees? If so, under what conditions? Can disputes, interpersonal conflicts, and insults be resolved or mended by the use of physical aggression? The majority of those interviewed consider it wrong to use physical force to resolve disputes or to mend harm caused by offenses against themselves, their

Table 13.7
The Use of Physical Force by Age Group

In a situation where one person insults another, is it right or wrong, in your opinion, for the person suffering the insult to harm the other physically:

São Paulo	Ages				
Actions	50+	35–49	25–34	16–24	Total
1. Only when someone insults your mother	18%	34%	18%	7%	14%
2. Only when someone flirts with your boy/girlfriend, husband/wife	14	24	10	6	15
3. Only when someone insults your boy/girlfriend, husband/wife	13	22	10	6	16
4. Only when they say that s/he is a robber	10	19	6	7	7
5. Only when the person says that he isn't a man, or she isn't a woman	8	18	7	2	6
6. In any situation	6	8	6	4	6
7. Only if the person says that s/he is a liar	5	12	4	2	4

Source: Núcleo de Estudos da Violência (Violence Studies Nucleus)/Ministerio da justicia (Ministry of Justice), 1999

reputations, or their family members. The youngest group appears to be less united in rejecting the use of physical force to mend harms and offenses. Thus this group appears to be inclined to accept certain forms of physical aggression as legitimate. One in three young people thinks it is right to strike someone who has offended his mother, one in four thinks it is right to strike someone who flirts with a girlfriend, and one in five thinks it is right to strike someone who calls his honesty into question. Among the youngest group, thus, we find some who are more liable to respond with force to insults and verbal abuse or behavior that they deem to be offensive. This is not surprising since they are not only more exposed to violence, but most frequently to violence in the form of verbal abuse: 30 percent claimed that they had been verbally abused in the twelve months prior to the survey. Given that this is also the group that says that it has the least self-control (as we will discuss later), it is possible that there are many opportunities for conflicts to turn into violent confrontations (see table 13.7).

When we compare the two groups, we note that the U.S. interviewees accept the use of physical aggression more than the Brazilian interviewees in situations where insults and offenses occur. This greater acceptance occurs in the southern United States as well as in

Table 13.8
Right and Wrong Use of Physical Force (By Age Group)

People have different ideas about what is right and wrong. For you, is it right to:

São Paulo	Ages				
Options	50+	35–49	25–34	16–24	Total
	Percentage that say that it is right				
1. Use violence in self defense	41	53	35	36	42
2. Use violence to protect your home	41	51	39	36	42
3. Use violence to defend your honor	39	40	31	34	52
4. Use violence to make people obey you	5	4	9	5	8

Source: Núcleo de Estudos da Violência (Violence Studies Nucleus)/Ministerio da justicia (Ministry of Justice), 1999

other regions. In the United States, there is less predisposition to assault someone because he flirted with the girlfriend/wife (10 percent of Southerners considered it right and 3 percent in the other states); however, the use of violence is more widely accepted when it is used to defend one's virility (right for 26 percent of Southerners and 18 percent of non-Southerners).[34] If the Brazilian survey interviewees do not present a greater acceptance of physical aggression in order to repair blows to their self-esteem than those interviewed in the United States, how do they behave in threatening situations?

Violence would be more acceptable when used to guarantee a person's physical integrity or residence than when used to defend one's honor. Yet, using violence to make others obey is rejected as wrong, corroborating the rejection of the use of corporal punishment in order to obtain "good behavior." There are some differences between the age groups: using violence to defend oneself or to defend one's house is more acceptable among the youngest than among the oldest, while using violence to defend one's honor is more acceptable among the older interviewees. This fact, along with the others, points to the differences in values among generations with respect to violence (see table 13.8).

We also measured whether the interviewees agree or disagree that one has the right to use violence in very specific situations. In general, the interviewees strongly agree that one has the right to take someone else's life to defend one's family, even more than defending one's own life. However, the interviewees reject the right to use fatal violence to

Table 13.9
Beliefs about the Use of Violence By Age Group

For each sentence I'd like you to say whether you agree, disagree or have no opinion:

São Paulo		Ages			
Options	50+	35–49	25–34	16–24	Total
			Percentage that agree		
Self defense					
A person has the right to kill in self-defense	42	47	38	42	40
A person has the right to kill to defend his/her family	42	46	40	41	42
A person has the right to kill to defend his/her possessions	21	26	18	18	24
Emotional Relationships					
A man has the right to assault another man who is trying to seduce his wife	11	17	9	7	11
If a man is unfaithful to his wife, he deserves punishment	14	20	15	12	10
A woman has the right to assault another woman who is trying to seduce her husband	11	18	8	7	10
If a woman is unfaithful to her husband, she deserves punishment	13	19	12	12	11
Weapons					
Having a gun in the home makes it safer	10	23	6	6	8
Carrying a weapon makes one safer	6	14	4	3	2

Source: Núcleo de Estudos da Violência (Violence Studies Nucleus)/Ministerio da justicia (Ministry of Justice), 1999

defend one's possessions (which differs from defending one's house) or to repair harm caused by disputes or amorous betrayals. Using violence to resolve emotional disputes or to repair harm caused by betrayal is another use of violence rejected by the majority of interviewees. Furthermore, they almost unanimously reject the notion that "violence can prevent violence." The majority of interviewees also reject weapons possession as a form of security, either for themselves or for their homes.

In general, the youngest group is once again more accepting of the right to kill in legitimate defense and also of killing in defense of one's possessions. The youngest interviewees also differ from the other groups by not unanimously rejecting the use of violence in emotional disputes, the use of violence to prevent violence, and the efficacy of using/possessing weapons. Almost one-fifth of young people strongly agree that a woman who is unfaithful to her husband should be hit. The data suggest that as one grows older, one rejects the use of violence in emotional relationships. This would be in line with what we have seen until now: the rejection of violence is less among the youngest, as a rule. This points to the possibility that the maturity process also involves developing more self-control over aggressive impulses.

On the topic of "beliefs about the use of weapons," there is one thing that stands out: among those who believe in the efficiency of weapons, we find the two extremes: the youngest and the oldest. This belief in the efficiency of weapons for self-protection is much less than that observed in the United States, where 37 percent of the interviewees in the South and 18 percent of the interviewees in the other states say that they strongly agree that "having a weapon at home makes the house safer." Young interviewees also reach this approval percentage (23 percent highly agree and 11 percent agree in part; 28 percent disagree). Thus, as referred to earlier, there is a series of beliefs that groups of young people maintain which increase their vulnerability to violent situations. These include believing that violence is right, that it is a type of retribution that works to repair harm to one's self-esteem; removing the traces of insults and offenses makes one more inclined to respond violently when provoked (see table 13.9).

Comparing the U.S. data to that of the Brazilian survey shows that the standard for what would be acceptable fatal violence in Brazil is similar to that in the United States: in the United States as in Brazil there is a greater consensus with regard to the right to defend one's family, followed by self-defense and, lastly, by defense of one's possessions. What differs is the degree of agreement: U.S. interviewees disagree more strongly than Brazilian interviewees with respect to the legitimacy of the right to use fatal violence. In the southern United States, killing in defense of one's family receives an 80 percent approval rating; 67 percent approve of this act in the other states. Seventy percent of Southerners approve of killing in self-defense, while 57 percent of the inhabitants of other states approve. Thirty-six percent of Southerners and 18 percent of the inhabitants of other states approve of killing in defense of one's possessions. Moreover, 54 percent of Southerners and 52 per-

Table 13.10
Self-Control by Age Group

With which of these situations do you, personally, agree:

São Paulo	Ages				
	50+	**35–49**	**25–34**	**16–24**	**Total**
Options	Percentage that always agree				
Talk to a child without yelling and hitting if you need to reprimand a child	56	52	47	56	70
Control yourself so as not to have a fight	54	45	48	54	72
If you have a serious problem with your husband/wife talk without getting upset	38	31	31	36	58
If hurt by someone, you think it was done on purpose	4	8	4	3	4
If insulted by someone, immediately begin a fight	3	8	3	1	3

Source: Núcleo de Estudos da Violência (Violence Studies Nucleus)/Ministerio da justicia (Ministry of Justice), 1999

cent of those who responded from other states agree that "it is often necessary to use violence to prevent violence." These data are used by Cohen and Nisbett to explore hypotheses regarding the relationship between believing in violence as a form of self-defense and legitimizing the use of violence as a form of social control. Cohen and Nisbett correlated this strong belief in the use of self-defense violence to the expectations that inhabitants of two areas of the country have with respect to their children's behavior (and the respective disciplinary practices) and with what they consider to be legitimate police violence.[35]

With respect to self-control, the Brazilian data confirm what we have already suggested: the consensus regarding the interviewees' capacity to deal with tense situations without losing control of their emotions increases with age. While only 45 percent of young people claim that they "always" manage to refrain from fighting, 72 percent of older people say they do. The oldest interviewees are more certain about always maintaining control in conflict situations. In conflict situations, the interviewees are generally more sure of their capacity to control themselves in front of a child than in front of a friend. The expressed majority also does not show hypersensitivity to situations that could be interpreted as risky, such as getting hurt or insulted by someone. Again,

Table 13.11
Justified Assaults and Violence

I will name a few situations that you may have witnessed and which may provoke a reaction in people. For each one, I would like to know whether you (a) agree or (b) do not agree but understand.

São Paulo	Ages				
	50+	**35–49**	**25–34**	**16–24**	**Total**
Options			Percentage A, B		
If someone cuts in line and someone yells at him/her	24, 45	28, 47	22, 48	21,51	24,42
Suppose someone seriously injures someone who was involved with his or her partner	13, 38	21, 35	7, 38	11, 44	12, 33
Suppose someone murdered the person who raped his/her daughter out of vengeance	35, 39	40, 38	32, 38	34, 44	34, 35
If someone causes fear in your neighborhood and someone kills him	29, 31	40,33	28, 28	24, 37	25, 27
If a group of people starts to kill "undesirable" people	13, 19	20, 21	11, 20	12, 18	9,19

Source: Núcleo de Estudos da Violência (Violence Studies Nucleus)/Ministerio da justicia (Ministry of Justice), 1999

we find the greatest sensitivity for responding negatively to the situations listed among the youngest interviewees (see table 13.10).

What type of solution/retribution or repair for harm done is approved for tense social situations that involve the potential for interpersonal conflict or even for provoking crimes? Various conflict situations and victimization scenarios were presented to the interviewees, who were asked to examine and evaluate the responses of the victims (or their relatives). The majority of interviewees would not approve of a more aggressive reaction (vengeance) as a response to a crime, but a considerable percent would understand an aggressive response. Consistent with what they consider to be one of the crimes most deserving of punishment, the "rape of a daughter," the aggressor could be punished with violent acts, even with death. More than one-third (35 percent) of the interviewees approve of death as a form of vengeance for someone accused of rape, while 39 percent of them "do not approve, but understand," this gesture. The "death of people who frighten their neighbors" is the second most highly approved situation (29 percent approve and 31 percent do not approve but understand), followed by "yelling at someone who cuts in line" (24 percent approve and 45 percent do not approve but understand). Also consistent with the pattern described earlier, the youngest are not only those who most approve of these actions but are also those who seem most predisposed to the elimination of "undesirable" people and the use of physical violence to repair harm to one's self-esteem. These answers confirm that among the youngest there is a group whose values and beliefs admit the use of violence as a way of repairing harm and resolving conflicts and disputes. But these answers also indicate that the group as a whole does not normalize this use of violence, and that some young people and those in other age groups emphatically reject it (see table 13.11).[36]

The answers of outright or doubtful (do not approve, but understand) approval with regard to retaliation suggest a substratum of authoritarian standards that one cannot ignore. Many forms of violence are extremely arbitrary and definitive. They do not allow for the possibility of reverting to retaliation, and their acceptance reveals not only the need for justice, but the need for revenge; this revenge comes in the form of eliminating those perceived as the source of aggression. This answer pattern would suggest that there is an acceptance of standards of justice in which each harm requires an equally severe penalty. This was tested by asking the interviewees to discuss the saying "an eye for an eye, a tooth for a tooth." The majority (50 percent) disagree with the phrase; 16 percent agree, and one-third are not familiar with the phrase, or simply do not know what it is about. The phrase is less known among the young—42 percent do not know what it is about. The 16 percent who agree with the phrase come from the two extreme age groups: the youngest and the oldest. In these two groups, one in five interviewees agrees with the phrase.

There may be various explanations for the apparent contradiction between the answers to this question and those to questions about retaliatory and aggressive behavior, to crimes and to the situations that they consider to be threatening. The eye-for-an-eye question asks the interviewees to discuss the sentence abstractly, without contextualizing it. In these conditions, it is plausible that the interviewees would have more emotional control over their answers, particularly if they are at all concerned with what they think they are expected to answer. They discuss the phrase rationally, without having to identify with either side. The question relating to approval/disapproval of specific behavior asks the interviewees to identify with one of the sides, arising from the suggestion that the interviewees may at some time have witnessed or reacted to specific situations. Not only are situations of aggression contextualized, but we ask the interviewees to put themselves in someone else's place. The answers suggest that this is what they did, and this resulted in answers that were controlled less by reason and more by emotion. The apparent contradiction among the different patterns of answer would stem from the differences in formulating the questions and of the type of task asked of the interviewees.

Conclusions

Are there indicators of a violent culture in Brazilian society? The survey data do not support this. The research data reveal that although people are exposed directly or indirectly of violence, a culture of acceptance or tolerance of violence is not developing. Nor is exposure to violence leading to alienation in the neighborhood or to estrangement between people. Trust between people is not lessening nor is intolerance for those who are different increasing. Furthermore, despite the fact that young people are more affected by it, violence does not seem to be affecting their values, expectations, and aspirations with respect to the future.

Contact with violence does not seem to be an element that leads to more violence because of a loss of sensitivity to it, or as a result of its becoming commonplace. The interviewees do not accept violence as a way of preventing violence, for paying back (punishing), for coercing, or for disciplining. For the interviewees, self-protection, defending the physical integrity of family members or of oneself, is the only acceptable form of violence. This acceptance is not as strong as that detected either in the southern United States or in the other states, which, in general are considered to favor the use of violence less.

In fact, all of the comparisons of the answer patterns about violence from the research conducted in the United States and in Brazil show that the Brazilians interviewed were more opposed to the use of violence when it comes to disciplining children; in the expectation that their children not retaliate when they are assaulted; and in their standards for the use of violence by adults in authority positions—for example, what a professor who is assaulted or what a policeman who is offended can do. Whereas the research from the United States reveals that participants accept violence as retaliation for aggression, the Brazilian interviewees reject the use of physical violence in those situations. This greater rejection of violence applies even to personal vengeance, such as in the hypothetical case involving a daughter who is the victim of a serious crime (rape). In general, exposure to violence in the home in the form of corporal punishment does not seem to affect the interviewees; it does not automatically become a perverse cycle. Interviewees who were victims of corporal punishment as children do not seem more disposed to using this type of violence with their children. Even among the few people who accept violence, there are signs that they also resort to it as an extreme answer when faced with situations of helplessness or lack of protection brought on by the failure of the criminal justice system, by impunity. Yet among the younger interviewees, who seem to reject certain violent behaviors less, there are no signs of a violent culture; they do not idealize or value young people who adopt violent behavior or use violence as a way of obtaining prestige and respect.

The data suggest, therefore, that if violence is growing in Brazilian society, the causes for this growth must be sought in other factors. This growth cannot be attributed to the existence of a specific type of violent culture or subculture.

TRANSLATED BY CLÉLIA F. DONOVAN

Notes

1. Facts from DATASUS (Departamento de Informática do Sistema Único de Saude), Minister of Health, Brazilian government.
2. The survey on which this study is based covered ten Brazilian capitals: Porto Alegre, São Paulo, Rio de Janeiro, Belo Horizonte, Salvador, Recife, Belém, Manaus, Porto Velho and Goiânia. Sixteen hundred people aged sixteen and over and of varying levels of education and economic conditions were interviewed. The interviewees were given closed questions (with a scale of attitudes) and open-ended questions. The data was collected between the end of March and the beginning of April 1999. The data allows for various cross-matching: by age, sex, education level, religion, type of family income, how long they have

lived in the city and (if migrants) their state of origin, and race. For the purpose of this study, the results are being presented in a way that highlights the breakdown by age, since the differences among the various age brackets seem to be more relevant, and because we are still in the process of conducting more sophisticated statistical analyses.

3. This review covered cultural factors that tend to be associated with violence, such as theories on the cultural impact of honor (Nisbett and Cohen, *Culture of Honor*), violence, exposure to violence (Hinton-Nelson et al., "Early Adolescents Exposed to Violence"), the causes attributed to violence, the "theories" of common sense (Everett and Price, "Students' Perceptions of Violence"), the consequences of exposure to violence (Singer et al., "Adolescents' Exposure to Violence"); the types of violence that are perceived to be justifiable, the use of corporal punishment, and lastly, the relationship between the evaluation and credibility of the institutions (the judges and the police) in charge of applying the laws against violence (Tyler and Degoey, "Collective Restraint in Social Dilemmas").

4. Sampson, "Neighborhood and Crime."

5. Singer et al., "Adolescents' Exposure to Violence."

6. Richters and Martinez, "Violent Communities."

7. Warner and Weist, "Urban Youth as Witness to Violence."

8. Fagan, *Adolescent Violence*.

9. For Baltimore, see Gladstein and Slater, "Inner City Teenagers' Exposure"; for Cleveland and Denver, see Singer et al., "Adolescents' Exposure to Violence."

10. Howard, "Searching for Resilience."

11. Rountree and Land, "Perceived Risk."

12. Meek and Ware, in "Maintaining Empathy," show that social workers who work in these areas have much difficulty in terms of empathy for the residents, as if the threat of neighborhood violence makes them less sensitive to the residents' problems. Assis, in "Crianças e adolescentes violentados," observed the same in relation to youth violators in Rio de Janeiro: "They reproduce the victim-perpetrator dyad," they are victims, and they also victimize.

13. Kpsowa et al., "Reassessing the Structural Co-Variates."

14. Liska and Bellair, "Violent Crime Rates and Racial Composition"; Taylor, "The Impact of Crime on Communities."

15. Putnam, "What Makes Democracy Work?"

16. Mithe, "Fear and Withdrawal"; Crane, "Epidemic Theory of Ghettos." Social capital is based on contact between members of a community in cooperative activities; the more such contact, the higher the solidarity among the people and the greater the public spiritedness. This greater trust among members of the community also has effects on the power the citizens feel with respect to politicians, particularly in the belief that they are able to control the politicians' actions.

17. Muller, Hunter, and Stollak, "Intergenerational Transmission of Corporal Punishment."

18. Fry, "Respect for the Rights of Others."

19. Assis, "*Quando crescer é um desafio social*."

20. Afolayan, "Consequences of Domestic Violence."

21. Mathias, Mertin, and Murray, "Psychological Functioning of Children."

22. Wall and Holden, "Aggressive, Assertive, and Submissive Behaviors." It was thought that children who suffer the most physical punishment were the most "difficult" children; for example, that aggressive or hyperactive children would

lead their parents to lose self-control. Muller's research showed that, on the contrary, a higher frequency of punishment causes children to be more active or aggressive (Muller, Hunter, and Stollak, "Intergenerational Transmission of Corporal Punishment").

23. Jaffe et al., "Similarities in Behavioral and Social Maladjustment."
24. Novy and Donohue, "Relationship Between Adolescent Life Stress Events."
25. Hemenway, Solnick, and Carter, "Child-Rearing Violence"; Henning et al., "Long-Term Psychological and Social Impact."
26. Emler and Reicher, *Adolescence and Delinquency*. See also Du Rant et al., "Factors Associated with the Use of Violence"; Sampson and Laub, "Urban Poverty"; and Forgatch and Stoolmiller, "Emotions as Contexts."
27. Garbarino, Kosteny, and Dubrow, "What Children Can Tell Us."
28. Astor, "Children's Moral Reasoning."
29. Hammond and Yung, "Psychology's Role."
30. Wilson and Daly, *Homicide*.
31. Nisbett and Cohen, "Self-Protection," 32, and *Culture of Honor*.
33. Nisbett and Cohen, "Self-Protection."
34. Ibid.
35. Ibid.
36. Nisbett and Cohen, in *Culture of Honor*, show that in the United States this approval rate is 47 percent in the South and 26 percent in other regions.

The Imaginaries

The Social Construction of Fear

ROSSANA REGUILLO

Urban Narratives and Practices

Society pushed the pendulum of modernity in one direction, almost to the point of self-destruction. Then the pendulum was pushed back, and a momentary equilibrium was reestablished.

—AGNES HELLER, 1996

Now there is nothing but victims, good or bad.

—OLIVIER MONGIN, 1999

I don't care who makes the laws of a society as long as I make its myths.

—AUTHOR UNKNOWN

The Day the World Ended

ACCORDING TO THE PREDICTIONS OF Nostradamus, the eclipse signaling the arrival of the Apocalypse would take place on August 11, 1999. All over the planet, people of the most varied beliefs and political affiliations prepared themselves to await the final collapse. From French designer Paco Rabanne, who foretold that the space station MIR would fall onto the Eiffel Tower, to the indigenous shamans who intoned cosmic litanies, there was no lack of predictions about the beginning of the end. In the small town of Paraíba, Brazil, a deputy liberated the only three prisoners housed in the small jail to give them a last opportunity to enjoy life, as he declared before being incarcerated for failure to perform his duties. In Koblenz and Magdeburg, Germany, the end of the world provoked suicides. In the province of Santa Fe, Argentina, bunkers were built to stockpile food and provide shelter during the final cataclysm. In Mexico, thousands flocked to archeological sites to purify themselves and reconcile themselves with the forces of nature, while in Peru dozens ascended to Macchu Picchu to await the UFOs that would pick them up to save them from the catastrophe. Thousands of faithful Catholics had blessings said over candles, which the Virgin of Fatima had predicted would be the only source of light during three days of darkness following the eclipse.

There was no darkness, no UFOs arrived, the food and other provisions were left for another day. What continued, nonetheless, was the violence, the structural deterioration, the floods and natural disasters whose effects are aggravated by the structural poverty of those they afflict. The wars continued, as did drug trafficking, with its lucrative and violent trade.

The reaction stirred up by the last eclipse of the millennium allows us to imagine the millenarian atmosphere that impregnated those times and that—beyond religious beliefs and magical thought—speaks above all of the fear with which individuals faced the signs of uncertainty that, apocalyptic or not, constitute the social, political, economic, and cultural panorama of the end of the twentieth century.

From Fragility to Risk

From the tribal community to the megalopolis, throughout the long voyage of history, social groups have sought out different mechanisms for facing fragility and defeating fear. From the magical amulet to the constitution of the state, the history of humanity has been the history of the long search to counteract the effects of forces that threaten the permanence, stability, and certainty of life in various ways.

In modern times, the fragility of bodies—plagued by illness, the unpredictable forces of nature, and the violence of other bodies—is met by science and the juridical apparatus of the state. The fragility of the social pact, constantly threatened by dissidence or rebellion, individual or collective rupture, is met by institutions of socialization (in its preventative phase), institutions to regulate conflict (in its political phase), and institutions of control (in its punitive phase).

The evidence of a progress that has turned against humanity, expressed primarily in the deterioration of the environment and the new threats brought about by progress itself, is met with the refounding of science and technology. Today, for example, the discourse on sustainable development takes on the appearance of a protective amulet against fragility. If Mary Shelley had to kill her creature to reestablish balance and signal the futility and risk of challenging nature, today the option can be less drastic: Frankenstein's monster can be dominated.

The fragility of the social body—threatened by poverty, backwardness, ignorance—is met with technology, with social and political engineering. In the moral sphere, the same social body that perceives the threat of corruption, the loss of sense, the transformation of values, and an uncontainable and amorphous violence responds with the expansion of mechanisms of vigilance, and the state loses its centrality in the exercise of legitimate violence.

Modern science responds to the fragility of the spirit and the mind with specialized disciplines; churches, with doctrines, commands, advice, and penance; the market, with material products and cultural offerings tailored to the needs of consumers plagued by diffuse ailments.

New risks pertaining to the current state of civilization and culture are added to the old and persistent frailties. These risks, according to Ulrich Beck, "generally remain invisible . . . so that they are only established in the knowledge (scientific or anti-scientific) of them, and in knowledge they can be transformed, broadened or reduced, dramatized or minimized, so that they are open to social processes of definition.[1]

There, where psychiatry and psychoanalysis, charismatic advice and faith, flourish, where institutions abound with attempts at responses, where technology cannot negate the effects of the sun's rays upon the wings of Icarus, and where political engineering shows itself incapable of going beyond mere discourse and bringing about a more just and humane world—there, in that territory, location of disappearances and vertigo, fear gathers force. Fear and, paradoxically, hope as well.

A fear, as Jean Delumeau would say, "liberated from its embarrassment," and a hope without a program.[2]

In contrast to the image of the valiant and dashing hero of chivalric literature, "capable of facing a thousand armies alone, without the slightest fear," or as opposed to a Don Quixote who feels the need to imagine an army of heavily armed soldiers to justify his daring where there are only flocks of sheep, fear liberates itself from its embarrassment and seems to constitute the only emotion capable of approaching salvation. "One must be afraid," is the watchword. Fear of the armies disguised as sheep, but above all, fear of not experiencing the saving fear and remaining exposed, without amulets, before enemy forces.

This is paradoxical, since it can be argued that society advances in knowledge capable of transforming the fragility of a calculated risk, a fundamental difference from the premodern periods of history.[3] But, by the same token, we can prove the breach between the so-called expert knowledges and the common citizen, for whom it should be enough—according to the principle of the social distribution of knowledge implicit in this theory—to have confidence in the idea that risks are controlled by expert knowledge.[4] Beck adds an issue that is relevant to this idea. For him, today, the sciences' monopoly on rationality is broken in the definitions of risk.

The rupture in the monopoly on legitimate knowledge adds to the multiplicity of logics, processes, and social knowledges that oppose themselves to scientific rationality and are rooted instead in a social rationality of historical and cultural density. Thus, while the distance between forms of knowledge grows and the reliability of modern institutions weakens, the forms of response that privilege the symbolic efficacy of myths and rites also grow. Hope appears in relation to the modern mechanisms to address contingency and reduce fragility. It is a multidimensional hope—contingent, precarious, expressed through faith, belief, and magical thought, centering its reestablishing power in an object, in a ritual, in nonreflexive confidence.

The Social Construction of Fear

"There are people who die of fear," says Norbert Lechner, while Delumeau asks, "Can civilizations, like isolated people, die of fear?"[5] The question is not irrelevant. Individual responses to consciousness of a present danger perceived as a threat to survival constitute an emotion whose effects vary according to each person and range from biochemical reactions to motor responses.

Fear liberates a type of energy that forms a defense against the perceived threat. This seems to imply that fear in people is a "natural," spontaneous, prereflexive action. This, in turn, would imply that the human organism is endowed with alarms that allow the individual to react "spontaneously" to a threat. It can be agreed that this is true.

Nonetheless, what makes animal life different from human life is that in the latter the natural alarm must be given form and adjusted to the conditions of the physical as well as social area, through complex processes of socialization that are not, as we know, homogeneous, but are rooted instead in differences of sex, class, gender, group—to cite only a few of the mediations that produce social differences and that at the same time are themselves products of social differences.[6]

Through socialization the individual learns to identify and differentiate the sources of danger, to use and control his or her own reactions, and, especially, to incorporate a combination of knowledges, procedures, and alternative responses to different threats perceived. Thus, what for one person represents a threat goes unnoticed by another.

A rat may detonate alarm mechanisms similar to those of an inhabitant of Milan in 1630 (the year of the terrible Italian plague), a citizen of the same city in the year 2000, or a turn-of-the-century citizen of any Mexican city. The agent that provokes the reaction is the same in the three cases, a rat; what changes is the perception of the threat. For the Italian in the midst of the plague, the rat will necessarily imply a threat of mortal consequences; but today it would not represent more than an immediate danger and unpleasant experience. The energy liberated by the presence of the rat will vary according to the adjustment of the alarm in each of the individuals in the example. Even if all three opt for the rat's annihilation (as a defense mechanism), what is in play—according to his perceptions of risk—is not the same.

We can complicate the example. Let us suppose for a moment that the two contemporaries, the Mexican and the Italian, share similar socioeconomic positions, educational levels, and access to the information world, but one of them belongs to a millenarian cult that is convinced that the end of the world will be announced by the return of certain plagues. Though this may seem a bit extreme, it serves to demonstrate that the millenarian will add one more element to his reaction to the rat: belief. For him, the rat is not simply a threat to health and cleanliness (as opposed to life, as in the case of the Italian). The millenarian's reading of the rat will be mediated by a magical-religious belief that can unleash differential reactions.

What this suggests is that even if we can recognize a biological constant—fear as the response to risk—it does not end there. It is, however, important to discuss the sociocultural dimensions that intervene in the process, and in order to do so it is important to point out that fear is always an individually experienced, socially constructed, and culturally shared experience.

Real people experience fear. The response depends on the individual; nonetheless, it is society that constructs the notions of risk, threat, and danger, and generates standardized modes of response, updating both—notions and modes of response—according to historical period. This means that contemporary society, in addition to facing its own demons, carries on its back the weight of demons inherited from the past. The notions and the forms of response are modalized in the territories of culture: that is, they acquire their specificity through the mediation of culture.

There, where society generates standardized perceptions and programs, culture does the finer work of establishing differences of perception and, at the same time, conferring upon the social actor the certainty of an "us" from which to interpret reality. An example will help to develop these issues.

Between the generic perception of the fear (volcanic eruption), and the generic response (evacuation)—both of a social nature—the cultural universe of the actors involved in the emergency mediates. The increased activity of the Mexican volcano Popocatepetl in recent years has laid bare the conflict between at least two systems of cultural representation: that of the state's civil protection agents and that of the largely indigenous and rural communities that live at the foot of the volcano. These communities have anthropomorphized the volcano, calling it familiarly "Don Goyo." As has been well documented by the University of Puebla Center for the Prevention of Regional Disasters, the inhabitants of the region experience more fear about abandoning their communities, their animals, and their way of life than they feel about the volcano itself and a possible eruption.

The beautiful and illuminating stories that anthropologist Julio

Glockner has collected at the foot of the volcano recount that the *tiemperos*—a sort of priest who reads time and interprets the appropriate symbols for planting and the harvest—have a gift for conversing in dreams with "Gregorio" or "Don Goyo" (and with his wife, "Rosita, the *volcana*," as the volcano Iztacihuatl is called). These tales speak above all to the persistence of a cultural matrix in which the word of a *tiempero* (that Don Goyo does not plan to do any harm) is more important than the zeal, discourses, and measuring devices of the governmental agents and scientists, who, paradoxically, are perceived as a threat.[7] The response has been different in the urban zones surrounding the volcano. There, people live clinging to measurements and the advisories; the volcano is perceived in that area as a real threat, and it inspires fear.

This long example underscores the fact that belonging to a particular cultural matrix not only modalizes fear but also helps generate in the individuals who share that culture the certainty that their alarms and modes of response operate according to the collective of which they are a part, including the sense that they are shared by the broad reference group. The social actors learn to be afraid and, in the course of culturization, learn to endow that fear with specific contents and to respond according to what is culturally expected of them, sometimes in total harmony with the common social discourse, sometimes in negotiation, and sometimes in frank conflict, according to the position that the culture of reference occupies in the general framework of society.[8]

Cultural differences are constitutive elements of fear.

The Domains of Fear

In the social sciences, the literature regarding fear from a sociocultural perspective is interesting but not abundant. Lechner has proposed a fundamental theme—what he calls the "authoritarian appropriation of fears"—that emphasizes the way in which the military dictatorships of the Southern Cone exploited the natural fears of society to affirm their domination. Fear of chaos and social disorder—represented in the glorious period of the dictatorships primarily by "communists" and the people of the "Left"—in good measure created the impunity with which these military governments held the complicity of the powerful classes and reduced the influence of intellectuals. Lechner's contribution, beyond his marvelous analysis of modern democracies, is in making visible the political dimension of fear.

Taking Lechner's analysis and ideas as a point of departure, the strategy of the political campaign of California Governor Pete Wilson ceases to be an anecdote and incidental fact for me and becomes a potent example of the mechanisms of the authoritarian appropriation of fears. In other texts I have signaled the way in which Wilson appealed to U.S. citizens' fear of migrants of Hispanic and primarily Mexican origin to win his state's election.[9]

The fear of disorder, of the deconstruction of the familiar, of the Other, of cultural contamination, and of the loss of tradition—all of these are found in the figure of the migrant, the best of scapegoats, who can trigger a political campaign or satisfy social actors' need for explicit recognition of social actors' sources of danger.

This last proposition linked to the political dimension of fear allows us to advance another step: in recognizing an authoritarian appropriation of fear, we can also find—this is of central importance—certain sociocultural constants. One of the most important of these is the profound need to name fears, that is, to find a way to explain, according to the rationality of the situation, the fears experienced.

From a psychoanalytical perspective, Rollo May has suggested that some explanations of reactions to fear can be attributed to the attempt to give meaning to the world of the disempowered, to try to find causality where disorder threatens, to reduce the dissonance generated by something incomprehensible.[10] In other words, it can be said that the generalized perception of crisis, the expanded representation that society is disintegrating, should have some form of explanation.

For instance, in the film *Alien*, for the passengers of the spacecraft that carries the alien life form, unbeknownst to them, the explanation given by the artificial intelligence that commands the mission—represented by an anthropomorphic robot that exalts the marvels that the human race could derive from contact with a distinct and superior life form—is not enough. It is far from an ethical valorization of protecting life. The crew of the spacecraft confronts, in different ways, the fear of a presence that threatens to annihilate not only physical life, but also the known rules for the exercise of violence. An allegory of the violence of conquest, the battle between Ripley and the monster can be thought of as society's battle with the stranger, the outsider who occupies the very center of one's own culture and threatens to annihilate the familiar and give birth to a different life. Governor Wilson's migrants take the place of the outer-space alien, easily installed in the scene of the disintegration of U.S. society, in a similar manner. From the shadows, the stranger, indecipherable, different, can carry out the transformation of the known world.

In the course of my investigation through methodological mechanisms to analyze representations of people, it constantly appears that evil comes from outside. Different social groups "need to causally identify the fears experienced."[11] From an anthropological perspective, Roger Bartra has called this need to endow fears with a recognizable face the "Jezebel syndrome." Bartra uses this marginal Biblical figure to "explain the forms in which the dominant power sustains the ideological configuration of society's Enemy (capital E) par excellence."[12]

Society responds to the invisible fears, to the systemic crisis, to the lack of confidence in institutions, to the diffuse perception of threats with the construction of figures, narratives, and characters that are transformed into its own executioners. This historical mechanism is amplified today by the presence, ubiquity, and velocity of information technology.

Mechanisms and Tales

For Ulrich Beck, society is changing from the community of misery of class society to the community of fear belonging to the society of risk. His proposal contains a daring and provocative affirmation: we are, according to Beck, "in an era in which solidarity surges out of fear and is converted into political force."[13] This is a risky affirmation because it implies that fear is a platform of social movements today.

Without a doubt, Beck makes this proposal thinking primarily of the environmental defense movements that, confronted with expanded perceptions of risk, have transformed their fear into a program of action. It can be agreed that perceived threats have given form to many of the so-called new social movements, which differ from traditional movements in that they propose different ways of exercising power rather than trying to take direct power.[14]

But, considering again only the part of the statement referring to fear as a form of action, the argument can be developed to suggest that if fear can be the unstable base of the action of social movements—which would suppose a minimal organicity—fear today overflows the margins of systemic as well as antisystemic movements and installs itself in all forms of sociality.[15] This facet of fear as a mode of social relation amplifies its political "effects." [16]

Beck's proposal would assume that fear is controlled and subjugated by the social movement. Although he does not develop this idea, the implication is that the cognitive domain of the social movement has such levels of reflexivity that it is capable of transforming the energy liberated by the perceived threat (environmental, economic, political, or cultural) into a program of action that tends toward institutionalization (laws, rules, organization). But this leaves aside very broad areas of social life in which fear does not leave its constitutive prereflexive form. Not all fears become social movements, but all become action.

As the context for (unequal and unbalanced) interconnection among the different regions of the planet, globalization puts the borders and frontiers of the traditional organization of the political and geographic coordinates of the world into crisis. It systematically "connects" movements and, in a relevant way, narratives. The complex background of turn-of-the-century fears configures the world as the realization of the local, and the local as the expression of an interconnected world.

An influential part of the business sector of Guadalajara, the city in which I live, recently organized an ambitious forum with international guests entitled "The Chiaroscuro of Human Rights," as part of a campaign against the State Commission for Human Rights, which they accuse of "defending criminals" and "destabilizing" the exercise of justice in the state. This forum was attended by panelists that included an Argentinean advisor to the military junta, a Chilean of the same stripe, and a Spaniard, director of the AVT (Association of Victims of Terrorism). The last, Juan Antonio Corredor Pérez, used images of children mutilated by ETA bombs and women crying in his presentation, and another series of visual aids that also appealed to the emotions of the audience. Corredor Pérez affirmed—in total ignorance of the Mexican situation—that "Mexico has become a paradise for terrorists since 1992" and that "it is probable that the EZLN will become, if it has not already, the ETA of Mexico."[17]

Independent of its real effects—which it is not my intention to negate—terrorism has become a narrative of global exportation. For the forum's participants, the appeal to subjectivity is sufficient: in the realm of images, as with nonreflexive discourse and causal explanation, everything is sufficient to provoke a reaction of fear that establishes automatic connections among unrelated phenomena.

The organizers of this forum and the majority of the participants share the same sociocultural affiliations and have the same kinds of fears. The most pronounced is the fear of social disintegration brought about from within by the internal enemy. This enemy has been found in what they call "leftist people," an explanation for the ills of society that today must be cured by the "defenders of human rights." But, besides their assignment of this localized identity, those supposedly internal enemies are also connected to the networks of global information. The ETA is thus a diffuse but unidentifiable enemy, cause of the disgrace of the Spanish people; a little push is enough for social actors to search and find the example at hand, in this case the indigenous movement in southern Mexico led by Subcomandante Marcos. Any contrary analysis is considered irrelevant to the logic of these social actors.[18]

The narratives of fear reposition themselves against the intended logos of modernity as a comprehensive discourse, opposing it with another rationality. The difference between the fears of the Middle Ages and those of contemporary society rests on the force with which fear circulates today in the form of planetary narratives, amplified by the media; the principal characteristic of these accounts is the reduction of the complexity and the silencing of question that demands of news reporting authenticity and truthfulness.

I believe that the media, especially television, has been capable of recovering the mythical speech of the people, in the sense of playing on the desire for experience and the need for a transcendent world that would surpass that which they have experienced and, paradoxically, be experienced through the story of fears in the media. Thus, I believe, far from being weakened, fears are reinforced in the intimidating amplification of the media's narration.

This would establish the difference between the fear provoked by the young murderers who massacred their teachers and classmate in Denver in 1999 and those provoked by the bandoleers, capable of the cruelest actions, who lurked in the path of travelers in the early twentieth century. The latter is an example of localized fear, whose agent is perfectly capable of being isolated from the rest; for that reason, the fear itself is avoidable. Narrated as what happened, by other travelers or by the survivors, fear can close in on itself. The case of Denver is different. In its media reproduction, fear assumes the face of any young person in any city; the account acquires a productive character and projects itself, like mythic speech, dislocates itself, and for that reason cannot be isolated. Its aperture allows for the juxtaposition of versions and anecdotes that bring one closer to one's own territory—localize the account. The future is projected and projectable from the media present.

Jesús Martín Barbero has said that "today the media constitutes at once the most sophisticated mechanism for the molding and co-opting of popular sensibilities and tastes, and one of the vastest combinations of historical mediations in the narrative, gestural, scenographic matrices of the popular world, as an environment of hybridization of certain forms of enunciation, certain narrative knowledges, certain dramatic and novelesque genres of the cultural mixtures of our countries."[19]

The media as "spaces of hybridization" have fundamentally transformed the forms of representation of the world by giving space to mestizo cultures; but they have gone beyond this to generate a new type of mestizaje, as Martín Barbero notes, in the genres that have been the crux of the story.

If modernity exerted itself by classifying discourse and giving it differentiated rules, the media has shuffled the cards. This situation, which is not new, has been captured in a particular way by the analysts of the reality show, a hybrid genre that has come to reinvent, for example, the aesthetic of violence.[20]

From another focus, that of a philosophical and cultural sociology of film, Olivier Mongin affirms that a displacement has been produced in the representation of violence and that it cannot be considered independent of the progressive but rapid disappearance of genre films. His analysis signals that the genre has had the function of containing fear.

According to Mongin, in the genre film "violence ordered a type of tale that opposed individuals and groups, with moments of violence that accompanied a more or less tragic evolution towards death."[21] The inevitable counterpoint is contemporary film that, upon abolishing the boundaries of the genre, gives way to a violence against which nothing can be done. The perfect example is Oliver Stone's *Natural-Born Killers*, where violence does not appear tied to any type of recognizable opposition, inasmuch as it appears not *between* social spaces, but rather emanates from a centerless center of society. Violence ceases to be the pre-text of narrated history to become the text and context of the narration. The restricting boundaries disappear.

If, as I believe, film is one of the most potent analyzers of social transformations and one of contemporary society's most efficient mechanisms of reflexivity, it is possible to think that fear assumes the same faces as this cinematic violence. That is, it is no longer a question of emotion produced by threats whose perception is constructed through tales ordered from a certain logic—whatever it may be—but rather of an omnipresence that cannot be contained. Fear is constituted in a more intense and simultaneously more paralyzing experience, to the degree in which no flight is possible if the sources that provoke it have ceased to obey—without annulling it—a Newtonian geography: above/below, left/right, East/West, center/periphery.

For that reason it is ever more necessary for social groups to endow their fears with recognizable faces, assisted in this operation by the media, specialists in the denomination of the world. When fear has a face it can be faced, psychoanalysts say.

The Other Constructed

At this end and beginning of a century—which re-edits (if they ever left circulation) ethnic and religious struggles, assists in the emergence of the new enemies, and seems to require the tranquilizing equilibrium of the cold war scheme of good and bad—the fear of the Other acquires, for analysis, a fundamental relevance. It is an Other constructed in the image and semblance of fear. There is an Other who can be blamed for all of the fears provoked by biogenetics, an Other who can be blamed for environmental deterioration, some Others responsible for society's insecurity and growing violence, an Other to whom the guilt for the loss of values and the moral deterioration of societies can be attributed.

Fear of the Other is one of the principal mechanisms instituted to channel the fear that, seen this way, transforms itself into another passion: hatred.[22] We hate that which threatens us. Fear is capable then of mobilizing emotional forces that in Spinozist philosophy are called "subjects."[23] It is not a question of empirical subjects, but of anonymous forces that operate in the intellect as "pre-existent subjects," that unleash affective networks, and that, still from a Spinozian perspective, will lose their bipolar character (affecting/affected) and be transformed into a tertiary relationship, where the appearance of a third contributes to compensate for the effects of fear.

For example, one can think of a person, an average inhabitant of a Latin American city, permanently exposed to discourses on urban violence. This person regularly consumes news in which persons similar to him or herself can be recognized in the victims of crime, for example: one of us, for whom we feel sympathy and solidarity. The subject force that affects one of us is constructed as a preexistent subject that substitutes anonymous and, for that reason, indiscernible forces to become a category accessible to the experience of the person. Urban crime (anonymous) is transformed, for example, into crimes that come from poor neighborhoods. The subject force that inflicts damage on the individual who affected one of us or allowed the Other to get away with his or her property is a third term, neither one of us, nor one of them. This perspective has considerable heuristic power, in that it breaks with the simplicity of the analysis of contemporary society from a focus on victims and victimizers. The density and complexity of the social fabric can only be apprehended in the intersubjective dynamic from which fears are constructed.

With these suppositions and a double objective, five hundred people were polled between 1998 and 1999. It was a question, on the one hand, of complementing the information obtained through in-depth interviews and discussion groups and following public debate in the media and, on the other hand, of experimenting with a closed instrument that while fixing the position of the respondents made an in-depth examination of their fears possible. The results surpassed expectations.

In the work preceding the poll, a combination of figures recurred in conversations with the women and men who had generously collaborated in this investigation. The same figures that had previously appeared endowed with an equally suspicious quantity of goodness now assumed the suspicious form of authentic incarnations of evil. Analysis determined that sixteen figures were alluded to at least once during the narratives of the participants. It is not my intention to recount the entire content of the poll, but to describe the elements that allow me to conclude what I have attempted to argue here.

The method was very simple. For each of the figures (which are in themselves a result) the participants were asked to signal if that figure seemed good, bad, or indifferent. In the second part of the poll, they were asked to explain in a single sentence the social function attributed to those figures, under the assumption that this would allow them to give content to the position and find—by absence, complementarity, or contradiction—the model of order to which the participants appealed upon assigning a function to the pre-existent subjects. Thus, for example, for the homosexual figure 49 percent of the participants chose the option "indifferent," which was not consistent with the kind of public debate that is developing in Guadalajara with regard to homosexuality.[24] But, in the analysis of the attributed functions, it was found that the majority of the responses signaled a high percentage of rejection by attributing to the homosexual figure the following attributes: depraved, egotistical, nonconformist, and amoral. From the combination of figures used in the poll, homosexuals and the poor were the only categories that generated responses of annihilation: the solution is to make them disappear, confine them, kill them.

Within the traditional terminology, the poll was formed around seven variables: place of application, age, gender, education, intended vote, occupation, and medium of communication habitually used. Three of these—place of application, age, and gender—were given from the beginning; the rest were considered found data. The underlying assumption is that these variables operate as moorings from which the world is interpreted. Although each variable added relevant differential information, age and education as well as habitual exposure to a mode of

Graph 14.1

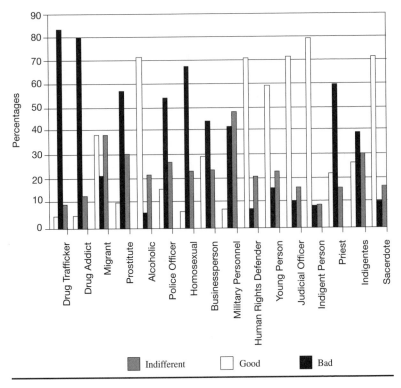

General Results

communication yielded the most interesting differences (see graph 14.1).

As graph 14.1 reflects, of the sixteen figures who appear in the poll, six were perceived negatively by more than 50 percent in the general responses: the drug trafficker (84.4 percent), the drug addict (81.6 percent), the alcoholic (68.2 percent), the judicial police officer (60.2 percent), the prostitute (58 percent), and the politician (54.8 percent).[25] In the positive responses, six figures exceeded 50 percent: the youth (81 percent), the indigenous person (72.2 percent), the business person (71.5), the human rights defender (71.6 percent), the priest (71.4 percent), and the soldier (59.8 percent).

None of these figures reached 50 percent in the "indifferent" category. Nonetheless, there are some figures that, for the way they have been scored by the participants, are susceptible to a quantitative read-ing organized according to indifference: the homosexual (49.2 percent), the migrant (39.4 percent), and the indigent person (31.6 percent). If, in the realm of the quantitative, they seem to be the ones that sparked less passion, the qualitative expressions signal that they probably call up the most emotional responses.

This is not the place to explore in detail the differences that the figures used in the poll yielded in the quantitative plan. Instead what is of interest is to recover some aspects of the qualitative dimension with regard to the analysis developed here.

The drug trafficker—constructed by the political and economic su-perpowers with the help of the media as a ubiquitous, all-powerful, ungraspable, and consequently invincible force—has penetrated the so-cial imaginary and installed itself as a force/subject emblematic of the sociopolitical deterioration of our societies. The figure of the drug traf-ficker is characterized in the poll through three clear axes: violence, illegality, and contamination.

Drug traffickers' principal function, associated with death, is to cor-rupt the social order. Their principal victims are the family and the youth. Their environment is not restricted to the local, making the drug trafficker a figure who operates from and in any place; in contrast to the perception of other figures, the drug trafficker's spoken portrait is variable—the same figure is described with boots and a mustache, of humble origins, and as an executive in a suit. Drug traffickers have the gift of appearing and disappearing on a whim. They are not for that reason peripheral or marginal enemies but rather are installed in the very center of power and corrode institutionality from that space.

Fear of the dissolution of the known structure, the deterioration and corruption of institutions, finds in the figure of the drug trafficker a tailor-made explanation. The sense of abandonment and defenseless-ness experienced by people faced with these evils finds its greatest ex-pression in the figure of the politician, who is, for 54 percent of the participants, a negative figure. Politicians' primary function is lying, fol-lowed by abuse and corruption. Instead of protecting and providing, they threaten and rob; they are perceived as the main persons responsible for what the participants call "social chaos."

Given the scant articulating power of formal politics, it is not surprising that people seek alternative mechanisms and options for responding to uncertainty. Among these mechanisms is the figure of the soldier, with a highly positive evaluation (59.8 percent); the participants attributed to soldiers two primary functions: protection and salvation. Given their attributes (integrity), soldiers seem to represent the only group capable of keeping watch over the politicians, police, drug traffickers, and criminals (and, to a much lesser extent, the guerrilleros). In the result of the poll, as in the in-depth interviews, there is a strong—and worrisome—consensus concerning the army as the alternative for "restoring order."

It seems to me that these three figures gather the general sense of the Other constructed in relation to society's hopes and fears. Although the movement that animates registration and analytical processes is unfortunately frozen in its discourse, the figures serve to account for the ways in which diffuse perceptions condense and fix social imaginaries with regard to the experience of vulnerability.[26]

Faced with the deterioration of institutions and, in a particularly relevant way, the loss of credibility of a good part of the institutional actors, the conflict diversifies.[27] Each social group, from its cultural affiliations and objective moorings, encounters the Other bearing its own fears. Fears are not outside the social: they are constructed and configured in contact between diverse groups.

By Way of Conclusion

Contemporary society's fears are not merely material for science fiction or secondary residue for research in the social sciences, in that they bear and configure their own program of action: to each fear (of certain spaces, actors, visions, and representations of the world), a few responses.

In the sociocultural area, these responses can be found in what I have called "urban survival guides," unwritten laws that prescribe and proscribe practices in the city in the growing visibility of the media—as spaces of domestication of chaos in its reductive, stereotypical, and stigmatizing purposes—and in the overwhelming success of self-help literature. They are also found in the tales that circulate and constitute urban myths with regard to AIDS, organ theft, kidnappings, the vulnerability of women, and so on; and ever more frequently, the appearances of Mary (the Virgin of the Metro in Mexico City, the Virgin of the Bridge in Guadalajara) and other turn-of-the-century miracles that express, more than belief, the need to count on supernatural help to face the chaos.

Fear is not only a way of talking about the world, it is also a way of acting.

TRANSLATED BY JENNIFER FRENCH

Notes

1. Beck, *La sociedad de riesgo*, 28.
2. Delumeau, *El miedo en el Occidente*, 16.
3. It would be necessary to subject to critical reflection the combination of assumptions in which, from the site of power, the calculus of risk is configured. In the field of economics, for example, the generation of wealth for the countries of Latin America has assumed the production of poverty as a calculated risk.
4. I use the expression "expert knowledges" in the sense that Anthony Giddens develops in *Consequencias de la modernidad*.
5. Lechner. *Los patios interiores de la democracia*; Delumeau, *El miedo en el Occidente*.
6. Paraphrasing Pierre Boudieu in regard to social structures, it can be said that mediations are simultaneously instituted (products of the social dynamic) and instituting (producers of the social dynamic). See Bourdieu, *La teoría y el análisis de la cultura* (Guadalajara: SEP/UdeG/Comesco, 1987).
7. Glockner, *Los volcanes sagrados*.
8. Fossaert, *La société*.
9. See Reguillo, "La memoria a debate," "El oráculo en la ciudad," and "Los lenguajes del miedo."
10. May, *La necesidad del mito*.
11. Reguillo, "La memoria a debate."
12. See Bartra, *Las redes imaginarias*. Jezebel is a figure from Apoc. 2:19–20 who misleads the slaves and teaches them to fornicate and eat meat sacrificed to the idols.
13. Beck, *La sociedad de riesgo*, 55. See also Bartra, *Las redes imaginarias*.
14. See Touraine, "Frente a la exclusión"; Melluci, *Nomads of the Present*; Castells, *La era de la información*; and Reguillo, "Notas críticas sobre los movimientos sociales.
15. This should be understood as society seen through the lens of communicative interactions. See Maffesoli, *El tiempo de las tribus*.
16. Wallerstein, *Impensar las ciencias sociales*.
17. Rossana Reguillo, "El oscuro objeto del temor," *Público*, September 16, 1999. [The Ejército Zapatista de Liberacíon Nacional, EZLN, known as the Zapatistas, is a pro-indigenous rights group active in Mexico since January 1, 1994. ETA, Euzkadi Ta Askatasuna (Basque Fatherland and Liberty), is a Basque separatist group considered by most to be a terrorist organization.—Translator]
18. Schutz, *El problema de la realidad social*.
19. Martín Barbero, "Los géneros mediáticos."

20. Mehl, "La vida pública privada"; Gómez Rodríguez, "Patrones en la construcción del reality show."
21. Mongin, *Violencia y cine contemporàneo*, 17.
22. The course of this argument is to a large extent inspired by Spinoza's philosophy of the passions. See Spinoza, *Ethics*.
23. Kaminsky, *Spinoza*.
24. The same poll will be carried out in Medellín beginning with the qualitative work, which will probably produce different figures as results.
25. The judicial police in Mexico are the investigative police, who have been found to be involved in numerous cases of corruption and torture. In Mexico, people generally distinguish between the judicials (*judas*) and the police (*tiras* or *cuicos*).
26. The actual poll is much more complex than can be described here.
27. For example, it has not ceased to amaze me that teachers—as articulating figures and figures of respect—have not been mentioned in conversations with the participants, and that the only explicitly female figure is that of the prostitute.

Imaginaries and Narratives of Prison Violence

YOLANDA SALAS

Prison life is worthless. In here man has no soul. This is
a living graveyard. We're here and we aren't, because
anyone can die here at any moment, from a stray bullet
meant for someone else.
　　Violence is when a human being doesn't organize
things. This is violence. To turn into an animal.
　　We pretend to be alive so they won't kill us.

—CARACAS PRISONER

THE VIOLENCE OF VENEZUELA'S PRISON crisis may be reaching its climax. Day after day the capital city's headlines report on the victims who routinely die as a result of confrontations between internal factions, the occurrence of riots and altercations in the different facilities, prisoners taking over the jails, and massive jailbreaks—even the discovery of an arms manufacturing workshop in one of the penitentiaries.

The threat or actual occurrence of blood strikes is happening with increasing frequency. The term "blood strike" implies self-mutilation, inflicting minor or serious injuries in an attempt to effect a favorable decision for an appeal in progress (as in the case of avoiding the transfer of prisoners from one prison to another or to encourage transfer to a prison closer to the prisoners' hometown or closer to their relatives, or the rapid implementation of the judicial benefits provided for in the new *Código Orgánico Procesal*).[1]

The use of a blood strike to attain one's rights is contradictory. Certainly, in our supposedly civilized world, the strike has achieved its place in the legal framework and emerges as a coercive breach in the realm of negotiations. A strike implies unemployment, the inactivity of the subject, and the cessation of physical work and activity. However, a blood strike calls for refection, in that the subject places his life in danger through an aggressive and violent act against his own body (an act that carries with it the shedding of blood), as a form of coercion directed toward a sphere that imposes order. What values underlie this act where life and death are (con)fused? A newspaper reports: "Twenty prisoners inflicted subcutaneous wounds upon themselves on various parts of their bodies, as a petition for the rights guaranteed them in the *Código Orgánico Procesal Penal*."[2] The media does its part as the televised images show the strikers' bloody bodies and the desperate lamentations of the prisoners' terrified mothers and wives posted in front of the bars, outside of the prisons. We are confronted with a penal population for whom life has a different meaning, a population that spills its own blood to convert it into a vindication that bursts forth as public spectacle before a society that consumes routine prison violence as it would a sports event.

An official spokesperson reported to the media that, toward the middle of October 1999, the number of victims of prison violence for the year was in the vicinity of 300 dead and 1,095 wounded, approximately one person deceased per day; similar results held for 1995 (239 violent deaths in the country's thirty-two prisons) and 1996 (213 deaths and 1,333 injuries).[3] Between 1993 and 1994, the prison tragedies or massacres almost surpassed the total number of deaths.

Here I approach prison violence through the incarcerated subjects' own narratives. Narration is to be understood in a broad sense: it includes oral testimonies from the prisoners, as well as the iconography of the altars and the religious images found in the prisons, for they form an integral part of the warrior imaginary that fortifies the spirit of the accused.

The most significant recurrent themes of these narrative expressions are offered as the great paradox of the Western civilizing and modernizing project. The texts presented here were documented in an investigation conducted in 1997 in one of the rundown prisons in the city of Caracas, Catia Prison, to explore representations and imaginaries of violence. The investigative work was primarily concentrated on two wings inhabited by approximately 170 inmates, some of whom were already serving their sentences, although the vast majority was in some phase of the judicial process.[4]

In this space, language, oral narrative, imaginaries, and representations of reality intensify violence as a way of life. Daily life becomes a fight for survival. Themes of death and vengeance predominate. The span between birth and death is shortened: between the two, life is combat and struggle. The protagonist subject is not recognized as a citizen, but as a warrior who, from prison, calls into question the notions of justice and civilization that have excluded him, relegating him to a space marked by its barbarism.[5]

Prison, Warriors, and Violence

The prisoner perceives himself as warrior within the confines of the prison grounds and behaves accordingly in his fight for survival within the penal community.[6] Accustomed to confronting death day after day on the street, the criminal has finely tuned his intimidating style. His body bears inscriptions, mostly battle scars and tattoos that indicate his affiliations and raise him in rank. These are bodies that reveal the reckless will of the warrior spirits. These are men possessed by the same imaginaries created in the collective, people incapable of feeling pain, given to fighting death itself to preserve their own lives. They say in their own words:

> We are already like warriors. Death doesn't surprise us, because we know that it's already close to us and we have already learned to live with it. Most of us aren't sure if we are going to leave this place, this sewer, alive. Here the most dangerous people are in charge—they are more violent people. Why? Because they are immunized against pain: they give them one hundred *peinillazos* and don't feel it.[7] They are shot once, twice, three times, and they seem like zombies. Why? Because of everything they have been through. That is violence. They are veterans, men who have lived through disasters in these places; they have spent their entire youths in these places. That is violence.

A warrior is a person who's immune to everything. They're people who have lived through unbelievable things, and now say, we'll deal with whatever comes along, like the saying goes. If that means fighting with death, then we fight with death. A warrior? A warrior is someone who eats whatever there is if there's nothing to eat. If there's nothing to wear, well, we just go barefoot, but tomorrow's another day.

The warrior is someone who protects his life, who has to kill to survive.

A social discourse emerges from their claims to justify and legitimize crime:

Progress sounds good, but it's not easy to go to work, to study, to get ahead . . . because most of us are poor, and we don't get the chance to make anything of ourselves. So then we have to fall back on crime, to steal to survive, even though it's not the best way. But it's the easiest, fastest way for somebody to help himself out a little bit.

We're not born breaking the law, we're pushed into it. Life makes us act this way. Criminals are always poor people like us, but the rich aren't criminals because they dress well and eat well. The same goes for the politicians. The politicians are even more criminal but they call them politicians. . . . They brought us up this way, taking money from us poor people.

Once a person has mugged and has had to kill to survive, he has to keep on fighting so he won't fall into prison's bottomless pit, where death is something else entirely. In jail you have to kill to save your own life.

The voices repeat themselves justifying their actions, while their youth is wasted in idleness and prison violence, with its rituals and practices that delineate territories and the distribution of power within the prison grounds. Meanwhile, corruption and complicity establish pacts between the empowered official sector and the transgressors themselves: firearms, drugs, steel-tipped shanks, and even grenades are introduced into the prison environment to increase its harshness and its barbarism.

We turned into robbers, murderers, violent guys. We killed, then this became a chain of events. They killed all my siblings, they killed all my friends. The pain never stopped. Death, escape. To the authorities we are murderers, but the prison wardens are bloodsucking leeches.

Criminals are born into the system where they grow up, at least those of us who live in the barrios. You get used to seeing other people breaking the law. All you need is a little push to do something wrong, you grow up seeing these things. I know people who started stealing shoes at twelve, and they're already bank robbers at twenty-five. And so you go from shoes to banks. There's another kind of evolution for the ones who just get worse, the scum of the neighborhood who do drugs in the street and make everybody nervous, even their own people. Everything is an evolution, you get there little by little, in stages, but in their case it's an involution.

As far as society is concerned we're dead. An ex-con has no life on the outside. What can we do? What does society make us to do? Steal. Society doesn't let you rehabilitate yourself and so you go on drifting the same way.

Religious Imaginary

In this scenario, the prison population reappropriates the traditional figure of the warrior within its imaginaries, a figure also found in popular religious imagery in which the warrior is symbolized by gods, religious figures, or saints.[8] Today this cult of possession by the savage warrior, with its pronounced African flavor, is led by María Lionza, spirit and queen (who enjoys the status of *alta luz* or high reverence), and embraces a number of "courts" or groups of spirits. These spirits are immediately recognized for their ethnic and bellicose origins (Black, African, Indian, Viking), for their magical and healing qualities (doctors, healers, and herbalists), for their proximity to the Catholic saints (the Celestial Court), and, more recently, for their role in behaviors that cross the threshold of transgression, as in for example, the *Malandra* Court (socially motivated outlaws or bandits) and the spirits *de baja luz*, among whose voices those of the guerilla soldiers of the 1960s are perceptible.[9]

In the semantic field of the savage warrior, the conduct of the spirits of African origin stands out, having exerted an Africanizing influence on the cult in question since the 1960s. Some of them rely on the fictionalized accounts of rebel lives generated in the Antilles. Popular mythology tells us that they were strong, virile warriors, trained for battle. Some of them, similar to the belligerent Viking spirits fighting for their lands, populated the American continent before Columbus. Memory, in this way, is infused with new subjectivities, which search for their raison d'être in fictionalized historical episodes. Human beings recognize and identify with spiritual images that incarnate struggle and survival, such as violent and lacerating gestures. It is the story retold from a field of meaning that exalts the heroic quality of the embattled.

To what situations is this way of representing memory responding, where the experiences and the histories of other peoples intersect in new configurations? These processes of restructuring identities are accompanied by a transformation of gesticulations, postures, and habits; by mutations in their own representations of themselves and their imaginaries. In this case, historical memory, which is not as stable and consolidated a structure as was once thought, reveals a dynamism that mobilizes in accordance with the change in perceptions, liberating the explosion of previously dormant cultural paradigms and psychological archetypes.

When the notion of the warrior is combined with other concepts and practices, such as crime, the rationale is made flexible, pretexts are sought within the ideals and causes that can in some way be associated with the criminals' own. In other words, the ethic of criminal violence emerges as the daily discourse of those who practice it and suffer from it.

The Social Dramatization of the Religious Imaginary: The Malandra Court

Imagery that elevates the delinquent to the heroic status of a socially motivated outlaw was found in the Catia Prison. The Malandra Court, inhabited by the spirits of "thieves from the past," is used to justify minor offenses and crimes in the shadow of a social discourse that praises a redistribution of wealth by taking justice into one's own hands.[10] The spirits of the Malandra Court who populate the collective memory of the criminals are those who in life stole from the rich with a certain gallantry in order to divide the spoils among the poor. Another interesting aspect of the spirits of the Malandra Court is the social control that they exert over the criminals, in particular in cases in which one of these spirits speaks through a medium to counsel and control the excesses of his fellow criminals. From the religious sphere, these spirits function as control mechanisms up to a certain point. Some mothers, aunts, grandmothers, girlfriends, or sisters of adolescents who are going down "the wrong path" of delinquency bring their relative or friend to a religious center, where certain spirits from the Malandra Court counsel the youth in order to save him or moderate his behavior. These spirits are also consulted by young and adult transgressors in the Catia Prison. They describe this phenomenon as follows:

> I see the spirits of the Malandra Court as normal people like us who died years ago. They were outlaws who would steal to help themselves and their families. Like some of us, they believed in God, in the saints, in spirits. As time went by, they were given the power to communicate with us, one way or another, to help us with information and advice and with messages like "Do this," "Hang out with those guys," and things like that. But they were also robbers, to put it that way, thieves, vicious people, but they still had their faith in God, the saints, and spirits. Faith is when you believe in what you can't see.

> The members of the Malandra Court were people who stole and gave to the people in their neighborhoods. They helped everybody. God Almighty speaks through our queen María Lionza, the mother. He makes her a channel for the malandro's spirit to come down and possess someone. Like the malandro Cheíto, from Petare. He stole, yeah, he would steal food and things like that and gave them out in the neighborhood. Then when he died, people began to worship him to the point where he began to come down and give people advice, even pointing them down the right path. I have also spoken with the malandro spirit Ishmael. Ishmael advises someone if he is doing a lot of drugs, if he isn't doing much of anything, if he talks back to his mother.

It's not that God allows anyone to steal, because God doesn't agree with anything like that. God's advice is not to get in trouble. . . . But what if it's to help your own family? And when there are people who steal because they need something, to help their mother because she is sick? They [the spirits of the Malandra Court] help in this sense. This is what the Malandra Court means. They're people just like everyone else, who give advice to others, they protect them from other malandros, from problems in the street and things like that.

Back in the old days, they helped themselves because there was a lot of misery, people were suffering, there was a lot of poverty. There weren't too many who went out to steal. Now it's not like that. Now everyone wants to steal to buy drugs, to have a good time, to have a few drinks. Now anyone can rob you, even though it might be a chain reaction, there are very few people who go as far as those people who helped so many others had in the past.

Back then the malandros weren't like the ones today. The earlier ones had *zumbao*, a really different way of walking, a really different way of talking, with much more respect. The spirits of the Malandra Court are *de baja luz* [of lesser reverence]. A way to acquire *luz* is through the faith people have in them. The spirits of *baja luz* are the ones who practically live by the people's thoughts and determination, who have kept them alive, because they were people who were as good as they were bad.

Kids today, we have a very wrong way of expressing ourselves. In the past people expressed themselves better, at least, in the past you could call them malandro. In the past, I could see holding up a jewelry store, a bank, or a shopping center. Now what you see is people stealing a pair of shoes, and shooting the guy twice for not wanting to give them up. If they steal that woman's wallet that had the family's grocery money in it, if they break into that woman's house and steal her television set, is this person a malandro? Excuse me, but you call that person a rat.

I call people who steal where there is money to steal, who steal when they have to, malandro. It's not that you have to steal, but at least, if you're going to steal, steal something that's worth it. I'm serving a sentence right now for armed robbery, assault, and battery. I went down April 9, robbing a tour bus on El Bosque Avenue, Chacao. Well, there's also a case of a guy doing time here for armed robbery, with a knife, for stealing two hundred *bolívares*. Do you believe that? You steal two hundred *bolívares* from a woman and get arrested for it?

Because we actually have a lot of kids who are envious. We aren't satisfied with what we have. We're living in a house that's falling down and we want to buy a pair of shoes that cost thirty, forty, fifty thousand *bolívares*. We do this out of envy and because today women like a man to dress in expensive shoes, expensive pants, an expensive shirt and a gun in your belt. Can you believe this? No, it's not possible. I didn't see these things before. I used to see these gun-slinging types and the women didn't pay any attention to them, they stayed away from them, kept their distance. They were shunned by practically everyone. Not now. Now if a woman sees a guy who isn't carrying a gun, he's a loser. He might have a job, he might be the working type, a simple guy, and it's hard for him to get a woman.

The young people today have practically gone crazy. They don't know what they're doing. I'm nineteen years old. Now I'm a prisoner. . . . I'm really paying for the mistake I made in life.

I don't think that people should steal, but you have to know how to steal. You know what I mean? Like my friend says, why is somebody going to ruin his life for a pair of shoes? I don't agree with that. At least, if I know that there is somebody, someplace, with a few million *bolívares*, and if I can get even a million, two million, I'll take them from him, and I'll take them and share them with my family, right?

Almost all of the politicians in this country have stolen something. And where are the politicians? They are walking the streets. Well, I see them as not doing much of anything.

In this study, based on the language and actions surrounding the typification of delinquency and crime, a mythification of the criminal as heroic, as religious, is found on the same level as the Robin Hood type of transgressor. Much as in the idealization of mugging and robbery, these facts tie in with the discrepancy between wealth and poverty, expressed through social injustice. It is important to point out that a mythic posture exists in this socially motivated thievery, for as this type of transgressor is exalted, the current social decomposition, which leads to a society in which one kills to steal a pair of shoes, is criticized. Being a warrior is a continuous battle, which does not belie the nuances of the struggle itself. The struggle transforms itself into disorder, fighting, brawling, rioting, and disturbances. Motives are converted into injustice, and survival is the objective of living this kind of corrupt existence.

The commonly accepted code justifies the offender's right to eliminate the victim if the life of the aggressor is in danger during the enactment of the crime. The power to make the decision regarding taking the life of the other, as in the case of homicide, appears to turn on whether there are obstacles in the way, if danger is lying in wait, and so it is with the right to steal. Equally permissible is the right to self-defense and murder during gang fights.

> Breaking the law is terrifyingly easy, terrifyingly easy because
> you go out on the street to look for money and you know as you
> leave you're ready to kill or be killed. You have to react if the
> police come. You can kill a police officer or you can kill the guy
> with the money or they can kill you. We look for the easiest life
> in the most difficult way.

Bolivar: The Political Dramatization
of the Religious Imagery

The overcrowding of offenders from marginalized areas adds to the violence hidden within disciplinary institutions; these depressed urban areas and their way of life are transferred to the vast majority of the prison campuses. Even though almost all of the negative aspects of the barrio are established in maximum security prisons, positive or dramatic values (like the anguish of the mother, the children, and other feminine figures who come on visiting days) momentarily reconfigure the environment. Heaped in dense human conglomerations, these prison populations share the sentence of accumulated blame in an indiscriminate manner; all transgressors share the same space, due to the absence of resources necessary to separate them in accordance with the severity of the crimes they committed.

Cells and hallways are used as housing and improvised communal dormitories. However, there is always a free nook to construct an altar to their most highly revered saints, gods, and spirits. Catholic religiosity harmoniously coexists with Cuban Santería and the María Lionza cult: the latter two share an ever-increasing intimacy of affinity. On these individualized and personalized altars, prints of the images of Jesús Nazareno carrying the cross, Cristo Crucificado (Christ on the Cross), Justo Juez (the Just Judge), Jesús Cautivo (the Captive Jesus) stand out, with their wounded and lacerated bodies, to visually remind them of the martyrdom lived by inmates in prison, referred to on a daily basis as "hell." Prints of Santa Barbara Guerrera and her African counterpart, Changó, along with the Virgen de las Mercedes, the Virgen de la Coromoto, and the Virgen de la Regla, share these spaces, invoking national identity and protection in combat.[11] The Holy Child of Antocha is also there, hiding Elegguá, the first of the warrior *orishas* of Cuban Santería, under his pyramidal mantel. Both the Catholic and the African represent the protection of the home and private space. Printed images of the Three Potencias, el Negro Primero, and other African figures are frequently found on these small altars, lit by candles with total disregard for the risk of fire, a factor further aggravated by the lack of space and the high quantity of flammable materials. The verbal references to the Viking spirits as well as Ochosi, *orisha* greater, son of Yemayá and patron of those who have problems with the criminal justice system, form part of this prison religious imagery.

As a result of the prison humanization program set in motion by the city of Caracas's Jacobo Borges Museum, workshops to encourage artistic creation were established for the benefit of the prison population, particularly in Catia Prison. Exercising an almost autonomous will, the population of this wing decided to open itself up to culture. Part of this pacifying transformation materialized symbolically in two altars, erected one in front of the other and placed at the far ends of one of the wing's hallways. At the extreme south end was the altar of the Virgen de las Mercedes, the patron saint of prisoners, with the face of Obatalá visually hidden but referenced in an inscription.[12]

The mural at the extreme north end, a sort of civic altar, is an excellent representation of the images and symbols that were modeling and inspiring the transformations carried out in the prison population. At the top of the painting is Bolívar, soldier, and the image of Che Guevara, each one showing his face, one at either extreme. Underneath each of them is inscribed: "Liberty is not begged for but won" and "It is better to be few and useful than an army and good for nothing." In between them are patriotic symbols alluding to freedom, such as two arms breaking the chains that bind them, in harmony with the Venezuelan national anthem, "Glory to the Valiant People Who Broke the Yoke." An emblem at the bottom reads: "Better perilous freedom than peaceful slavery."[13] Other symbols of freedom were added later, such as the dove and the North American Statue of Liberty. They come together in this mural as the emblematic figures of one of the "warrior wings," as the most violent sectors of this well-known Venezuelan prison are called.

The elevation of Che Guevara to a place of honor beside Simon Bolívar places the reading of the mural on a revolutionary battlefield. Under this mythologizing focus of battle, both personages, converted into paradigmatic heroes, transfer freedom-fighting attributes between themselves. The hero par excellence of the 1960s Latin American guerilla soldiers is crowned in the prisoners' collective memory as inspiration and exemplary guide. Both crime and minor offences are infused by their influence. The slogans implicit in the 1960s revolutionary battle and the wars for independence legitimize transgression by giving it an ideological basis of social struggle in order to break with the norm. The criminal act is then protected under the license offered by myth and a magical vision of history.

Prison Violence as Public Spectacle

The frequent massacres that stem from riots and decapitations form part of the news broadcasts' repertoire. It is fitting to ask oneself what is happening on the level of global society when criminal violence is transformed into public spectacle. Are these public representations of violence limited to denouncing the human rights violations? Or is there an underlying desire to differentiate and distance ourselves from this uncivilized and barbaric society that we have not been able to urbanize or civilize? It is fitting to ask oneself what feelings are evoked among the television audience that watches tumultuous crowds of grieving mothers and women positioned behind the front gates of the prison waiting to hear the names of the deceased. They wait for their turn to visit, still with a glimmer of hope bound up with the life of a prisoner, son or relative. For some, rightful punishment is represented there, for others, the familiar pain of transgression. Whether it be the public representation of punishment or anguish as a lesson, the effects of prison violence have exceeded the limits of privacy, of what was kept hidden; they are openly exposed as evidence of a society that becomes more uncivilized with every passing day.

The voices of the warrior spirits included in the religious imagery answer this need for differentiation: Vikings and Africans are also representations of the primitive and the barbaric. They are spirits who are "crude, dirty and who don't like to bathe." In them, untamed nature is part of man himself: the hide of the hunted animal is confused with the flesh of man. The animal is the essence of humanity. The garment ceases to be clothing and the symbol of a cultivated appearance. It is not even protection against the inclemencies of weather. The hide that recovers the barbaric spirit in its verbal and visual representation is the emblem of the dark and shadowy side that modernity has wanted to repress and hide. The voice that these representations emit is the recognition and legitimation of the barbarian: it is not repressed;, it is not hidden; it is, in fact, the opposite—the prisoner venerates it and looks to it for strength; he keeps it as a model of the warrior and the fighting man.

> The Viking court, the Vikings, is like saying something warlike, something strong. They're huge, hairy, they have the horns and the skins of the animals they hunt. They're assassins, warriors. They have no laws. They make the laws themselves. They're strong, they like things to be strict. They run knives over their tongues, they cut themselves.

Life and death are not opposites in this context. On the contrary, they are drawn closer together all the time. Life's plan is to fight to survive and to resist so as to forestall death, which they push aside with an outstretched hand that holds a gun. The life-death pair of opposites acquires a different representation in the day to day, and in the style expressed in the indigenous mythologies and ancient cultures. There, life grows old, and the almost dead womb of the old woman offers life. The life cycle is completed—birth, life, and death—in order to transform itself and be reborn. The concept of the heroic changes in uncivilized violence: life is worth nothing because the ideal of transcendence has been lost; on the contrary, it deprives one of the fight for survival in the present moment. The motivation and ultimate end for action is to not die at that moment. Valor is centered in the defense of the ephemeral. Bravery is intrepid, suicidal, self-destructive. The barbarous spirits are recognized, spoken to, and prayed to. They shape imaginaries, even as they train the body for the fight. They are appealed to for protection so that the combatants' own blood may not be spilled during confrontations with their enemies.

In the diagnostic process of the Venezuelan prison crisis, aggravated by prison overcrowding, the fact that the streets are overpopulated by the poor, by frustration, by discontent, is also ignored, owed in particular to the concept of easily acquired wealth (imparted by a corrupt elite) or the idea of easily attainable well-being (offered by a consumer ideology).

A nation's prison and criminal justice systems do not fail and collapse by themselves. Before this can happen, the concepts of right and wrong must be dissolved and their lines blurred. It is for this reason that so many inmates have, in their own way, attested to the fact that crime was the most expeditious occupation open to them to allow them to have at least the minimum required for survival. It is because of this that the zeal for taking justice into one's own hands and the right to kill fall within the inmates' codes, should their lives be in danger. In the same sense, society has denied them an adequate space to cultivate their abilities and their right to a life worth living.

> Society lives outside these walls. It's the person who criticizes the fact that somebody commits a crime, but doesn't ever criticize the people who take the bread out of the poor peoples' mouths, out of the mouths of the children who are already going through so many bad things. It's not my fault that children are going hungry. All of Venezuela and the rest of world knows who is to blame: the government, the people who bankrupted the country.

How they starve people to death.

How they kill children through malnutrition.

A criminal is someone who kills for a pair of shoes. A criminal is someone who kills the father of a family. But the worst criminal is the one who starves this country's children to death.

In Venezuela, as in many Latin American countries, notions of civilization and the neglect of the principles of the social contract are called into question from its prisons. In recent decades delinquency and crime have become the most evident forms of the system's destabilization, as the guerrilla soldiers were in the 1960s. This has been mythologized by the tricks that memory plays with history, and its heroes are the objects of exaltation or popular devotion.[14] Embroiled in this cult, the delinquent sees himself as a warrior in a scenario that exalts savage resistance, the primitive, and the guerrilla, even allowing himself to meld the liberating political action of Bolívar with his own liberation aspirations.

"Margin" and "periphery" are not merely abstract concepts elaborated by the social sciences, but active social spaces inhabited by a segment of the population that numerically exceeds the center. This margin, however, is not as homogeneous as it is generally thought to be. The criminals and criminality that reside therein do not represent the majority: they are the margins of the margin who have received the rules of conduct from the center and have interpreted them in their own way, translating them into terms of conflict.

The mythologized delinquent is converted into a symbol of social protest by protecting himself with the ethic of a righteous criminal, who, in theory, exclusively steals from the poor's enemy class. Within the juvenile population of Caracas's barrios, the criminal embodies the opportunity for rapid gain that allows for the consumption of material goods that grant status and prestige. The malandro's attributes elicit admiration among adolescent peers, particularly young girls. The motivation for the heroic is found in the acquisition and illegal consumption of the goods offered by the market.

TRANSLATED BY HEATHER HAMMETT

Notes

1. *Código Orgánico Procesal* is a body of laws pertaining to the judicial process.—Trans.
2. *El Nacional*, October 21, October 15, June 10, 1999.
3. *El Nacional*, August 29, 1999. Official figures have revealed that 144 violent deaths occurred in the prisons during 1995, and 208 in 1996.
4. The fieldwork was carried out in the now demolished Catia Prison, under the cultural program executed by the Jacobo Borges Museum. Over the course of eight months a workshop on oral history was conducted to compile a biography of the religious spirits and divinities linked with the practices of possession by African American religious cults. Approximately fifteen hours of audio tape were recorded and were complemented by video tape recordings filmed by cinematographer Mario Crespo. The partial transcriptions and the indices of the content extracted from the recordings were the subject of revision and reflection by the same prison population. Some of the recordings were made in the wings where the prisoners resided, which allowed for partial observation of their routine.
5. Despite the fact that sovereign states planned to centralize and monopolize violence by creating armies and armed bodies of police to defend the geopolitical borders and to impose civil order, another society has developed in their midst, the uncivilized, who are armed and organized not to follow the path of political revolution, but to impose and establish the domination of violence and an uncivilized society. The maximum power exercised by the gangs, the cartels, or the groups of mercenary assassins, for example, far from doing away with violence, ends up restoring it and configuring a new sense of the heroic and the warrior, even based upon self-destructive principles. For a more in-depth look at uncivilized society, see Keane, *Reflections on Violence*.
6. It is important to point out that the classification of "warrior" for the inmates on the wings who rely on a history of violent confrontations and deaths attributed to them was a form found in the Catia Prison, used as much for the members of the prison administration as for the inmates themselves. I have also heard this expression used by the inmates of other prisons interviewed by the media, thus its usage is fairly generalized. The opposite of the "warrior" is the "*paisa*," the prisoner who, in some form or another, reconciles himself to the disciplinary norms and has more communication with the prison officials. *Paisa* is a contraction of the word *paisano*, which has the possible meanings of "farmer" or "civilian."
7. *Peinillazos* refers to the act of whipping someone. In this case, it would be one hundred lashes.—Translator.
8. In other studies I have pointed out the presence of what I have called a popular ideology of the savage-warrior to encompass an existent semantic field in a Venezuelan cult, in which María Lionza is the central figure. See Salas, "Las desarticulaciones de una modernización en crisis." The theme of popular religious imaginaries and, especially the semantic field of the savagery and the Africanization of spirits has been discussed in Salas, "Nuevas subjetividades," 261–278. See also Salas, "Una biografía de los 'espíritus'."
9. "Malandro" is also used for the criminal who dedicates himself to assaults, robbery, mugging, and committing crimes. Due to the environment in which he is raised, a malandro is also associated with drug use.
10. Eric Hobsbawn is an obligatory reference for studies on socially motivated banditry for his pioneer book *Primitive Rebels*. He uses a comparative methodology

to establish the connection between the emergence of socially motivated out-laws and particular social conditions. For him, the outlaw is a prepolitical form of protest, linked to pastoral, agricultural, and rural societies. Based on tradi-tional forms of authority, these societies perceive themselves to be threatened by transformation. Paul Kooistra, in *Criminals as Heroes,* proposes a sociologi-cal analysis: if the social banditry is a remnant of the past and a phenomenon foreign to modernization, why does it continue to emerge in the present day? This author analyzes how a group of criminals are not condemned by the whole of society but are converted into heroes in their own time or immediately there-after. Kooistra asks himself what rule underlies this phenomenon and finds that people are brought to this type of life by having been victims of injustice or by having committed an act condemned by the state but not necessarily by the community. In order to understand how these criminals are molded into he-roes, Kooistra proposes to determine whom they revere as paradigmatic heroes, so as to be able to understand the social interpretations surrounding their un-governability and transgressions. This author finds a gap between the real bi-ography of the criminal and his heroic idealization. Upon offering itself as a space where injustice reigns supreme, the social system opens itself up to a field prone to the spontaneous creation and consumption of symbols of justice out-side of the law.

11. Changó, *orisha* greater, god of fire, lightning, thunder, and war, patron of war-riors and storms, appeared frequently in prison iconography, along with prints of other Africans also perceived to be warrior spirits. Obatalá, *orisha* greater, is a syncretized being that combines several deities, including the Virgen de las Mercedes. The Catholic legend explains that when Spain was under Arab rule, San Pedro Nolasco experienced a vision of the Virgin who insisted that he found a religious order to redeem the Christian captives in the Saracen prisons. In 1218, the Order of the Redemption of the Captives was founded, under the protection of the Virgen Santa María de las Mercedes. Obatalá, for her part, has various forms, some of them syncretized with Jesús Nazareno, who is shown as a primitive, bellicose, intrepid, and combative male like Changó.

12. This altar was collectively constructed, to be inaugurated September 24 in a cultural act attended by the inmates' relatives and the members of the prison administration.

13. It is important to emphasize that this emblem was found to be a countersign, written in graffiti on the walls of the cells of other prisoners in other wings, along with other writings such as *"jálame calle"* (Give me a hand back to the street), uniting the cry of physical freedom with that of protest.

14. In the public sector, the devotion to the warriors as social fighters is present not only in some of the religious centers dedicated to spiritualist devotion, but also in the barrios of Caracas such as the 23 de Enero, where the custom of raising flags to commemorate some of their dead is kept alive (*El Universal,* February 21, 1997).

We Are the Others

SUSANA ROTKER

*I dedicate this story to the 247 official deaths and to the
other thousands dead (unofficially but dead just the
same) of February 27, 1989.*

          —JOSÉ ROBERTO DUQUE, *Salsa y Control*

I WAS IN BUENOS AIRES ONE NIGHT in February of 1989 when I received
the news that forty people had died in Caracas during protests against
an increase in public transportation prices. I was with another Caracas
native watching the news on television and I remember his comment
with complete clarity: forty deaths is a civil war. A few hours later, the
total had doubled; it continued to escalate until it included thousands
of wounded and an undetermined—or, rather, never acknowledged—
number of deaths. These figures say nothing. It was only later that I
began to understand what the population experienced during those days,
thanks to *El día que bajaron de los cerros* (The day they came down from
the hills), published in 1989 by Ateneo de Caracas, an anthology of
chronicles written by a group of journalists during the February 27 up-
rising and the turbulent days that followed, which includes photographs
of the same period.

    Reading the chronicles by Fabricio Ojeda, Roberto Giusti, Eliza-
beth Araujo, and Régulo Párraga, one is fascinated and disconcerted
by the surging forth of a protest as popular as it was spontaneous. Without leaders or organizers, the people began to take to the streets—

Lecuna, Bolívar, and Francisco Fajardo Avenues; the mob also appeared on Rómulo Gallegos Avenue, in La Urbina, in Catia and El Silencio, in areas where the well-to-do live, like Las Palmas, burning trucks and tires, sacking bakeries and supermarkets, stealing food. On the night of February 27, 1989, the sounds of shots were heard throughout the city for the first time, and the hospitals and morgues could not keep up.

The latent fear that the upper classes of Caracas had always had became a reality or, rather, had begun to become a reality: the fear of the day that the people from the poverty-stricken hills that surround the capital would come down and take the city, fed up with their misery. The confusion that began February 27 lasted for several days; days that were unforgettable because of the intensity of the military repression, because of the images of smiling young people carrying immense pieces of stolen meat, or televisions, or stuffed animals, of women holding up supermarkets, sometimes with the help of a supportive policeman. On February 27, 1989, the tenuous thread that maintained the unity of the social fabric—the Rousseauian social contract of citizens conscious of their rights and, above all, their obligations to the community—began to unravel. While it is true that countries do not change from one day to the next, there is no doubt that this day marked a before and after for the entire society. José Ignacio Cabrujas explained:

On February 27, Venezuela lived an ethical collapse that left many people stupefied. It was . . . an explosion that translated into a sacking, but it is not a revolutionary sacking. There is no slogan. It is a dramatic sacking: the people robbed places in the middle of a delirious happiness. There is no tragedy at the beginning of the process. The image of a happy Caraqueñan carrying half a cow on his shoulder has stayed with me. But it wasn't a starving man looking for food—it was a Venezuelan joker whose face corresponded to a very particular ethic: if the President is a thief, so am I; if the State lies, so will I; if the power in Venezuela is a leadership of troublemakers, what law will stop me from walking into the butcher shop and taking half a cow? Is it wit? No, it is drama, a great human conflict and a great ceremony. That day of play ends in a monstrous, cruel ending, the laughter ends with blood. It is the most Venezuelan day that I have lived.[1]

It is already known that in Venezuela, the principal exporter of petroleum to the United States, only 20 percent of the population perceives their monthly income as sufficient with regard to purchasing the minimum quantity of food and the basic quantity of services; that is to say that even today, on the eve of the new millennium, eighty out of every one hundred Venezuelans do not enjoy minimal water and electrical services or have enough to eat.[2] So, where does violence begin? As the order that its editors chose for the book demonstrates, violence begins with social injustice, abuse, and political corruption—*El día que bajaron de los cerros* opens with a chronicle about Carlos Andrés Pérez's pharaonic presidential takeover. During that time, the strategy of social representation adopted by neoliberalism began to take hold: neutralization of the poor and their protest, the criminalization of poverty, in order to secure a market logic that no longer has any use for those who are not consumers.[3]

The chroniclers' gaze, although disconcerted, is that of an intermediary "we"; the writers do not count themselves among the rebels, and, even though they fear them deep down, their gaze accords them a certain political justification. The stories are born of a plural and fragmented gaze that may have inaugurated a way of narrating a decade. In these chronicles, individuals' names are unimportant; the chroniclers crisscross a city taken first by the people, then by the military, writing individual stories that occur almost simultaneously in various parts of the city. It is a voice that is plural, disorganized, frightened, and certainly not epic; the urban references are those of street and highway names—the outside is no longer a space of civil interaction but one of vulnerability and danger—rather than the usual references to the landscape of a modern city (advertisements, lights, construction materials—metals, concrete, glass, wire—and satellite antennae). This outside space is that of "the discontent [that] boiled over in the streets, came down from the hills, and penetrated commercial centers and supermarkets" (Ojeda, 33), that of men in uniform who pillaged, the shots that "really killed" (Párraga, 61), the fear, the laughter of the people dividing food and drink amongst themselves like war booty, the old women of honorable stature creeping into the fruit store (Giusti, 37), the lies of the official sector, the military's disproportionate force, the dead in the streets. Like flaneurs, the chroniclers wander around the occupied city, telling individual human stories without a totalizing spirit and, more than once, serving as civil servants (they are asked for transportation, information), since the police and the army are perceived as the enemy, given to arbitrary and excessive repression.

When I say that the writing of these chronicles inaugurates a decade, I refer not only to the narrators, but also to that which is represented: the alarming symptoms of a society in decay. The lesson that when the marginalized in consumer society lose control they go out to burn cars, stores, and televisions (scattered markers of consumerism in a hostile and unconquerable territory: capital) will remain in the urban imaginary. Not everything can be attributed to February 27, 1989—given that, lamentably, many other countries share these types of images and logic—but it is a milestone at which notice is taken of a situation in a volcanic state. The society was too accustomed to subalterns who live "their subordination with 'normality,' dominated by a naturalizing vision of social hierarchies, and a relationship to the State that is . . . expressed more frequently in terms of clientelism or paternalism than in terms of citizenship, rights and obligations."[4] However, the actions undertaken by the poor are no longer understood as expressing the desire for an end to the already intolerable state of affairs, but instead as simple riots or barbaric uprisings. It is the "proof" that the problem of the poor has to be resolved through the intensification of law and order.[5] The problem, of course, is that common citizens, regardless of their social class, have little or no faith in the representatives of law and order, who are perceived as active parts of generalized violence.

I am worried because of the implications that it has today, that solidarity amongst the people is completely casual and passing in these texts (there is no organization of neighborhood communities, small affiliations, nor are there visible leaders, only a population that asks itself what is happening, like the journalists, the reader, as a shared "we"). I am worried by talk of "getting even" or the repetition of the word "rematch," perhaps the one that was most often repeated in the last presidential election debates. *El día que bajaron de los cerros* corresponds to an apocalyptic perception without the hope of a future and the sensation that if civil society ever functioned, little remains apart from political weakness. And when there is no solidarity, no civil society, no faith in institutions or political parties, when there is no faith in a project for the future, what is left, aside from a group of people sharing a geographic space, distrusting one another and waiting for their chance for revenge or for self-defense?

I have spoken of the "we" used by the chroniclers of 1989: I am referring to that which is found in the middle, not on the side of a corrupt and squandering class ultimately responsible for social violence (of its origin), nor on the side of the masses that burn tires in the streets. Sympathy brings this textual "we" closer to the people, but the photographs tell another story: the people are the "others." In effect, the photographs create fear: they capture the loss of control, the dirtiness, pain, hatred, poverty.[6] They cry out, perhaps without wanting to, for law and order; only a few, taken by Tom Grillo, manage to capture the desperation of the poor, seen through his lens as victims of a violence stronger than they are rather than as victimizers of the city's peace. These texts do not consist of a paternalistic representation of the poor or of social injustice; unlike the case of the *costumbrista* chroniclers of the nineteenth century, these chronicles of violence do not organize a system of coherence. Even in giving a voice to those who normally do not have one, they do not manage to normalize them or appropriate them into the orders of writing and thought.

Fernando Coronil and Julie Skurski explain that the fear of the masses came to stay that day. "Borders were no longer solely located at the nation's outer edges but had become internalized, turning into the arteries that irrigate the country with poor people. Wherever there were people at the margins—the *marginales*—a threat was seen. Caracas, once the showcase of modernity, appeared fragmented by the slums that surround it, as well as by those that grow like wild grass in the multiple ravines that crosscut the city."[7] For the elite, including the middle classes, fear had come to stay.[8]

Ten years after the day that they came down from the hills, more people in the city carry weapons every day, trust in legal and judicial institutions is practically nonexistent, personal security is an obsession: going out into the street is always risking one's life. In Venezuela two hundred robberies are committed daily (eight per hour) and eight rapes are reported each day, a figure that may be 80 percent higher, since the majority of rapes go unreported. In the metropolitan area there are forty deaths each weekend. Ten years after February 27, one can say, as did the friend that I met up with in Buenos Aires, that the capital of Venezuela lives a stealthy civil war every weekend.[9]

Us

According to Plato (in *The Laws*), original, foundational violence is the violation of the right to control one's property. For Rousseau, wealth corrupts as much as abject poverty does. Both extremes threaten justice, as he clearly states in *The Social Contract*: no citizen should be rich enough to buy another, nor should anyone be so poor as to be forced to sell himself. It is not necessary to go back to Plato or Rousseau. José Roberto Duque, the only chronicler who, ten years after February 27, speaks from the same "we" that is fed up with the excesses of authority, says it much better: "Ever since the concept of property was invented, there have been bloody battles over the possession of goods. Territorial conflicts tend to be much more traumatic, and can occur between nations as well as between common people, without many differences with respect to cruelty."[10]

His is the knowledge imparted by experience. Duque, also author of the book of stories *Salsa y control*, is probably the spokesperson for the majority of the victims of urban violence today. Citing him simplifies the need to explain the current situation. In "Para subir al cielo basta toparse con la autoridad" (Running into the authorities is all it takes to get to heaven), he states, for example: "The fact that walking in the streets is risky in certain cities, because of thugs and thieves is something that is very well known and frequently spoken of. But there are other risks: coming across one of those who impart justice, especially if it is someone that one does not know when, in a crucial moment, one does not have time to demonstrate that one is free of guilt" (*El Nacional*, January 3, 1998).

Or: "A horrendous crime may not transcend nor hurt many people. It depends on how much stock is taken in the victim: justice does not exist for the poor, much less for the marginalized and for families lost in forgotten villages" ("La bulla de los inocentes" [The innocents' uproar], *El Nacional*, May 2, 1999). Reading these kinds of statements, so commonplace and mundane, one asks what is left of the notion of citizenship. In societies in which this feeling of injustice is experienced, perhaps it is necessary to ask oneself about the effect of social ties, or how group bonds function with regard to individuals. Or perhaps it is necessary to redefine the notion of what it is to be a citizen: the parameters designed or dreamed in the constitutions written after the Wars of Independence no longer function. The reality is very different from that which was conceived by the thinkers who fostered independence in the United States, the French Revolution, and the U.S. Constitution.

Week after week, for months, Duque waged a unique crusade in "Guerra nuestra" (Our war)—published until just a few months ago in *El Nacional*—the only column written with a profound knowledge of what occurs in the poor neighborhoods of Caracas, the only one with a profound knowledge of a logic that does not come from the middle class and the elite.[11] In his texts he denounces institutional corruption, especially that of the police, judges, lawyers and doctors; but police abuses have been his most recurrent theme. The text published exactly one decade after that February 27, entitled "Vidas no tan paralelas" (Not-so-parallel lives), and its headline, provide a great deal of food for thought in regard to the community base today: "Perhaps they had few things in common, but something as definitive as death is capable of linking together the most distinct beings," he writes, leaving murder at the hands of the police as the only social equalizer. "Guerra nuestra" has told horrible stories, like that of the family in "La bulla de los inocentes" that claims their son's body only to find that his genitals have been mutilated and that the cornea from one of his eyes is missing:

> One could understand the missing cornea; Doctor Jack Castro had already explained that when someone dies, their family members have three hours to come and submit a letter that prohibits the extraction of organs. It's okay—maybe someone needed the cornea. But as for the rest . . . I don't know, I don't know. A lot of people in the world have no balls, but, as far as I know, no one has ever had a testicle transplant. The furthest that science has gone is cloning sheep, so it will be very hard to explain that cruel act.

In the same text, Duque writes of prisons, stating, almost casually: "A strike has broken out in the El Dorado jail. Nothing special: fifty inmates have declared a blood strike. And what's that? Well, you cut yourself, and if they don't respond to your petitions, you bleed to death. The inmates had already patented the act of sewing their lips together in order to force a hunger strike; the only problem was that in addition to being unable to eat, they were also unable to speak."

Duque's texts are about humor, no escape, the lack of solidarity apart from a family's weeping (when it is already too late), cynicism; his techniques include a multiple gaze that takes in multiple stories throughout the country and the nonconformist voice, and in the process, he confronts the tendency to criminalize the poor. Sometimes one imagines Duque as the journalist who had to spend the whole night of February 27, 1989, in the 23 de enero barrio, unable to enter his house because no one was home, valiantly writing everything that he saw in his notebook, waiting for the military to confuse him with a sniper or for the snipers to confuse him with the police, vulnerable, exposed although inside a building, too close to the horror without having looked for it, and with a sense of humor on the battlefield. Perhaps the most discouraging of these chronicles is one of the last ones published in *El Nacional*, "El Super agente 004," in which he writes:

> In this column I do not usually tell the end of the story at the beginning so that the reader is obliged to follow the thread of the narrative, but this time I'm going to cross that damned line; the reader will decide if he wants to keep reading until the end. At any rate, this story is similar to many of those that preceded it, so it will no longer surprise anyone. Basically, an officer of the Municipal Police of Plaza, in Guarenas, shot and killed a child in the presence of fifty people, and the next day tried to convince the press that the incident had been a fight and that the youngster was a criminal.

"El Super agente 004" is a meditation on habits, on how human beings end up adapting to everything. The reader is implicated in this as well: we already know that when something is repeated day after day, even mass murders, one responds with boredom. Cicero warned that if we were forced to watch or hear about horrible events all of the time, the constant flux of horrible impressions would rob even the most delicate among us of all respect for humanity; the problem, of course, is not the flow of information, but the excess of our everyday lives.

Is there no limit to the horror, no point at which daily violence will create a need for community? Norbert Lechner, reflecting on how we can arrive at these levels of tension, explains that social marginalization is tolerated because it is seen as a necessary transitional stage in the process of modernization, associated with notions of progress and well-being. "That implies . . . that social exclusion will not be institutionalized as a type of apartheid."[12] But is it not necessary to speak of apartheid when we try to understand urban violence, an apartheid that, in the case of Venezuela, affects 80 percent of the population? Is the civic dimension of citizenship not perhaps defined on the basis of feelings that unite a community, which at the same time starts from one premise, the "right to have rights," as Hannah Arendt summarized it?[13]

The Others

I return to Lechner:

> As the horizon of an integrated community vanishes, a situation of rootlessness and helplessness is revealed and any type of sacrifice loses meaning. Tendencies toward fragmentation and exclusion become intolerable, and the search for an alternative mechanism of social cohesion reemerges. . . . It is the experience of social disintegration that determines the revindication of democracy, offering it its concrete significance. In this sense, the revalorization of democracy in Latin America fundamentally means the longing for a restored community.[14]

Perhaps rethinking the terms of democracy is beyond me, because I am not a sociologist or political scientist. But as a reader and a citizen, I try to find some sense or form in this desired community. While reading, I look for the answers that no one has, trying to reconstitute a moral space, an ethical space in which to rethink writing, culture, and, in fact, my relationship with my peers today. I try to reconstruct a definition of citizen responsibility, of personal responsibility. For now, I am left with a minimal premise, given that the concept of solidarity (today so often replaced in intellectual debate by the idea of tolerance) seems only a practical joke on militant human rights organizations; not criminalized like the poor, but certainly not idealized in the media, they are presented as a little out of style, like sixties radicals. I am therefore only left with a premise as innocent as it is impossible: not that we love each other, but that no one suffer or be hurt. Starting from there, it is necessary to think of a new philosophy of the subject (which I call responsibility), as Roland Barthes did nearly twenty years ago in an interview on violence: "We should not allow ourselves to be intimidated by this morality of the collective superego, diffuse in our society, with its values of responsibility and of political commitment. We must accept the scandal of individualist positions"[15]—that is, the scandal that each one of us ceases to accuse the status quo (the political parties, the government, the entrepreneurs, repressive organisms, the mass media) and begins to question him or herself in regard to everyday ethics.

The Others

There is a chronicle by Fabrico Ojeda entitled "Pánico bajo techo" (Panic under cover) in *El día que bajaron de los cerros* in which he announces and summarizes the state of Caracas in the 1990s: "A new virus, the syndrome of the riot, attacks the nerves of members of Caracas's middle class, those who still have valuable objects in their homes. Now everyone fears that the 'popular fury' will enter their estates and homes to take what is left" (Ojeda, 69).

In this same text he tells the story of the former prison director and, at that time, prefect of Caracas, Dunia Farías: "She dreamed of the multitudes attacking her apartment and decided to call the National Guard, the Minister of Defense, the PTJ, the Disip, the Metropolitan Police, and every friend that she had in the government to protect the area from the hypothetical hordes that—according to her imagination—were preparing an assault on the residential area."

When, accompanied by a patrol of soldiers, the prefect realized that it was just a figment of her imagination, "she had no other option than to lower her face and offer apologies for her lamentable mistake when she arrived at her building and the neighbors looked at her with a mixture of pity and astonishment" (Ojeda, 69).

But the virus of fear of the masses had been sown forever, the terror not only of muggings on the streets but of criminals, kidnappers, or assailants who raid houses. And it is here that the 80 percent who suffer like no one else come to be seen as criminals in the making, as the enemy: the middle class always believes that they themselves suffer the most. The voice is no longer that of José Roberto Duque's "we," but that which looks upon passersby as the "other" to be feared. As Jesús Martín Barbero put it:

> The order of the cities is constructed with the uncertainty that the "other" produces in us, which inoculates us each day with distrust for he who passes by me on the street. . . . I ask myself if that other, converted into a threat on a daily basis, does not have a great deal to do with our political culture, with the growth of intolerance, with the impossibility of that social pact that is spoken of so frequently, that is, with the difficulty of recognizing oneself in the difference of what the other thinks, in what the other likes, in what he has on his life, esthetic or political horizons.[16]

There are few cases of this distrust as extreme as that of another writer who, also publishing in the pages of El Nacional, is the diametric opposite of José Roberto Duque. I am referring to Marcos Tarre Briceño, author of various police novels, salesman of security and protection manuals, creator of the Internet site called Condición Amarilla [The yellow condition], a space in which Central and South America, "currently the most violent region in the world," can learn to define a "clear and effective politics in regard to crime," and especially so that the citizen, "the victim *par excellence*," learns to "face this situation."[17] For Tarre, the citizen lives in Santa Rosa, in Lima, and similar neighborhoods with economic power. He speaks to these privileged citizens—the punished middle class—so that "anyone" will have "the means to act positively and proactively in the face of a problem and the ability to explain to their sons and daughters, children or adolescents, all of the unpleasant and absurd things that they live, see or hear on a daily basis."

Tarre is not proposing the creation of the figure known in the United States as the neighborhood watch member—the neighbor who spontaneously arms himself for self-defense purposes—but he does recommend that his readers ask for professional help from his security company. In his weekly column, provocatively entitled "No sea usted la próxima víctima" (Don't be the next victim), he offers statistics of muggings, assaults, and rapes, and he speaks of kidnappings (generally attributed to Colombians) and, of course, of children addicted to drugs. I obtained the following disheartening statistics from Tarre:

> In 1996 13.5 homicides were committed each day. In 1998 this number fell to 8.9. The unofficial figures seem to indicate that we are at higher levels in the first half of 1999 than last year, arriving at eleven or twelve homicides each day. In terms of muggings, 101 cases were registered each day in 1996. Now, in the first half of 1999, the figure has risen to close to eighty reports each day. In regard to robbery, 234.5 were reported daily, falling to 136.5 in 1998. In the first half of the year, theft, the most frequent crime in the country, had risen to 200 cases per day. According to these figures, last year at this time homicides had risen 22 percent, muggings 31.14 percent and robberies 46.5 percent. Taking into account these three indicators, we can see that criminality has risen 33.2 percent in the first half of 1999 in comparison to 1998.

The Tarre phenomenon is very curious, given that his credentials are not conventional: he is the author of *Colt Comando, Sentinel 44, Operación Victoria, BAR 30, En Caso Extremo, Manual de Seguridad y Prevención Comunitaria*. This writer has the rank of honorary commissioner for Disip (the secret police); he is a ballistics instructor for the police, and a consultant for organizations and governing bodies. This character, so different from Duque, offers talks and seminars in business and industry; he is an extreme character. I understand his fear, not only because I have lived it (I don't know anyone who has not been mugged at least once), but because fear is the daily companion of Caracas's inhabitants. But many of his columns make my hair stand on end. "Guardaespaldas, escoltas y espalderos (II)" (Security guards, escorts, and bodyguards), for example, tells the story of the kidnapping of an entrepreneur and then moves on to offer an etiquette handbook for bodyguards. Among his pieces of advice, learned in the top-gun business, is a warning to the vulnerable entrepreneur: escorts "should not be diverted or distracted from their work, doing small favors such as: 'Please, go for a second and cash a check,' carrying briefcases, packages, cell phones, opening doors, etc. . . . It is assumed that . . . if one has the money to hire a group of escorts, one will also have a personal administrator or assistants to take care of such things."

Other pieces of advice: the guards should use the formal form of address with relatives and friends; they should wear clothing that does not make them stand out in the social circles of the person who is protected, pay attention to the hands (and not the faces) of those who come near them, not show that they are armed, be ready to deal with provocations and offensive behavior without losing control, and avoid conversations with the public. If it were not for the fact that knowledge of different "classes of firearms, revolvers, pistols, submachine guns, rifles, assault weapons, etc.," in addition to lacrimogenic gases and similar weapons, is required, the manual would seem quite similar to one of the biggest best-sellers of recent years, *La nueva guía de comportamiento, etiqueta y urbanidad* (The new guide to behavior, etiquette, and urbanity) by Marisela Guevara, in which one is given advice on everything from how to treat domestic help to the use of a handkerchief to blow one's nose since using one's hand is in poor taste.[18]

Of course, Tarre's chronicles do not have the hilarious and frivolous tone that one can encounter in this manual, although the success of this renovated version of Carreño's advice in this age and in the context of these social conditions alone merits consideration. If I compare them, it is because both Guevara and Tarre have their own way of re-thinking the urban subject, the definition of this new citizen with which I am concerned. In "Niños pequeños y riesgos escolares" (Small children and scholastic risks), Marcos Tarre tells of his experience during one of the security workshops for children that he offers to the families that can pay for them; his intention is not to create elegant citizens, but to keep them alive:

> The club's board of directors was enthused by the notion of giving personal security tips to its members' children, and the workshops were scheduled as part of the vacation activities. We asked if any of them had been the victim of criminals. Immediately, many of the boys and girls, anxious to participate, raised their little arms:
>
> My mom was walking down the street and a thief ripped off the gold chain that she was wearing . . .
>
> We gave an explanation for each comment: This is called an *arrebatón*. It occurs frequently in the streets, and because of this it is better not to wear jewelry, necklaces or chains.

This lesson in civility in schools concerns me, that the ABCs should now be accompanied by learning how to discern, for example, the difference between "criminals, antisocial people, petty thieves, slackers, gangs, or the mentally disturbed," terms that I take from this same text. In "El síndrome del estrés post traumático en los niños" (Post-traumatic stress disorder in children), he states:

> Mr. Andrés Paredes took his two small children downstairs as he did every morning at 6:30 A.M. to take them to school before continuing on to his work. He walked out to building's uncovered parking area in El Paraíso. The gate had stopped working a few months earlier. When he got to his parking spot, Andrés Paredes' heart jumped. He could only understand that his white Toyota Sky was not there. He thought back quickly: Yes, he had parked it in this spot himself the night before. There was no doubt. They had stolen it! Beaten by this cruel reality, by what it meant for his family to be left without a vehicle, knowing that it was not insured and that there was no money to replace it, Andrés Paredes sat on the curb of the parking lot and cried silently. His five-year-old daughter, upset, frightened, repeated: "Don't cry, Daddy, please don't cry." His son, who was younger, who didn't understand what was happening, also cried.

This is an everyday narrative of the middle class. That of José Roberto Duque, "Un tiro en la nuca por ofender a la autoridad" (A shot in the back of the neck for offending the authorities), is no less bitter. In this piece he tells the story of a young man named Boris Alberto who got involved in a lovers' quarrel and was shot by a policeman. The family brought him from hospital to hospital until they finally found someone who would tend to him and operate on him. The doctor who performed the surgery called Boris's mother "in order to give her some words of encouragement" in the following manner:

> "How many children do you have, ma'am?"
> "Eight."
> "Well, get used to the fact that there won't be more than seven, because this one doesn't count anymore."

Duque concludes: "The words of a doctor; imagine what a sicario would say."[19]

Social identity is constituted to a large degree by memories, myths, the symbolic order. And it is also formed by the ways in which it is written: narrative provides the coherence that reality generally lacks. When I read these chronicles, I cannot help but ask myself what is chosen for representation and if that reinforces fear, if it helps to combat injustice or to reestablish the minimal social pact that seems to have been lost; none of these things legitimates violence. I also ask myself how empathy functions, an element without which I cannot see how our societies can get out of these abysses: the lack of the bonds of solidarity, of empathy, of civic consciousness and adequate hermeneutic tools to read the text written by the cities in the present. However, far above all else, what strikes me is the lack of a clear sense of personal responsibility for others. I propose that the discussion of ethics and responsibility be reinserted into literary and cultural studies. In the face of so much violence, I appeal to individual conscience, asking myself how willing we are, as privileged people, to change the terms and if, as the privileged members of the academy, we do or do not think of making ourselves responsible for others.[20]

TRANSLATED BY KATHERINE GOLDMAN

Notes

1. Cabrujas, "La viveza Criolla." There had previously been uprisings in the Dominican Republic and Brazil; Caracas itself held the memory of the acts of violence that led to the overthrow of dictator Pérez Jiménez at the end of the 1950s and of the subversive and repressive violence of the 1960s.
2. "Sólo 20% de los hogares gana más de Bs. 500 mil" (Only 20 percent of households earn more than five hundred thousand bolívars), Emilce Chacón, in *El Universal*, October 17, 1999. The article cites the figures offered by the Central Office of Statistics and Information (Oficina Central de Estadística e Información) for the first quarter of 1999.
3. According to Bauman, the poor are brutalized and isolated; in contrast to the way the poor were seen a few years ago—as individuals who could be transformed into cheap labor—the current free-market culture sees them as nonconsumers and, therefore, superfluous. Bauman, "Morality Begins at Home: Or the Rocky Road to Justice," in *Postmodernity and Its Discontents*, 61.
4. Jelin, "La construcción de la ciudadanía," 120.
5. Bauman, "Morality Begins at Home," 61.
6. Originally published in the newspaper *El Nacional*, the photographs were taken by Sandra Bracho, Tom and José Grillo, Oswaldo Tejada, Jacobo Lezama, Dimas Ibarra, and Fraso.
7. Coronil and Skurski, "Dismembering and Remembering the Nation," 328.
8. In "*Insolencias de lo prohibido*," a talk given at Wellesley College in April 1999,

in the context of the colloquium "El Caribe a fin del milenio," I analyzed the birth of the new urban subject: the *víctima-en-potencia* (the potential victim).

9. The image of a civil war each weekend is nothing more than an image of the discourse created by the media: obviously the murders and violence occur indistinctly, all the time, but the newspapers report the weekend's statistics on Mondays. This practice, which is not effectively counterbalanced by the daily police beat in the newspaper, creates a distortion effect in that it is perceived as reality.

10. "Una de invasores" (One about the invaders), March 21, 1999; this chronicle, like those that follow, formed part of the series "Guerra nuestra" (Our war), in *Siete Días*, a section of *El Nacional*, Caracas. The quotes will be marked in the text only with the date of publication in parentheses from this point forward.

11. Duque has taken "Guerra nuestra" to a newspaper of a more popular nature than *El Nacional*, Caracas's *El Mundo*, which was the newspaper that offered the most opposition to the government for a few months and, for that reason, became much more sought after by the middle class than before; its director, Teodoro Petkoff, left *El Mundo* because of governmental pressure, and Duque did the same a few months later.

12. Lechner, "Modernización y modernidad," 69.

13. Arendt, *The Origins of Totalitarianism*.

14. Lechner, "Modernización y modernidad," 69.

15. Barthes, "Opiniones sobre la violencia," 214.

16. Martín Barbero, "Comunicación y ciudad," 80.

17. See *http:www.seguridadaldia.com*.

18. Marisela Guevara, *Nueva guía de comportamiento, etiqueta y urbanidad* (Caracas: Los libros de El Nacional, 1998). According to the publicity for the book, which occupies the number-three spot among the ten top-selling books, ten years after February 27, 1989:

    Few things provoke as much panic as submitting oneself to the scrutinizing gaze of others. If you do not know what to do when seated at a table set with various sets of silverware, if you stutter each time you have to offer your condolences to the loved ones at a funeral, if you are nervous about what wedding invitations should say or how to behave in a condominium meeting, simply take a look at this book so that your doubts may be appeased and, above all else, so that you can become a more polite, elegant and self-satisfied citizen.

19. The term *sicario* refers to teenage boys who are trained to be hired killers, most of whom carry out their work knowing very well that they themselves will eventually become the victims of violence.

20. Bauman put it well in "Morality Begins at Home": "We do not know what justice is, but we know it when an injustice is committed" (62). I do not know if assuming our responsibility is the new categorical imperative ("preserving human life," as Bauman adds), but I know that sitting around and waiting for the paternalist state or the free market to solve the problem, while we learn the difference between a mugging and an *arrebatón* or watch our friends die, will not solve much. Neither resignation nor the comfort of indifference helps.

Citizenship and Urban Violence

CARLOS MONSIVÁIS

Nightmares in the Open Air

THE STRUCTURE OF THE UNDERSTANDING of urban violence has been created, through personal experience, the conversion of the sum of collective and individual experiences, in determinism, and the somewhat literary version, which converts urban violence into melodrama. Certainly discourses, reports, and academic analyses on the topic may be tinged with melodrama or formulated in that literary or paraliterary genre. Thus the image of the defenseless city, like the bound victim's body awaiting the knife thrust. So it is in the case of the metaphors used in nineteenth-century serial novels to refer to the vulnerable, which is how the majority of people see themselves, even if they don't use the word. Thus the idea of new crimes and new forms of violence. What is more, melodrama selects subterranean, or not so subterranean, Christian metaphors. Violence is our cross. Citizens, precisely because we are not who we might be, are Christlike figures, assaulted, beaten, or murdered for the sins of the system or our carelessness, or for our inability to hire a bodyguard, or for our abstention from the practice of our rights as citizens.

Interference

The Christ metaphor is indispensable in melodrama. There is no mother who may not be Jesus Christ in the melodramas, and there is no honest person who may not be confused with a politician, who may also be confused with Christ. On a fundamental level, the melodrama of violence is theology. On another, it is a soap opera without secrets. I believe that whether it is accepted or not, soap opera is a literary genre devised to understand life's processes. On a third level, melodrama is the provisionally effective exorcism that converts lamentably real and multiform violence into something comprehensible, that frees us from the obligations of civic intervention, that disassociates itself from democratic transformations, from the construction of civil society, and from the compromises confronting the phenomenon of inequality, most commonly noted in Mexico and Latin America.

Without melodrama, one would never understand, in most cases, that somebody is a victim in the making or has already been a victim. One would then have to derive a different understanding from society. In a strict sense, the translation of urban violence to the melodramatic idiom complies with the very useful and not to be underestimated function of facilitating the assimilation of a tragic landscape. In another harmful sense, melodrama's influence hinders citizenry, makes them propitiatory victims at celebrations of their own impotence, convinced of fatalism's powers. As a result, up to now, citizens have failed in their zealous campaigns and attempts to mobilize the population against violence. In Mexico, we have had a particularly melodramatic campaign in which white ribbons were worn as a sign of solidarity against violence. Remarkably, this was not even melodrama, but a mute cry for help. And the antiviolence campaigns amount to soap opera commentators' meetings. That which serves to assimilate also serves to calm. "What would we do if it was our turn here, between one assault and another?" Melodrama is acted out in every meeting, in the metamorphosis of the real, in the theatrically representable, in live suffering transformed into theater. How is this effected? The subject is discussed interminably, I suppose, in São Paulo or in Bogotá or in Caracas, and naturally in Mexico City. If any topic that can guarantee that the meeting will make sense to the participants, it is violence.

And when violence is discussed, each participant adopts a role and is converted into a soap opera character. Violence, as it is socially interpreted, is the great soap opera from which we cannot free ourselves, but that never reprises our roles; we continue saying the same things with the same words, since we do not have scriptwriters. Endless conversations take place, even as the participants' anxiety levels increase as they offer undoubtedly true information. "They assaulted me"; "they took my sister in a taxi so that she could take out money with her ATM/credit card"; "they killed an acquaintance of mine"; "they cleaned out my neighbors' house." This unquestionably true information is then lodged in a limitless space that is only comprehensible by way of melodrama. Shifted to this space, violent anecdotes disarm, inhibit, terrorize, give rise to minimal bouts of resistance, and, at the end of the day, nullify civic volition.

Melodramatically, many obtain arms, and by so doing, feel as though they were living in a movie. The possession of the weapon gives them the conviction that no other object would give them. The use of the firearm, however, is something almost phantasmagoric. Melodramatically, the unnerving insistence is such that society as a tangible presence disappears and only the individual remains, isolated, or with his terrorized family. In our case we could say "poor Mexico, so close to the criminals, so far from the opportunity for collective action."

Despite what others may claim, I insist that the majority of people in large cities are law abiding. Violence has been delineated and the corruption localized. Nevertheless, if violence is undeniable and ever increasing, the melodramatic intrusion comes in the language of broadcasters and reporters (not the state), who are the great translators of urban violence and fortify through their jargon the passion of these years.

Determinism achieved its own canonization with the boom of neoliberalism. Margaret Thatcher affirmed that "there is no other path," and "alternatives do not exist." This is a viewpoint that has been stated in many different ways since 1989. If no other alternatives exist, the world arrives at that end of history that is the adoption of fatalism as the sole ideology. And fatalism itself encompasses practically every theme, from the economic system to the fight against violence. Accept neoliberalism, because there is no other alternative; admit that we are victims, because we do not have the ability to stop being victims.

The political parties, and naturally the government, use the favorite discourse of determinism: the nebulous promises, the abstract threats, the apocalyptic scenarios. Ultimately, the melodrama par excellence is the apocalyptic daily reality assumed to be the end of the world, and the end of the world as daily reality, divested of sense in both instances. What really happens, which is sufficiently tragic, becomes blurred or clouded by the strength of melodramatic pretexts.

I believe that we do not insist enough on the role that determinism plays as the ideology of the "not other." I believe that this time is dominated by determinism and that we have spent exactly ten years in an atmosphere without exits. Not that the ones we had before 1989 were many or significant, but alternatives are now simply decreed as abolished or exterminated, and this affects everything. In regard to the problem of urban violence, the feeling that there is no escape precedes any project.

The effects on behavior of the ideology of a narrative genre are notable. The behavior of the city is governed by the representations of victimology, which, more than a judicial science, has been transformed into a repertoire of clamorings and tremblings. The citizens—and they hardly are citizens—wake up daily to find that they have been transformed into potential victims. Urban vitality is dissolved into a mere shadow of its former self; fear, which I recognize as a legitimate feeling, becomes the most reliable psychology, the only one that offers a sense of security to those inhabiting it. The change suffered by society results in one feeling confident in one's fear, not in one's valor.

The sectors most affected by the convictions of melodrama are the criminal element and the police force. Seeing assailants on the news or in the chronicles and police reports is sufficient to confirm that their fixed psychology is that of film and television. There are innumerable examples of this. I believe that Jorgé Zepeda could tell the story of the criminal from Jalisco who kidnapped a family and then asked that television cameras be brought in to record the whole incident and requested that a reporter be brought in from Televisa. Complaints against society are expressed, the cries multiply, and at the end the accused is allowed to leave with someone. Was it his mother? Yes, it was his mother. It was a fantastic melodrama. Evidently all of his steps brought the assailant, who, in addition, had fled during a police chase and was seeking refuge, to this point. It was obvious that he only felt real in the presence of the cameras.

Melodrama's power, which is to say the power of the seduction of fatalism, which adopts theatrical forms and expressive speech, is also part of the determinist genre, as it places itself in service to the negation of exits. In holding up banks or taxis during kidnappings, the perpetrators behave as if they were the characters in a movie or soap opera that has yet to be filmed. The most common characteristic of assaults in Mexico City is that the assailant chastises the victim. Moreover, the assailant morally chastises the victim because there has to be a minimal rationalization. Because the victim has money, given that the assailant has to obtain something and the victim can provide it to the assailant, who will take this money and convert it into material possessions, when the perpetrator doesn't have it, and so on, and so on. Part of the assailant's melodramatic conviction is the moral chastisement of the victim, not only because he cannot defend himself, but because he has no way of morally justifying himself. And in having possessions, the victim is different from the assailant, who does not have them and thus has to acquire them at the price of crime, which is a risk. Meanwhile, the victim runs only the risk of being murdered, which is a minor risk in comparison to the major risks run by the criminals.

It is not a question of a televised or cinematographic education in violence, about which so much has been said; it is the sensation that violence is the road to a fuller reality, that of melodrama, the knowledge of which is no consolation, nor does it serve any great purpose. The important thing is to determine to what extent the notion of free will has been abolished in society in the past few years. There is no faith in autonomy as a philosophical or judicial concept, except for the social belief in the will of autonomy. Since violence is inevitable, any solution that is not extreme is discarded a priori, and the religious myth of the human being's fatal condition returns, and extreme punishments are considered the only effective measures—because they extend and propel melodrama. The death penalty is conceived of as a melodramatic solution that also has the advantage of not allowing the character to return. Therefore, preventive measures tend to be ineffective almost before the fact, because they are dissolved in a monitoring melodrama, and in the clerical sermons that so abound. For example, the democratization of the clerical sermon is the assailant's chastisement of the victim; the political melodrama is the cloud of promises. The repressive melodrama of the police, which is really only part of the problem in regard to the composition of violence; the judicial melodrama, the extremely harsh punishments for those who cannot afford to pay the most expensive criminal defense attorneys. There is also the melodrama of the good conscience, whereby one alleviates one's guilt by discharging anti-governmental fury during after-dinner discussions; and the melodrama of the community that takes justice into its own hands through lynchings.

I am not saying that many of the results of these actions are melodramatic—quite to the contrary, they are savage and terrible; but the ethical sense of these actions, which falters or is weakened as a result of this sort of action, is melodramatic. The ethic that is ultimately diluted by melodrama becomes a form of complicity with violence.

The melodrama that is the most difficult to describe is that of the community that takes justice into its own hands. During the last decade in Latin America, the destruction of the apparatus of justice, or the destruction of the faith in that apparatus, has led to the rise in lynching in Venezuela, Colombia, Ecuador, Bolivia, Central America, and, naturally, Mexico. Yes, melodramatic action can be perceived. Five years ago in a town in Vera Cruz (one which was not necessarily poor, because it had high-tension wires), a forty-six-year-old woman was raped and murdered, and the likely murderer was found, a twenty-eight-year-old young man who was detained by a group and brought to the village's town square. The first thing that the lynch mob did was rent video equipment to record what was to be, from that point on, the broadcast of a live soap opera.

Once the equipment had been obtained, they proceeded with the trial, which lasted approximately five minutes. One segment of the population did not want to participate and moved away, distancing itself. The other remained to witness the execution, the burning at the stake. The video that was later distributed lasts about forty-five minutes. The entire process is seen: collecting the wood, lighting the fire. The most shocking thing is that young children and teenagers can be seen contemplating the auto-da-fe as if they were watching a horror film. There is a transpositioning of planes here.

What grieves me in particular is that the children did not react in horror. I do not understand this extreme moral turpitude. After thirty minutes, the fire went out but the condemned man was still alive, his lynched body now charred. The fire was relit. I felt that the only human element in all of this was the agonized cries of this man whose guilt or innocence we will never know. At the end of the auto-da-fe the only person arrested was the man responsible for filming it. There was no other act of justice. This example is only one of many. Each year there are between forty and fifty lynchings; some of the victims are burned and some are not. There was also an attempt in the center of Mexico City to lynch a police officer, who was saved only by the arrival of a special police unit. Three months ago there was an attempt to lynch a person because the town was falling prey to criminal violence and petty crime; the streets were patrolled by "deathwishers." People get lost and enter a town for reasons that have nothing to do with crime; but the deathwishers enter at dawn and detain them, as in the instance of one man who was bound to a flagpole for ten hours. He was insulted and left to be burned with lit cigarettes by the women.

All of this has the action of a savage fury and a fundamentally melodramatic conception. The people involved feel as if they were acting in an inquisition or a horror film. It seems to me that this lack of distinction between the real and the melodramatic, even though it may come from horror, is an integral part of the atmosphere of violence.

TRANSLATED BY HEATHER HAMMETT

References

Adorno, Sérgio. "A gestão filantrópica da pobreza urbana." *São Paulo em Perspectiva.* São Paulo, 1991.

———. "A gestão urbana do medo e da insegurança: violência, crime e justiça penal na sociedade brasileira contemporânea." Thesis, Departmento de Sociología de FFLCH/University of São Paulo, 1996.

———. "Consolidação democrática e políticas de segurança pública no Brasil: rupturas e continuidades." In Jorge Zaverucha, ed., *Democracia e instituições políticas brasileiras no final do século XX.* Recife: Bagaço, 1998.

———. "La precoce esperienza della punizione." In J. de S. Martins, ed., *L'infanzia negata. Omicidi, prostituzione, mallatie e fame dei bambini brasiliani.* Chieti Scalo: Vecchio Faggio, 1991.

———. "O gerenciamento público da violência urbana: a justiça em ação." In Paulo Sérgio Pinheiro et al., eds., *São Paulo sem medo. Um diagnóstico da violência urbana.* Río de Janeiro: Garamond, 1998.

Adorno, Sergio, and Paulo Sérgio Pinheiro. "Violência contra crianças e adolescentes, violência social e Estado de Direito." *São Paulo em Perspectiva. Revista da Fundação SEADE* 7, 1 (1993): 106–118.

Adorno, Sergio, Renato Sérgio de Lima, Dora Feiguin, Fanny Biderman, and Eliana Bordini. "O adolescente e a criminalidade urbana em São Paulo." *Revista Brasileira de Ciências Criminais* 6 (1998): 189–204.

Adorno, Sergio, Renato Sérgio de Lima, and Eliana Bordini. *O adolescente na criminalidade urbana em São Paulo* (The adolescent in urban crime in São Paulo). Brasília: Ministerio de Justicia, Secretaría de Estado para los Derechos Humanos, 1999.

Afolayan, J. "Consequences of Domestic Violence on Elementary School Education." *Child and Family Behavior Therapy* 15, 3 (1993): 55–58.

Alba, R. D., et al. "Living with Crime: The Implications of Racial/Ethnic Differences in Suburban Location." *Social Forces* 73, 2 (1994): 395–434.

Alves, M. *State and Opposition in Military Brazil.* Austin: University of Texas Press, 1985.

ACTIVA. "Actitudes y normas culturales frente a violencia en ciudades seleccionadas de la región de las Américas." Proyecto APTIVA. Washington: Organización Panamericana de la Salud, 1996.

Araújo, Braz José de, ed. *Crianças e adolescentes no Brasil: diagnósticos, políticas e participação da sociedade*. Campinas: Fundação Cargill, 1996.

Area de Análisis Político del Instituto de Estudios de la Revolución Democrática. "Ley de Seguridad Pública." *Coyuntura* 69–70 (March–April 1996): 39–41.

Arendt, Hannah. *The Origins of Totalitarianism*. New York: Harcourt, Brace and World, 1973.

Ariès, Phillippe. *L'enfant et la famille sous l'Ancien Régime*. Paris: Éditions du Seuil, 1973.

Assis, Simone. "Crianças e adolescentes violentados: passado, presente e perspectiva de futuro. *Cadernos de Saúde Pública* 10, 1 (1994): 126–134.

———. "Iniciativa de Ley contra la Delincuencia Organizada." *Coyuntura*, IERD 72 (1996): 26–28.

———. "*Quando* crescer é um desafio social. Estudo sócio-epidemiológico sobre violência em escolares em Duque de Caxias, Rio de Janeiro." Master's thesis, Escuela Nacional de Salud Pública, 1991.

———. "Situación de la violencia juvenil en Río de Janeiro." Paper presented at "Taller sobre la violencia de los adolescentes y las pandillas [maras] juveniles" (Workshop on Youth Violence and Youth Gangs). Oficina Panamericana de la Salud (OPS/OMS). San Salvador, El Salvador, May 7–9, 1997.

Astor, R. "Children's Moral Reasoning about Family and Peer Violence: The Role of Provocation and Retribution." *Child Development* 65, 4 (1994): 1054–1067.

Aubusson de Cavarlay, Bruno. "La place des mineurs dans la délinquance." *Les Cahiers de la Sécurité Intérieur* 29 (1997): 17–38.

Azaola Garrido, Elena. "Notes on Juvenile Delinquency in Mexico: Programa de Acción Niños en la Calle." Paper presented at "Rising Violence and the Criminal Justice Response in Latin America: Towards an Agenda for Collaborative Research in the 21st Century." University of Texas, Austin, May 6–9, 1999. http://lanic.utexas.edu/project/etext/violence/memoria/session_1.html.

Bailleau, Francis. "Délinquance des mineurs: question de justice ou d'ordre social?" *Les Cahiers de la Sécurité Intérieur* 29 (1997): 77–88.

Baker, Pauline, and John Ausink. "State Collapse and Ethnic Violence: Toward a Predictive Model." *Parameters, U.S. Army War College Quarterly* 26, 1 (1996): 19–31.

Barone, C. "Involvement in Multiple Problem Behaviors of Young Urban Adolescents." *Journal of Primary Prevention* 15, 3 (1995): 261–283.

Barthes, Roland. "Opiniones sobre la violencia" In *El grano de la voz: Entrevistas 1962–1980*. Trans. Nora Pasternac. Mexico: Siglo XXI, 1983.

Bartra, Roger. *Las redes imaginarias del poder político*. Mexico: Océano, 1996.

Bauman, Zygmunt. *Postmodernity and Its Discontents*. New York: New York University Press, 1997.

Beato, Cláudio. "Determinantes da criminalidade em Minas Gerais." *Revista Brasileira de Ciências Sociais* 13, 37 (1998): 74–87.

Beck, Ulrich. *La sociedad del riesgo: Hacia una nueva modernidad*. Buenos Aires: Paidós, 1998.

Benítez, Raúl. "La ONU y el proceso de paz en El Salvador: 1990–1992." *Análisis Político* 17 (September–December 1992): 84.

Benjamin, Walter. *Para una crítica de la violencia y otros ensayos*. Madrid: Taurus/ Alfaguara, 1991.

Birnbaum, Pierre, Jack Lively, and Geraint Parry, eds. *Democracy, Consensus, and Social Contract*. London: Sage, 1978.

Black, Jan K. *United States Penetration of Brazil*. Manchester: Manchester University Press, 1977.

Bledstein, Burton J. *The Culture of Professionalism: The Middle Class and the Development of Higher Education in America*. New York: Norton, 1976.

BNM Archdioceses of São Paulo. *Torture in Brazil (Brasil Nunca Mais)*. New York: Vintage Books, 1986.

Boltvinik, Julio. "Evolución heterogénea de la pobreza en México. 1970–1995." Paper presented at "Confronting Development: Assessing Mexico´s Economic and Social Policy Changes," University of California at San Diego, 1999.

———. "La agudización de la pobreza en el régimen neoliberal." Paper presented at the Secretaría de Formación Política del Partido de la Revolución Democrática, Neoliberalismo y resistencia popular, Mexico, 1999, 81–88.

Bourdieu, Pierre. *Outline of a Theory of Practice*. Cambridge, U.K.: Cambridge University Press, 1977.

Brant, Vinicius Caldeira, et al. *São Paulo. Trabalhar e viver*. San Pablo: Brasiliense, 1989.

Brunner, José Joaquín. *Globalización cultural y posmodernidad*. Mexico: Fondo de Cultura Económica, 1998.

Cabrujas, José Ignacio. "La viveza Criolla. Destreza, mínimo esfuerzo o sentido del humor." In *La cultura del trabajo*. Caracas: Cátedra Fundación Sivensa-Ateneo de Caracas, 1996.

Calderón, Fernando, and Mario DosSantos. *Hacia un nuevo orden estatal en América Latina. Veinte tesis sociopolíticas y un corolario*. Santiago de Chile: Fondo de Cultura Económica/FLACSO, 1991.

Camacho, Alvaro, and Guzmán Camacho. *La violencia y la multiplicidad de las violencia*. Cali: Department of Social Sciences, University of Valle, 1990.

Cárdia, Nancy. "A violência urbana e os jovens." In Paulo Sérgio Pinheiro, ed., *São Paulo sem medo. Um diagnóstico da violência urbana*. Río de Janeiro: Garamond, 1997.

Castells, Manuel. *La era de la información. Economía, sociedad y cultura*. Vol. 2., *El poder de la identidad*. Mexico: Siglo XXI, 1999.

Castoriardis, Cornelius. *The Imaginary Institution of Society*. Trans. Kathleen Blamey. Cambridge, Mass.: MIT Press, 1987. (In Spanish: *La institución imaginaria de la sociedad*. Vol. 2. *El imaginario social y la institución*. Trans. Mario Aurelio-Galmarini. Barcelona: Tusquets, 1989.)

Castro, Myriam Mesquita Pugliese de. "Assassinatos de crianças e adolescentes no Estado de São Paulo." *Revista Crítica de Ciências Sociais* 36 (1993): 81–102.

Catherine V. and Michel M. *Security and Democracy*. Le Forum. Analytical College on Urban Safety 1993 Report. S.E.P.C. Saint-Armand, France: Analytical College on Urban Safety, 1994.

Causas de Mortalidade, Brasil. Ministério da Saúde, Governo do Brasil. *www.datasus.gov.br* (1999).

Center of Study and Prevention of Violence (CSPV). *Youth Violence: An Overview*. Boulder: Institute of Behavioral Sciences, University of Colorado, 1994.

Centro de Derechos Humanos Fray Francisco de Vitoria OP. "Informe anual. La situación de los derechos humanos en México, noviembre de 1997–octubre de 1998." Mexico, 1998.

———. "Informe anual. La situación de los derechos humanos en México, noviembre de 1996–octubre de 1997." *Revista Justicia y Paz* (Mexico) 46 (1997).

———. "Informe anual. La situación de los derechos humanos en México, diciembre de 1995–octubre de 1996." *Revista Justicia y Paz* (Mexico) 43 (1996).

Centro de Derechos Humanos Fray Bartolomé de Las Casas. *Acteal: Entre el duelo y la lucha.* Mexico, 1998.

———. *La legalidad de la injusticia.* Mexico, 1998.

Centro de Derechos Humanos Miguel Agustín Pro Juárez. "Informe anual sobre violaciones a los derechos humanos en México." Mexico, 1998, 1999.

Centro de Estudos de Cultura Conteporânea (CEDEC). *Mapa de risco da violência: cidade de São Paulo.* San Pablo: CEDEC, 1995.

Centro Internacional de Investigación Clínico-Psicológica, CEIC. *Del Colombiano Valiente y Aguerrido al Colombiano de la Violencia y la Barbarie.* Casa editorial RAFUE, 1999.

Certeau, Michel de. *The Practice of Everyday Life.* Trans. Steven Rendall. Berkeley and Los Angeles: University of California Press, 1984.

Chevigny, Paul. *Edge of the Knife: Police Violence in the Americas.* New York: Vintage, 1995.

Chiappe, Domenico, and David González. "Los delitos aumentan y la denuncia disminuye." *El Nacional* (Caracas), November 14, 1999.

CISALVA. *Dimensionamiento de la violencia en Colombia.* Faculty of Health, University of Valle, Cali / Interamerican Development Bank, Documents of Network Centers, R–339, Washington.

Cohen, Albert. *Delinquent Boys: The Culture of the Gangs.* Glencoe, Ill.: Free Press, 1955.

Cohen, D., and R. Nisbett. "Self Protection and the Culture of Honor: Explaining Southern Violence." *Personality and Social Psychology Bulletin* 20, 5 (1994): 551–567.

Cohen, Stan. "Human Rights and Crimes of the State: The Culture of Denial." *Australian and New Zealand Journal of Criminology* 26 (July 1993): 97–115.

Colburn, Forrest D. "Crime in Latin America." *Dissent* 45, 3 (summer 1998): 27–30.

Comisión Mexicana de Defensa y Promoción de los Derechos Humanos. *Las consecuencias de la militarización.* May 1997.

Coronil, Fernando, and Julie Skurski. "Dismembering and Remembering the Nation: The Semantics of Political Violence in Venezuela." *Comparative Studies in Society and History* 23, 1 (January 1991): 288–337.

Corradi, Juan E., et al. *Fear at the Edge: State Terror and Resistance in Latin America.* Berkeley: University of California Press, 1992.

Correa, Mariza. *As ilusões da liberdade.* Bragança Paulista: FAPESP/CDAPH-IFAN, 1998.

Crane, J. "The Epidemic Theory of Ghettos and Neighborhood Effects on Dropping Out and Teenage Childbearing." *American Journal of Sociology* 96, 5 (1991): 1226–1259.

"Crime and Violence as Development Issues in Latin America and the Caribbean." Challenge of Urban Criminal Violence Seminar (OPAS, BID, World Bank, UNESCO, HABITAT). Pamphlet. Rio de Janeiro, March 1997.

Crovi, Delia. *Cultura política, información y comunicación de masas.* Mexico: Asociación Latinoamericana de Sociología, 1996.

Davis, Mike. *Ecology of Fear: Los Angeles and the Imagination of Disaster.* New York: Henry Holt, 1998.

Dellasoppa, Emilio, Alicia Bercovich, and Eduardo Arriaga. "Violência, direitos civis e demografia no Brasil na década de 80: o caso da área metropolitana do Rio de Janeiro." *Revista Brasileira de Ciências Sociais* 14, 39 (1999): 155–176.

Delors, Jacques. "¿Qué clase de educación para el Siglo XXI?" *Revista de la Internacional de la Educación* (1996): 6.

Delumeau, Jean. *El miedo en el Occidente (Siglos XIV–XVIII): Una ciudad sitiada.* Madrid: Taurus, 1989.

DeVries, Hent, and Samuel Weber. *Violence, Identity, and Self-Determination.* Stanford: Stanford University Press, 1997.

Diógenes, Glória. *Cartografias da violência. Gangues, galeras e o movimento hip hop.* San Pablo: Anna Blume; Fortaleza: Secretaría de Cultura y Deporte, 1998.

Donziger, S. R., ed. *The Real War on Crime: The Report of the National Criminal Justice Commission.* New York: Harper Perennial, 1996.

Dresser, Denise. "Bringing the Poor Back In: National Solidarity as a Strategy for Regime Legitimation." In Wayne A. Cornelius, Ann L. Craig, and Jonathan Fox, eds., *Transforming State-Society Relations in Mexico.* San Diego: University of California at San Diego, 1994.

Duque, José Roberto, and Boris Muñoz. *La ley de la calle. Testimonios de jóvenes protagonistas de la violencia en Caracas.* Caracas: Fundarte, 1995.

DuRant, R., C. Cadenhead, R. Pendergrast, et al. "Factors Associated with the Use of Violence Among Urban Black Adolescents." *American Journal of Public Health* 84, 4 (1994): 612–617.

Emler, N., and S. Reicher. *Adolescence and Delinquency.* Oxford: Blackwell, 1995.

Estrategia Social Consultores. *Marco legal de la seguridad ciudadana en Venezuela.* Caracas: Estrategia Social Consultores, 1999.

Everett, S., and J. H. Price. "Students' Perceptions of Violence in the Public Schools: The MetLife Survey." *Journal of Adolescent Health* 17 (1995): 345–352.

Fagan, Jeffrey. *Adolescent Violence: A View from the Street.* Research in Progress Seminar Series. Washington: Office of Justice Program, National Institute of Justice, January 1998.

Faria, Wilmar. "A Montanha e a pedra: os limites da política social e os problemas da infância e da juventude." In *O trabalho e a rua: crianças e adolescentes no Brasil urbano dos anos 80.* San Pablo: UNICEF/FLACSO/CBIA, 1992.

Fazio, Carlos. *El tercer vínculo. De la teoría del caos a la teoría de la militarización.* Mexico: Joaquín Mortiz, 1996.

Feldman, Allen. *Formations of Violence. The Narrative of the Body and Political Terror in Northern Ireland.* Chicago: University of Chicago Press, 1991.

Felson, R. B., et al. "The Subculture of Violence and Delinquency: Individual versus School Context Effects." *Social Forces* 73, 1 (1994): 155–173.

Fitoussi, Jean Paul, and Rosanvallo, Pierre. *La nueva era de las desigualdades.* Buenos Aires: Manantial, 1997.

Forgatch, M., and M. Stoolmiller. "Emotions as Contexts for Adolescent Delinquency." *Journal of Research on Adolescence* 4 (1994): 601–614.

Fossaert, Robert. *La société: Une théorie générale.* Vol. 1. Paris: Editions du Seuil, 1977.

Foucault, Michel. *Discipline and Punish: The Birth of the Prison.* New York: Vintage, 1979.

———. *História da sexualidade.* Rio de Janeiro: Zahar, 1984.

Franco, Jean. "La globalización y la crisis de lo popular." Trans. Nora López. *Nueva Sociedad* 149 (May–June 1997); also *http://www.nuevasoc.org.ve/n149/ens.htm* (2001).

Franco, S. *El Quinto: No Matar. Contextos explicativos de la violencia en Colombia.* Bogota: Tercer Mundo Editores, 1999.

Fry, D. P. "Respect for the Rights of Others Is Peace: Learning Aggression versus

Non-Aggression Among Zapotecs." *American Anthropologist* 94 (1992): 621–639.

Fundação Getulio Vargas. *Ernesto Geisel*. Río de Janeiro: Fundação Getulio Vargas, 1997.

Fundação Instituto Brasileiro de Geografia e Estatística (IBGE). Departamento de Estatísticas e de Indicadores Sociais. *Participação político-social no Brasil, 1988: Brasil e grandes regiões*. Río de Janeiro: IBGE, 1990.

———. *Anuário Estatístico do Brasil, 1970–1991*. Río de Janeiro: IBGE, 1991.

Fundação Sistema Estadual de Análise de Dados (Seade). "Pesquisa de condições de vida na Região Metropolitana de São Paulo." San Pablo: Seade, 1988 and 1998.

———. *O jovem e a criminalidade urbana em São Paulo*. San Pablo: Seade; Nev/USP, 1998.

———. *Vinte anos no ano 2000: estudos sociodemográficos sobre a juventude paulista*. San Pablo: Seade, 1998.

Garbarino, James. "The American War Zone: What Children Can Tell Us About Living with Violence." *Journal of Developmental and Behavioral Pediatrics* 16, 6 (1995): 431–435.

———. "Children's Response to Community Violence: What Do We Know?" *Infant Mental Health Journal* 14, 2 (1993): 103–115.

Garbarino, James, K. Kostelny, and N. Dubrow. "What Children Can Tell Us About Living in Danger." *American Psychologist* 46, 4 (1991): 376–383.

García Canclini, Néstor. *Consumidores y ciudadanos*. Mexico: Grijalbo, 1995.

Garretón, Manuel Antonio. "La democracia entre dos épocas. América Latina, 1990." *Revista Paraguaya de Sociología* 28, 80 (January–April 1991): 23–37.

———. "Situación actual y nuevas cuestiones de la democratización política en América Latina." *Sociedad civil en América Latina: representación de intereses y gobernabilidad*. Caracas: Nueva Sociedad, 1999.

Gelles, R. "Poverty and Violence Toward Children." Special issue: "The Impact of Poverty on Children." *American Behavioral Scientist* 35, 3 (1992): 258–274.

Giddens, Anthony. *Consecuencias de la modernidad*. Madrid: Alianza, 1993.

Girard, René. *La violencia y lo sagrado*. Caracas: Ediciones de la Biblioteca Central de Venezuela, 1972.

Gladstein, J., and E. J. Slater. "Inner City Teenagers' Exposure to Violence: A Prevalence Study." *Maryland Medical Journal* 37 (1988): 951–955.

Gladstein, J., E. Rusonis, and F. Heald. "A Comparison of Inner-City and Upper Middle Class Youths' Exposure to Violence." *Journal of Adolescent Health* 13, 4 (1992): 275–280.

Gómez Rodríguez, Gabriela. "Patrones en la construcción del reality show en México: Algunas estrategias de discurso." Precis of "La construcción de la violencia televisada: el caso de Ciudad Desnuda Jalisco," M.A. thesis, University of Guadalajara, 1999.

González, Carlos Mario. "Autoridad y autonomía." In *Cuadernos pedagógicos*. Medellin: National University of Medellin, 1996.

Gregori, Maria Filomena. *Meninos nas ruas: a experiência da viração*. Ph.D. diss., University of São Paulo, 1997.

Hammond, W. R., and B. Yung. "Psychology's Role in the Public Health Response to Assaultive Violence Among Young African-American Men." *American Psychologist* 48, 2 (1993): 142–154.

Hardt, Michael, and Antonio Negri. *Empire*. Cambridge, Mass.: Harvard University Press, 2000.

Hartless, J., J. Ditton, G. Nair, and S. Phillips. "More Sinned Against Than Sinning: A Study of Young Teenagers' Experience of Crime." *British Journal of Criminology* 35, 1 (1995): 114–133.

Heller, Agnes. *Una revisión de la teoría de las necesidades.* Introduction by Angel Rivero. Barcelona: Paidós, 1996.

Hemenway, D., S. Solnick, and J. Carter. "Child-Rearing Violence." *Child Abuse and Neglect,* 18, 12 (1994): 1011–1020.

Henning, K., H. Leitenberg, H., P. Coffey, P., et al. "Long-Term Psychological and Social Impact of Witnessing Physical Conflict between Between Parents." *Journal of Interpersonal Violence,* 11, 1 (1996): 35–51.

Hinton-Nelson, M. D., et al. "Early Adolescents Exposed to Violence: Hope and Vulnerability to Victimization." *American Journal of Orthopsychiatry,* 66, 3 (1996): 346–353.

Hobsbawn, Eric. *Primitive Rebels: Studies in Archaic Forms of Social Movement in the Nineteenth Century and Twentieth Century.* Manchester, U.K.: Manchester University Press, 1959.

Howard, Donna E. "Searching for Resilience Among African-American Youth Exposed to Community Violence: Theoretical Issues." *Journal of Adolescent Health* 18, 4 (1996): 254–262.

Huggins, Martha. *Political Policing: The United States and Latin America.* Durham, N.C.: Duke University Press, 1998.

———. "Reconstructing Atrocity: How Torturers, Murderers, and Researchers Deconstruct Labels and Manage Secrecy." *Human Rights Review.* Forthcoming.

———. "Violencia Institucionalizada e Democracia: Ligacoes Perigrosas." Lecture, Center for the Study of Violence, University of São Paulo, November 21, 1992.

Ibarra, Darío. "¿Rumbo a la 'colombianización' de México?" *Uno más Uno* (São Paulo, México), October 23, 1999.

Jabri, Vivienne. *Discourses on Violence: Conflict Analysis Reconsidered.* Manchester, U.K.: Manchester University Press, 1996.

Jaffe, P., D. Wolfe, S. Wilson, and L. Zak. "Similarities in Behavioral and Social Maladjustment Among Child Victims and Witnesses to Family Violence." *American Journal of Orthopsychiatry* 56, 1 (1986): 142–146.

Jankowiski, Martin Sanchez. *Islands in the Street: Gangs and American Urban Society.* Berkeley: University of California Press, 1991.

Jelin, Elizabeth. "La construcción de la ciudadanía: entre la solidaridad y la responsabilidad." In Elizabeth Jelin and Eric Hershberg, coords., *Construir la democracia: derechos humanos, ciudadanía y sociedad en América Latina.* Caracas: Nueva Sociedad, 1996.

Jenkins, P. "School Delinquency and School Commitment." *Sociology of Education* 68, 3 (1995): 221–239.

Jessor, R. "Successful Adolescent Development in High-Risk Settings." *American Psychologist* 48, 2 (1993): 117–126.

Kaminsky, Gregorio. *Spinoza: la política de las pasiones.* Barcelona: Gedisa, 1998.

Keane, John. *Reflections on Violence.* London: Verso, 1996.

Klein, M. W. *Street Gangs and Street Workers.* Englewood Cliffs, N.J.: Prentice-Hall, 1971.

Kooistra, Paul. *Criminals as Heroes: Structures, Power, and Identity.* Bowling Green, Ohio: Bowling Green State University Popular Press, 1989.

Kpsowa, A. J., et al. "Reassessing the Structural Co-Variates of Violent and Property Crimes in the U.S.A.: A Country-Level Analysis." *British Journal of Sociology* 46, 1 (1995): 79–103.

Kratcoski, Peter C. "Youth Violence Directed Toward Significant Others." *Journal of Adolescence* 8, 2 (1985): 145–157.

Kupersmidt, J., P. Griesler, M. DeRosier, C. Patterson, et al. "Childhood Aggression and Peer Relations in the Context of Family and Neighborhood Factors." *Child Development* 66, 2: 360–375.

Kymlicka, Will, and Wayne Norman. "El retorno del ciudadano. Una revisión de la producción reciente en teoría de la ciudadanía." *La Política* (Paidós, Spain), October 1997, 7.

Laclau, Ernesto, and Chantal Mouffe. *Hegemony and Socialist Strategy: Towards a Radical Democratic Politics.* Trans. Winston Moore and Paul Cammack. London: Verso, 1985.

Lahalle, Annina, et al. *Jeunes délinquants et jeunes en danger en milieu ouvert.* Toulouse: Editions Érès, 1994.

Langguth, A. J. *Hidden Terrors.* New York: Pantheon, 1978.

Laurell, Asa Cristina. *La reforma contra la salud y la seguridad social.* Mexico: Era/ Friedriech Ebert Stiftung, 1997.

———. "Social Policy Issues in Latin America." In Göran Therborn, ed., *Globalization and Modernities.* Stockholm: Forskningsradsnamdnden, 1999.

Le-Blanc, Marc, Evelyn Vallieres, and P. McDuff. "Adolescents' School Experience and Self-Reported Offending: An Empirical Elaboration of an Interactional and Developmental School Social Control Theory." *International Journal of Adolescence and Youth* 3, 3–4 (1992): 197–247.

Le Breton, Dennis. *La sociologie du risque.* Paris: Presses Universitaires de France, 1995.

Lechner, Norbert. *Cultura política y democratización.* Santiago de Chile: CLACSO/ FLACSO, 1987.

———. *Los patios interiores de la democracia. Subjetividad y política.* Mexico: Fondo de Cultura Económica, 1990.

———. "Modernización y modernidad: la búsqueda de ciudadanía." In Vania Salles and Francisco Zapata, comps., *Modernización económica, democracia política y democracia social.* Mexico: Centro de Estudios Sociológicos, El Colegio de México, 1993.

Lernoux, Penny. *Cry of the People.* Hammondsworth, U.K.: Penguin, 1979.

Levi, Giovanni, and Carl Schimitt, eds. *História dos jovens.* San Pablo: Cia. das Letras, 1996.

Lifton, Robert. *The Nazi Doctors: Medical Killing and the Psychology of Genocide.* New York: Basic Books, 1986.

Lipovetsky, Gilles. *La era del vacío.* Barcelona: Anagrama, 1986.

Liska, A., and P. E. Bellair. "Violent Crime Rates and Racial Composition: Convergence over Time." *American Journal of Sociology* 101, 3 (1995): 578–610.

Lockner, Julio. *Los volcanes sagrados. Mitos y rituales en el Popocatepetl y la Iztacihuatl.* Mexico: Grijalbo, 1996.

López Obrador, Andrés Manuel. *FOBAPROA: Expediente abierto.* México: Grijalbo, 1999.

López Rivas, Gilberto, Jorge Luis Sierra, and Alberto Enríquez del Valle. *Las fuerzas armadas mexicanas a fin del milenio. Los militares en la coyuntura actual.* México: Fifty-seventh Legislature, Parliamentary Group of the PRD, 1999.

Maffesoli, Michael. *El tiempo de las tribus.* Barcelona: Icaria, 1990.

Martín Barbero, Jesús. "Los géneros mediáticos y la identidad cultural de los pueblos." Paper presented at the Third International Conference on Culture and the Media, Salamanca, 1999. Mimeograph.

———, comp. "Comunicación y ciudad: entre medios y miedos." *Pre-textos*. Cali: Editorial University of Valle, 1996.

Martinez, Pedro, and John E. Richter. "The NIMH Community Violence Project: II. Children's Distress Symptoms Associated with Violence Exposure." Special issue: "Children and Violence." *Psychiatry: Interpersonal and Biological Processes* 56, 1 (1993): 22–35.

Martinez, Ramiro, Jr. "Latinos and Lethal Violence: The Impact of Poverty and Inequality." *Social Problems* 43, 2 (1996): 131–146.

Martuccelli, Danilo. "Reflexões sobre a violência na condição moderna." *Tempo Social. Revista de Sociologia da USP* 111 (1999): 157–175.

Mathias, J., P. Mertin, and A. Murray. "The Psychological Functioning of Children from Backgrounds of Domestic Violence." *Australian Psychologist* 30, 1 (1995): 47–56.

May, Rollo. *La necesidad del mito. La influencia de los modelos culturales en el mundo contemporáneo*. Buenos Aires: Paidós, 1992.

McAlister, A. *Juvenile Violence in the Americas: Investigative Studies in Research, Diagnosis, and Prevention*. Washington: Pan-American Health Organization, September 1998.

Meek, Harriet W., and Philip Ware. "Maintaining Empathy in a Threatening Environment." *Psychodynamic Counseling* 2, 1 (1996): 67–90.

Mehl, Dominique. "La vida pública privada." In Isabel Veyrat and Daniel Dayan, eds., *Espacios públicos en imágenes*. Barcelona: Gedisa, 1997.

Melluci, Alberto. *Nomads of the Present. Social Movements and Individual Needs in Contemporary Society*. Philadelphia: Temple University Press, 1989.

Miller, W. B. "Gangs, Groups, and Serious Youth Crime." In D. Shichor and D. Kelly, comps., *Critical Issues in Juvenile Delinquency*. Lexington, Mass.: Lexington Books, 1980.

Mills, C. Wright. "Situated Actions and Vocabularies of Motive." *American Sociological Review* 8, 1940.

Misse, Michel. "As ligações perigosas. Mercado informal legal, narcotráfico e violência no Rio." In L.A.M. da Silva, org., *Contemporaneidade y Educação. Revista semestral temática de Ciências Sociais e Educação* 2, 1 (1997).

Mithe, Terance. "Fear and Withdrawal from Urban Life." *Annals* (AAPSS) 539 (1995): 14–27.

Molinar, J., and J. Weldon. "Electoral Determinants Consequences of National Solidarity." In Wayne A. Cornelius, Ann L. Craig, and Jonathan Fox, eds., *Transforming State-Society Relations in Mexico: The National Solidarity Strategy*. San Diego: University of California at San Diego, 1994.

Moneta, Carlos. *Fuerzas Armadas y gobierno constitucional después de Las Malvinas: hacia una nueva relación civil-militar*. Mexico: CLEE, May 1986.

Mongin, Olivier. *Violencia y cine contemporáneo. Ensayo sobre ética e imagen*. Barcelona: Paidós, 1999.

Monsiváis, Carlos. "De no ser por el pavor que tengo, jamás tomaría precauciones. Notas sobre la violencia urbana." *Letras libres* 1, 5 (May 1999): 34–39.

———. *Los rituales del caos*. México City: Era, 1995.

Muller, Robert T., John E. Hunter, and Gary Stollak. "The Intergenerational Transmission of Corporal Punishment: A Comparison of Social Learning and Temperment Models." *Child Abuse and Neglect* 19, 11 (1995): 1323–1335.

Muncie, John. *Youth and Crime. A Critical Introduction*. London: Sage, 1999.

National Committee for Injury Prevention and Control. "Injury Prevention:

Meeting the Challenge. A Report of the National Committee for Injury Prevention and Control, 1989." New York: Oxford University Press, 1989.

Newburn, Taylor. "Youth, Crime, and Justice." In Mike Maguire, Rod Morgan, and Robert Reiner, eds., *The Oxford Handbook of Crimonology.* 2d ed. Oxford, U.K.: Clarendon Press, 1998.

Nisbett, R., and Dove Cohen. *Culture of Honor: The Psychology of Violence in the South.* Boulder, Colo.: Westview Press, 1996.

Novy, D., and S. Donohue. "The Relationship Between Adolescent Life Stress Events and Delinquent Conduct, Including Conduct Indicating a Need for Supervision." *Adolescence* 20, 78 (1985): 313–321.

O'Donnell, Guillermo. *Contrapuntos. Ensayos escogidos sobre autoritarismo y democratización.* Buenos Aires: Paidós, 1997.

O'Donnell, Guillermo, J. Hawkins, R. Catalano, R. Abbott, et al. "Preventing School Failure, Drug Use, and Delinquency Among Low-Income Children: Long-Term Intervention in Elementary Schools." *American Journal of Orthopsychiatry* 65, 1 (1995): 87–100.

O'Keefe, Maura. "The Differential Effects of Family Violence on Adolescent Adjustment." *Child and Adolescent Social Work Journal* 13, 1 (1996): 51–68.

Oliver, Lucio, Eduardo Ruiz, Irene Sánchez, and Raquel Sosa. "Neoliberalismo y política: la crisis mexicana." In *Estudios Latinoamericanos.* No. 4. Mexico: Centro de Estudios Latinoamericanos de la Facultad de Ciencias Políticas y Sociales de la UNAM, 1995.

Oquist, Paul. *Violencia, conflicto y política en Colombia.* Bogotá: Instituto de Estudios Colombianos, 1978.

Osofsky, Joy D. "The Effect of Exposure to Violence on Young Children." *American Psychologist* 50, 9 (1995): 782–788.

Paixão, Antônio Luiz. "Crime, controle social e consolidação da democracia." In Guillermo O'Donnell and F. W. Reis, eds., *A democracia no Brasil. Dilemas e perspectivas.* San Pablo: Vértice; Editora Revista dos Tribunais, 1988.

———. "Crimes e criminosos em Belo Horizonte (1932–1978)." In Paulo Sérgio Pinheiro, ed., *Crime, violência e poder.* San Pablo: Brasiliense, 1983.

Palacios, Marco. "El espejo colombiano." *Letras libres* 5 (May 1999).

Pan-American Health Organization. "Situación de Salud en las Américas. Indicadores Básicos." *Programa Análisis de Situación de Salud,* Division of Health and Human Development. Washington: Pan-American Health Organization, 1998.

Pecaut, Daniel. "Presente, pasado y futuro de la violencia." *Revista Análisis Político,* no. 3 (January–April 1997): 29.

Perrot, Michèle. "Les échanges à l'intérieur de la famille. Approche historique." In François de Singly, ed., *La famille. État des savoirs.* Paris: La Découverte, 1997.

Pile, Steve, and Michael Keith, eds. *Geographies of Resistance.* London: Routledge, 1997.

Pinheiro, Paulo Sérgio. "Police and Political Crisis: The Case of the Military Police." In Martha K. Huggins, ed., *Vigilantism and the State in Modern Latin America.* New York: Praeger, 1991.

———. "Polícia e crise política: o caso das polícias militares." In *A violência brasileira.* San Pablo: Brasiliense, 1982.

Pinheiro, Paulo Sérgio, Sérgio Adorno, Nancy Cárdia, et al. *Continuidade autoritária e construção da democracia. Relatório final de pesquisa.* 3 vols. San Pablo: NEV/USP; FAPESP, 1999.

Pizarro, Eduardo. *Insurgencia sin revolución. La guerrilla en Colombia en una perspectiva comparada.* Bogota: Tercer Mundo Editores/IEPRI, 1996.

Pocock, J.G.A. "The Ideal of Citizenship Since Classical Times." In Ronald Beiner, ed., *Theorizing Citizenship*. New York: State University of New York Press, 1995.

Prado, Jorge, and Maria Helena de Mello. "Os adolescentes e jovens como vítimas da violência fatal em São Paulo." In Paulo Sérgio Pinheiro, ed., *São Paulo sem medo. Um diagnóstico da violência urbana*. Río de Janeiro: Garamond, 1998.

Przeworski, Adam, et al. *Democracia sustentable*. Buenos Aires: Paidós, 1998.

Putnam, Robert. "What Makes Democracy Work?" *IPA Review* 47, 1 (1994): 31–34.

Rangel, Alfredo. *Colombia: guerra en el fin de siglo*. Bogotá: Tercer Mundo Editores/Universidad de los Andes, 1998.

Reguillo, Rossana. "El oráculo en la ciudad: creencias, prácticas y geografías simbólicas. ¿Una agenda comunicativa?" *Diálogos de la comunicación*, no. 49. Lima: FELAFACS, 1997.

———. "Imaginários globais, medos locais: a construçao social do medo na cidade." In *Lugar Comum* (Río de Janeiro), forthcoming.

———. "La memoria a debate." In *Secuencia*, no. 43. Mexico: Instituto Mora, 1999.

———. "Los lenguajes del miedo. Nuevos escenarios ¿nuevos?" In *Renglones*, no. 35. Guadalajara: ITESO, 1996.

———."Notas críticas sobre los movimientos sociales: una perspectiva gramsciana." In *Iztapalapa*. No. 30. Mexico: National Autonomous University of Mexico-I, 1993.

Richters, J., and P. Martinez. "Violent Communities, Family Choices, and Children's Chances: An Algorithm for Improving the Odds." Special issue: "Milestones in the Development of Resilience." *Development and Psychopathology* 5, 4 (1993): 609–627.

———. "The NIMH Community Violence Project: I. Children as Victims of and Witnesses to Violence." Special issue: "Children and Violence." *Psychiatry: Interpersonal and Biological Processes* 56, 1 (1993): 7–21.

Rorty, Richard. *Contingencia, ironía y solidaridad*. Barcelona: Paidós, 1991.

Rotker, Susana "Crónica y cultura urbana. Caracas: la última década." *Estudios* (Universidad Simón Bolívar) 11 (1993): 122–130.

Rountree, Pamela Wilcox, and Kenneth C. Land. "Perceived Risk Versus Fear of Crime: Empirical Evidence of Conceptually Distinct Reactions in Survey Data." *Social Forces* 74, 4 (1996: 1353–1876.

Rubio, Mauricio. *Crimen sin sumario. Análisis económico de la justicia penal colombiana*. Bogotá: Universidad de los Andes, 1996.

Salas, Yolanda. "Las desarticulaciones de una modernización en crisis: revueltas populares y la emergencia del caudillismo en Venezuela." *Montalbán* 29 (1996): 55–76.

———. "Nuevas subjetividades en el estudio de la memoria colectiva." In *Venezuela: Tradición en la modernidad. Primer simposio sobre Cultura Popular*. Caracas: Ecquinocio. Ediciones de la Universidad Simón Bolívar y Fundación Bigott, 1998.

———. "Una biografía de los espíritus en la historia popular venezolana." *INTI Revista de Literatura Hispánica* 45 (1997): 163–174.

Salla, Fernando Affonso. *As prisões em São Paulo*. San Pablo: AnaBlume/FAPESP, 1999.

Sampson, R. "Neighborhood and Crime: The Structural Determinants of Personal Victimization." *Journal of Research on Crime and Development* 22 (1985):7–40.

Sampson, R., and J. Laub. "Urban Poverty and the Family Context of Delinquency: A New Look at Structure and Process in a Classic Study." Special issue: "Children and Poverty." *Child Development* 65, 2 (1994): 523–540.

Sampson, R., S. W. Raudenbush, and F. Earls. "Neighborhoods and Violent Crime: A Multilevel Study of Collective Efficacy." *Science* 277 (1997): 918–924.

Sanjuán, Ana María. "La actual coyuntura venezolana." In *Las relaciones entre Colombia y Venezuela: Análisis de su coyuntura y propuestas para el futuro.* Bogotá: Tercer Mundo Editores, 1999.

———. "La criminalidad en Caracas: percepciones, realidades y política." Paper presented at the Urban Violent Crime Seminar (Banco Interamericano de Desarrollo). Río de Janeiro, 1997.

———. *Notas técnicas sobre violencia.* Caracas: Banco Interamericano de Desarrollo, 1999.

Savater, F. *Etica, política y ciudadanía.* Mexico: Grijalbo, 1998.

Scarry, Elaine. *The Body in Pain: The Making and Unmaking of the World.* New York: Oxford University Press, 1985.

Scheper-Hughes, Nancy. *Death Without Weeping: The Violence of Everyday Life in Brazil.* Berkeley: University of California Press, 1992.

Schutz, Alfred. *El problema de la realidad social.* Buenos Aires: Amorrortu, 1995.

Scott, Marvin, and Stanford M. Lyman. "Accounts." *American Sociological Review* 33, 1 (1968): 46–62.

Scruton, David L., ed. *Sociophobics: The Anthropology of Fear.* Boulder: Westview Press, 1986.

Secretaría de Formación Política del Partido de la Revolución Democrática. *El fraude electoral en el estado de Guerrero*, México City: Secretaría de Formación Política del Partido de la Revolución Democrática, 1999.

Sen, Amartya. *Bienestar, justicia y mercado.* Barcelona: Paidós, 1997.

Sheridan, Alan. *Michel Foucault: The Will to Truth.* New York: Tavistock, 1980.

Short, F. *Gang Delinquency and Delinquent Subcultures.* New York: Harper and Row, 1968.

Silva, A.P.S. *O jovem no conflito com a lei na cidade de Ribeirão Preto (SP): 1986–1996.* Master's diss., Ribeirão Preto, FFCL de la Universidad de San Pablo, 1998.

Simon, J. "Governing Cities Through Crime." Paper presented at Coloquio de MOST/UNESCO, "Management of Social Transformations," Geneva, October 1996.

Singer, M., et al. "Adolescents' Exposure to Violence and Associated Symptoms of Psychological Trauma." *Journal of the American Medical Association* 273, 6 (1995): 477–482.

Skidmore, Thomas. *The Politics of Military Rule in Brazil, 1964–1985.* New York: Oxford University Press, 1988.

Skonick, Jerome, and James Fyfe. *Above the Law: Police and the Excessive Use of Force.* Ontario: Macmillan, 1993.

Skykes, Gresham, and David Matza. "Techniques of Neutralization: A Theory of Delinquency." *American Sociological Review* 22 (1957): 664–670.

Solimano, Andrés, Felipe Sáez, Caroline Mosere, and Cecilia López, eds. *Ensayos sobre paz y desarrollo. El caso de Colombia y la experiencia internacional.* Bogotá: World Bank/Tercer Mundo Editores, 1999.

Sosa Elízaga, Raquel. *Conciencia colectiva y control social en Emile Durkheim.* Mexico: Dirección General de Publicaciones, National Autonomous University of Mexico, 1988.

———. "Descomposición política, militarización y resistencia popular en México." In Margarita López Maya, ed., *Lucha popular, democracia, neoliberalismo: protesta popular en América Latina en los años de ajuste.* Caracas: Nueva Sociedad/Universidad Central de Venezuela, 1999.

———. "Violencia política na América Latina: contradicao ou consequencia da política neoliberal?" *Cadernos do CEAS* (Salvador de Bahía, Centro de Estudos e Ação Social) 173 (1998): 11–20.

———. "Violencia política y terrorismo de Estado." In Ruy Mauro Marini and Márgara Millán, coord., *La teoría social latinoamericana. Cuestiones contemporáneas, IV.* Mexico: Ediciones El Caballito, 1996.

Spinoza, Baruch. *Etica.* Mexico City: Fondo de Cultura Económica, 1958.

Starobinski, Jean. "1789 et le langage des principes." *Preuves* 203 (January 1968).

Taussig, Michael. *Shamanism, Colonialism, and the Wild Man: A Study in Terror and Healing.* Chicago: Chicago University Press, 1987.

Taylor, Ralph. "The Impact of Crime on Communities." *Annals* (AAPSS) 539 (1995): 28–45.

———. "Poverty and Adolescence." In P. B. Edelman and J. Ledner, comps., *Adolescence and Poverty: Challenge for the 1990s.* Washington: Center for National Policy Press, 1991.

Tejada *de Redacción.* Antioquia, Colombia: University of Antioquia, 1989.

Thrasher, F. *The Gang: A Study of 1303 Gangs in Chicago.* Chicago: University of Chicago Press, 1928.

Touraine, Alaine. "Frente a la exclusión." In *Sociológica* 18 (January–April 1992) (Mexico, National Autonomous University of Mexico-A).

Toussaint, Florence. *Democracia y medios de comunicación: un binomio inexplorado.* Mexico: La Jornada Ediciones/Centro de Investigaciones Interdisciplinarias en Ciencias y Humanidades, National Autonomous University of Mexico, 1995.

Tuan, Yi-Fu. *Landscapes of Fear.* New York: Pantheon, 1979.

Tyler, R. T., and P. Degoey. "Collective Restraint in Social Dilemmas: Procedural Justice and Social Identification Effects on Support for Authorities." *Journal of Personality and Social Psychology* 69, 3 (1995): 482–497.

Ugalde, Luis, et al. *La violencia en Venezuela.* Caracas: Monte Avila Editores/ Universidad Católica Andrés Bello, 1994.

Vallejo, Fernando. *La virgen de los sicarios.* Bogota: Alfaguara, 1994.

Varas, Augusto. *Transición a la democracia.* Santiago de Chile: Asociación Chilena de Investigación para la Paz, 1984.

Verbitsky, Horacio. *The Flight: Confessions of an Argentine Dirty Warrior.* New York: New Press, 1996.

Vermelho, L., Jorge Mello, and H. P. Maria. "Mortalidade de jovens: análise do período de 1930 a 1991 (a transição epidemiológica para a violência)." *Revista Saúde Pública* 30, 4 (1996): 319–331.

Vianna, Herbert. "O funk como símbolo da violência carioca." In G. Velho and M. Alvito, eds., *Cidadania e violência.* Río de Janeiro: UFRJ/ FGV, 1996.

Villa, Víctor. *Pre-ocupaciones.* Antioquia: Secretary of Education and Culture, Collection of Antioquean Writers, n.d.

Wall, J., and E. Holden. "Aggressive, Assertive, and Submissive Behaviors in Disadvantaged, Inner-city Pre-school Children." Special issue: "Impact of Poverty on Children, Youth, and Families." *Journal of Clinical Child Psychology* 23, 4 (1994): 382–390.

Wallerstein, Immanuel. *Impensar las ciencias sociales.* Mexico: Siglo XXI, 1998.

Warner, B. S., and M. D. Weist. "Urban Youth as Witness to Violence: Beginning Assessment and Treatment Efforts." *Journal of Youth and Adolescence* 25, 3 (1996): 361–377.

Werthamer-Larsson, L., S. Kellam, and L. Wheeler. "Effect of First-Grade Classroom Environment on Shy Behavior, Aggressive Behavior, and Concentration

Problems." Special issue: "Preventive Intervention Research Centers." *American Journal of Community Psychology* 19, 4 (1991): 585–602.

Weschler, Lawrence. *A Miracle, a Universe: Settling Accounts with Torturers*. New York: Pantheon, 1987.

Wieviorka, Michel. "O novo paradigma da violência." *Tempo Social. Revista de Sociología de la Universidad de San Pablo* 9, 1 (1997): 5–41.

Wilson, M., and M. Daly. *Homicide*. Ontario: McMaster University, 1988.

Wirth, Louis. "Urbanism as a Way of Life." In John Friedl and Noel Chrisman, eds., *City Ways: A Selective Reader in Urban Anthropology*. New York: Thomas Y. Crowell, 1975.

Yablonsky, Lewis. *Gangsters: Fifty Years of Madness, Drugs, and Death on the Streets of America*. New York: New York University Press, 1997.

———. *The Violent Gang*. New York: Macmillan, 1966.

Zaluar, Alba. *Condomínio do diabo*. Río de Janeiro: Revan e UFRJ, 1994.

———. "Teleguiados e chefes: juventude e crime." *Religião e Sociedade* 15 (1990): 54–67.

———. "Violência e crime." In Sérgio Miceli,, org., *O que ler nas ciências sociais brasileiras.* Vol. 1. San Pablo: Sumaré, 1999.

Zizek, Slavoj . *The Sublime Object of Ideology*. London: Verso, 1989.

Zuleta E. *Colombia: Democracia y Derechos Humanos*. Bogotá: Altamira, 1988.

Contributors

SÉRGIO ADORNO is associate professor in the department of sociology at the University of São Paulo and researcher at the Center for the Study of Violence in São Paulo (Brazil.) He is the author of *Os aprendizes do poder (o bacharelismo liberan na politica brasilera)* (1998) and *Nos limites do direito, nas armadilhas da tradição: a revolução descolonizadora na America Latina* (1993), as well as a series of studies that includes "La delincuencia juvenil en San Pablo," "Justicia criminal y violencia urbana," "Ciudadania e administação da justicia criminal," "La precoce experienza della puniozione," and "A gestão filantropica da pobreza urbana."

JESÚS MARTÍN BARBERO received a Ph.D. from the University of Lovaina and completed postgraduate work in anthropology and semiotics in Paris. A well-known contributor to current studies of political cultures, he was founder of the department of communication sciences at the Universidad del Valle (Cali, Colombia) as well as the president of the Latin American Association of Researchers in Communications. Martín Barbero is currently professor and researcher at ITESO in Guadalajara, Mexico. He is the author of many books, including *Comunicación masiva: discurso y poder* (1978), *De los medios a las mediaciones. Comunicación, cultura y hegemonía* (1988), and *Televisión y melodramas* (1992) and coauthor of *Los ejercicios del ver* (1999) and *Contemporaneidad latinoamericana y análisis cultural* (2000).

NANCY CÁRDIA received a Ph.D. in social psychology from the London School of Economics and Political Science; she is the coordinator of the Center for the Study of Violence in São Paulo, Brazil. Her areas of investigation include attitudes, values, and behaviors toward violence and the criminal justice system, the violation of human rights, authoritarianism, violence, and political culture. Her publications focus on the topics of violence and youth, death squads, judicial systems, and urban and school violence.

ALBERTO CONCHA-EASTMAN received a master's degree in epidemiology from the Universidad del Valle (Colombia), and an M.S. in epidemiology from the University of London. He has been visiting professor at the Rockefeller Center for Latin American Studies of Harvard University and advisor of various governmental and nongovernmental organizations in the areas of public health and epidemiology. He is coeditor and coauthor of *La violencia urbana: nuevos retos iniciativas* (1998) and *Ciudad y violencias en América Latina* (1994). Concha-Eastman has directed his research at the Pan-American Health Organization in Washington toward the epidemiological processes of urban violence, poverty, and public health.

JOSÉ ROBERTO DUQUE has worked as a writer and reporter for the Venezuelan newspapers *El Universal, 2001, El Nacional,* and *El Mundo* and for the magazine *Imagen.* He is the author of the weekly column "Guerra nuestra," a series of chronicles that denounce the violation of human rights and urban violence in general. He has won literary prizes from the Universidad Central de Venezuela and the Venezuelan Society of Authors and Composers. Duque is the author of *Salsa y control, Guerra nuestra,* and *La ley de la calle* (1995), an anthology of testimonials, chronicles, interviews, and reporting on violence in Caracas coauthored with Boris Muñoz.

MARTHA HUGGINS is Roger Thayer Stone Professor of Sociology at Union College in Schenectady, New York. She has studied the problem of crime and police violence in Brazil for the last twenty-five years. She is the author of numerous articles on criminology and of *From Slavery to Vagrancy in Brazil: Crime and Social Control in the Third World* (1984), *Vigilantism and the State in Modern Latin America: Essays on Extra-Legal Violence* (1991), and *Political Policing: The United States and Latin America*, winner of two awards for the best book of 1998. Huggins is currently finishing *Working in Violence: Police Torturers and Murderers Reconstruct Brazilian Atrocity* with Mika Harito-Fatouoros and Philip Zimbardo.

CARLOS MONSIVÁIS's writings on topics such as popular mythology and the urban chronicle include political, historical, and literary essays, as well as criticism of film and visual art. He is the most distinguished cultural essayist of contemporary Mexico. Monsiváis's many books include *Días de guardar* (1970), *Amor perdido* (1976), *Nuevo Catecismo para indios remisos* (1982), *Entrada libre: crónicas de una sociedad que se organiza* (1988), *Escenas de pudor y liviandad* (1986), *Los rituales del caos* (1995), and *Parte de guerra* (1999).

JOSÉ NAVIA has explored the faces of urban and rural conflict in Colombia since 1985 as a journalist for the newspaper *El Tiempo*. His chronicles cover youth violence and the diverse effects of the activity of guerrillas, paramilitary forces, gangs, and drug-traffickers upon indigenous and rural communities. He has been a correspondent in the peace negotiations between the Colombian government and the Revolutionary Armed Forces of Colombia (FARC.) He received the National Prize for Journalism from the Bogotá Journalists' Circle in 1992 and again in 1996. Navia is the author of *El lado oscuro: crónicas urbanas* (1998.)

EDUARDO PIZARRO is a sociologist at the Institute of Political Science of Paris and director of the Institute for Political Studies and International Relations of the University of Colombia and of the magazine *Análisis Político*. He has served as a member of the Commission for the Study of Violence, the Commission for the Study of the Reintegration of Guerrilla Groups, and the Commission for the Reform of Political Parties. He is the author of *Las FARC: de la defensa a la combinación de todas las formas de lucha* (1991) and *Insurgencia sin revolución: la guerrilla colombiana en perspectiva comparada* (1996).

ROSSANA REGUILLO received a Ph.D. in the social sciences with specialization in social anthropology at the University of Guadalajara. Professor of cultural studies since 1994, she has taught in Bolivia, Colombia, Brazil, Guatemala, Nicaragua, El Salvador, and Uruguay. Focusing on the subject of urban violence, her books discuss the processes of youth culture and the dynamic between the city and the communications media. Among them are *En la calle otra vez* (1995), *La construcción simbólica de la ciudad; Mapas nocturnos; diálogos con la obra de Jesús Martín Barbero* (1998), *Pensar las ciencias sociales hoy: reflexiones desde la cultura* (1999), and, with Cristina Padilla, *Quien nos hubiera dicho, Guadalajara, 22 de abril* (1993.)

SUSANA ROTKER received a Ph.D. at the University of Maryland. She was professor of nineteenth-century literature and of Latin American thought and cultural studies at Rutgers University, where she also directed the graduate program of the department of Spanish and Portuguese. Rotker won the Casa de las Américas Prize and fellowships from the Social Science Research Council (New York) and the Wilson International Center for Scholars (Washington, D.C.). She is the author of *Cautivas: Olvidos y memoria en la Argentina* (1999), *Los transgresores* (1991), and *Fundación de una escritura: las crónicas de José Martí*, which has been published in a revised version as *The American Chronicles of José Martí: Journalism and Modernity in Spanish America* (2000). She also edited various works, including *Ensayistas de Nuestra América: Siglo XIX* (1994) and a series of studies on political-cultural processes and the formation of modernity, the city, and the Latin American journalistic chronicle.

YOLANDA SALAS received a licenciada in letters at the Universidad Católica Andrés Bello and is a Ph.D. candidate in literature at the University of Indiana at Bloomington. She has been director of research of the Rómulo Gallegos Center for Latin American Studies Foundation and is currently president of the Institute of Ethnomusicology and Folklore in Caracas, Venezuela. Her research focuses on the construction of identities, collective memory, popular religiosity, and imageries. Her publications include *El cuento folklórico en Venezuela* (1985), *Bolívar y la Historia de la conciencia popular* (1987), *Ideología y lenguaje en la literatura de la modernidad* (1990), and, forthcoming, *Manuel Piar: el héroe e los múltiples rostros.*

ALBERTO SALCEDO, whose major field of study is social communication, Universidad Autónoma del Caribe (Barranquilla), is a film and television director at the Universidad del Rosario of Bogotá, as well as the author of *Los golpes de la esperanza* and *De un hombre obligado a levantarse con el piel derecho y otras crónicas*, and coauthor of *Diez juglares en su patio*. His work has earned him the Premio Internacional de Periodismo Rey de España and the Premio al Mejor Documental in the II Jornada Iberoamericana de Televisión (Cuba).

ANA MARÍA SANJUÁN, a social psychologist, received a doctorate in political science from La Universidad Central de Venezuela; she is coordinator of diverse research projects in the areas of urban violence, citizen security, human rights, and youth. She is the author of numerous articles on violence, such as "Caracterización de las muertes violentas en el Area Metropolitana de Caracas," "La criminalidad en Caracas: diagnóstico situacional," and "Ciudadanía, violencia y pobreza en Venezuela."

RAQUEL SOSA ELÍZAGA, magister in Latin American Studies, Ph.D. in history, is a professor and researcher at the Center for Latin American Studies of the Division of Graduate Studies of the Faculty of Political and Social Sciences of the Universidad Nacional Autónoma of Mexico and was president of the Latin American Association of Sociology (1995–97). She is the author of numerous studies on the subject of violence, such as "América Latina, perspectivas de su reconstrucción," "Violencia política y terrorismo en América Latina: un ensayo sobre lo que puede ser nuestro futuro," and "Descomposición política, militarización y resistencia popular en México" and of *Conciencia colectiva y control social en Emile Durkheim* (1988) and *Los códigos ocultos del cardenismo* (1996).